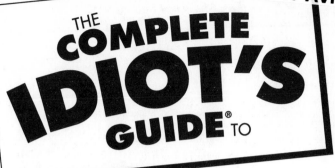

THE COMPLETE IDIOT'S GUIDE® TO

Finding Mr. Right

by Josie Brown and Martin Brown

ALPHA

A member of Penguin Group (USA) Inc.

In memory of our mothers, Maria and Ruth. If they had not found the men of their dreams, we would not have been able to help so many others find their Mr. Right.

ALPHA BOOKS

Published by the Penguin Group

Penguin Group (USA) Inc., 375 Hudson Street, New York, New York 10014, USA

Penguin Group (Canada), 90 Eglinton Avenue East, Suite 700, Toronto, Ontario M4P 2Y3, Canada (a division of Pearson Penguin Canada Inc.)

Penguin Books Ltd., 80 Strand, London WC2R 0RL, England

Penguin Ireland, 25 St. Stephen's Green, Dublin 2, Ireland (a division of Penguin Books Ltd.)

Penguin Group (Australia), 250 Camberwell Road, Camberwell, Victoria 3124, Australia (a division of Pearson Australia Group Pty. Ltd.)

Penguin Books India Pvt. Ltd., 11 Community Centre, Panchsheel Park, New Delhi—110 017, India

Penguin Group (NZ), 67 Apollo Drive, Rosedale, North Shore, Auckland 1311, New Zealand (a division of Pearson New Zealand Ltd.)

Penguin Books (South Africa) (Pty.) Ltd., 24 Sturdee Avenue, Rosebank, Johannesburg 2196, South Africa

Penguin Books Ltd., Registered Offices: 80 Strand, London WC2R 0RL, England

International Standard Book Number: 978-1-59257-895-5
Library of Congress Catalog Card Number: 2009923293

11 10 09   8 7 6 5 4 3 2 1

Interpretation of the printing code: The rightmost number of the first series of numbers is the year of the book's printing; the rightmost number of the second series of numbers is the number of the book's printing. For example, a printing code of 09-1 shows that the first printing occurred in 2009.

Printed in the United States of America

Note: This publication contains the opinions and ideas of its authors. It is intended to provide helpful and informative material on the subject matter covered. It is sold with the understanding that the authors and publisher are not engaged in rendering professional services in the book. If the reader requires personal assistance or advice, a competent professional should be consulted.

The authors and publisher specifically disclaim any responsibility for any liability, loss, or risk, personal or otherwise, which is incurred as a consequence, directly or indirectly, of the use and application of any of the contents of this book.

Most Alpha books are available at special quantity discounts for bulk purchases for sales promotions, premiums, fund-raising, or educational use. Special books, or book excerpts, can also be created to fit specific needs.

For details, write: Special Markets, Alpha Books, 375 Hudson Street, New York, NY 10014.

Publisher: *Marie Butler-Knight*

Editorial Director: *Mike Sanders*

Senior Managing Editor: *Billy Fields*

Development Editor: *Lynn Northrup*

Senior Production Editor: *Janette Lynn*

Copy Editor: *Lisanne V. Jensen*

Cartoonist: *Barbara Slate*

Cover Designer: *Kurt Owens*

Book Designer: *Trina Wurst*

Indexer: *Angie Bess*

Layout: *Ayanna Lacey*

Proofreader: *Laura Caddell*

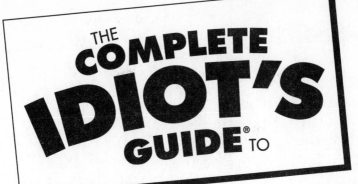

Finding Mr. Right

Contents at a Glance

Contents

Foreword

If you have opened your heart to the true possibility of finding your very own Mr. Right, then this is the right book for you.

I don't believe there is just one special someone waiting out there for you. There are several. But two things need to happen first in your life, which will make all the difference between failure and success in your search for Mr. Right.

First, you must bring to this quest an open heart.

Without an open heart, opportunity can knock day and night, but you won't hear it because you have closed your heart and mind to the possibility of finding your soul mate. Women tell me all the time how astounded they were to discover that once their heart opened, once they set their intention on finding a meaningful relationship worthy of the future they desired, guys they thought they would never meet actually came into their lives.

Why this remarkable change? It's simple:

Opportunities come to those who believe that what they want in life can and will happen.

Second, you must be prepared for when opportunity knocks.

Like other books in *The Complete Idiot's Guide* series, *Finding Mr. Right* is the perfect go-to source because the information presented here is done in a clear and concise manner. Whether it's dispelling common myths about the identity of Mr. Right, or laying out a variety of clear-cut warning signs that you are in a relationship with Mr. Wrong, Josie and Martin Brown give refreshingly honest and candid views of what you must do if you are to have a happy and lasting relationship.

I've known the Browns for fifteen years, both as personal friends and professional colleagues. In fact, I've worked with them on a number of my books: *Mars and Venus on a Date, Mars and Venus Starting Over,* and *Mars and Venus Book of Days.* Both as journalists and essayists, they bring wonderful insights to the study of relationships.

Beyond all their professional work in the field of relationship writing, their own relationship is the sort that others strive to have: they are open and honest with each other in their communication, and they are loving and supportive partners.

Forming and keeping a happy relationship has never been easy. Whether it's a Bonnie and John Gray, or a Josie and Martin Brown, we who work in the world of relationships know that commitment is an ongoing process of emotional growth.

From the moment you first meet your Mr. Right, to the day you decide to make a commitment to one another, you'll encounter some inevitable bumps along the road to happiness—not the least of which is learning to avoid the pitfalls of a previous failed relationship.

Take this book as a roadmap for your journey. I have no doubt that it will place you eye-to-eye and heart-to-heart with your Mr. Right, and give you the essential skills with which to build the lasting and loving relationship that you were always meant to have.

—John Gray, Author, *Men Are from Mars, Women Are from Venus*

Introduction

Is there really a "Mr. Right"? The answer is an emphatic *yes*. In fact, there are probably several Mr. Rights hoping at this moment that they will get the chance to meet you.

Unfortunately, there are many Mr. Wrongs as well. We're guessing that you've already met your fair share of those. And we'll take a further guess that at least one of those Mr. Wrongs left you brokenhearted. It hurt when you found out that he just wasn't that into you. And it certainly didn't matter that you were so very much into him—which is why that relationship left you disillusioned and fully determined never to feel that miserable again. Besides, it's easier (on your heart and soul) to find fault in a relationship than to take the riskier steps to make it work.

It's perfectly understandable that you'd want to shield yourself from any additional pain. But what you *don't* want to do is put up a force field so strong, so thick, and so high that you can't connect with the one or more men out there who can make you happy. Why? Because the wall that keeps out all those Mr. Wrongs will also keep out your Mr. Right.

And that's why you're reading this book, right? You are ready, at this very moment, to open your heart to the right man. You're ready to let your guard down and break down that wall—or at least take down enough bricks to see who's out there and who's trying to look in. You've yanked those blinders off so that you can take a relationship—the *right* relationship—beyond light flirtation, one-night stands, and all those doubts that have you declaring, "Sure, I like him … *but* …" You're reading this book because you're not only ready to take a chance on love again, but you're also open to taking that much bigger step that will actually lead you to making a commitment. You want to make sure, however, it will be to some guy who is willing to put it all on the line for you, too.

So that you end up with a man who will love, cherish, and appreciate you, we're going to give you answers that are open and honest. We're also going to give you the emotional tools to gain insight into what makes you happy and emotionally fulfilled and show you how to fine-tune your instincts about the men you encounter so that you can discern the role they'll play in your happiness—both immediately, and more importantly, in the long term.

When you asked whether Mr. Right existed, we said yes. Now we want you to ask yourself this much more important and relevant question: "Who is *my* Mr. Right?"

Ultimately, only *you* can answer that question.

Are you feeling stumped? Well, here's the good news: by the time you finish this book, you'll know your Mr. Right when you meet him. Your answer will be based on these criteria that are unique to you and you alone:

1. Your ideal of who your Mr. Right is—the traits that make him desirable to you

2. Your universe—your life—as it exists right now

3. Your resolve to move beyond any self-imposed boundaries that previously held you back from finding your soul mate

Are you ready to step out from behind that wall and see all the possibilities out there? Good—because Mr. Right is waiting for you on the other side!

How This Book Is Organized

Part 1, "Let's Talk About You …" examines society's archetypes of the perfect man, and how they may have influenced your own perceptions about the man you hope to marry. You also learn to assess your own dating behavior, which is often influenced by the emotional baggage carried by each of us. Plus, you learn to identify your relationship priorities.

Part 2, "How to Tell Mr. Wrong from Mr. Right," points out the many types of Mr. Wrongs: those men who don't have the desire to commit. You discover what red flags indicate when a guy is just not right for you, and learn the importance of timing in the quest for your Mr. Right.

Part 3, "Finding Your Mr. Right," explores which traits best embody your Mr. Right. You also learn of some unlikely places you're likely to run into him, and get tips on the best ways to attract him online. Plus you pick up some new insights on flirting, and learn what to say and how to act in order to feel right at home with any group of guys.

Part 4, "**Is He Mr. Right?**" gives you a clear idea of things you should—and shouldn't—do on a first date, as well as warning signs of what constitutes overbearing behavior on your part. You also learn when and if a male friend will make a good lover, and discover the traits found in all caring lovers. You examine your feelings as to whether he's truly the right guy for you; and if not, get a closer look at the emotions that surround a breakup.

Part 5, "**Keeping Mr. Right**," recognizes that, with your engagement, you've taken on all kinds of new challenges. Here you learn the right communication tools to keep you on track, as well as tips on how to negotiate his (and your) emotional ups and downs. Assess how well you handle relationship stress, and learn the difference between emotional and physical intimacy. Address any doubts you have for long-term happiness with your Mr. Right, and learn how to deal with the stress of planning your wedding. Gain the insights for a lifetime of love with your Mr. Right.

Extras

In the scope of our lives, the importance of finding that one special someone cannot be overstated. To give you new and various perspectives on finding your Mr. Right, we've added a number of fun and interesting sidebars in each chapter. Look for the following boxes:

He's a Keeper if …

Stay love-savvy with these helpful reminders that define the kinds of guys who could be your Mr. Right.

Dating 911

These cautions keep you from making any major dating faux pas that send Mr. Right in the opposite direction.

He Said, She Said

These helpful statistics, interesting quotes, and miscellaneous bits of information bring you new insight and understanding of the art of love, lust, and relationships.

Acknowledgments

We'd like to thank the following friends and colleagues whose insights and guidance were instrumental in the creation of this book:

First, to two of our dearest friends: Richard C. Levy, the man of a million ideas, for his concept and vision for this book; and John Gray, the man who redefined loving relationships for countless millions, for being a mentor and devoted supporter of our work.

Also, we want to thank our team at Alpha Books: Mike Sanders, (the original Mr. Right) for his steady hand of leadership, and for welcoming us to the CIG family of authors; and Dawn Werk, for her energy and brilliance in the critical area of book promotion. To Lynn Northrup, for her wit, talent, patience, and most of all her succinct editing efforts on our behalf; and to Lisanne Jensen and Jan Lynn for catching us each time we slipped.

It doesn't take a village to write a book, just a support team of caring, thoughtful, and dedicated individuals.

Trademarks

All terms mentioned in this book that are known to be or are suspected of being trademarks or service marks have been appropriately capitalized. Alpha Books and Penguin Group (USA) Inc. cannot attest to the accuracy of this information. Use of a term in this book should not be regarded as affecting the validity of any trademark or service mark.

Let's Talk About You ...

Before you discover Mr. Right, you have to know more about yourself. Your own strengths and weaknesses may surprise you. Assessing them in advance lets you break through any emotional walls holding you back and gives you the skills you'll need in your quest to find Mr. Right.

Is your Mr. Right made of flesh and blood, or is he a composite character constructed from various myths and impressions that you've collected from your earliest years up to the present? Have you undermined your own efforts in finding a lasting relationship, and have you unknowingly committed a variety of dating faux pas?

We explore those issues and much more in this first part. The simple truth is that we can meet a potential soul mate far more frequently than we would ever imagine. Without a clear vision of our desires and expectations, love can seem very far away—when in reality, it's closer than we ever thought possible.

The Mythical Mr. Right

In This Chapter

- ◆ Do you have misconceptions of Mr. Right?
- ◆ Busting the myths of an ideal man
- ◆ How your personal growth changes your perception

At this very moment, like millions of other women, you are searching and hoping that someday soon—perhaps even today—you will at last find your Mr. Right.

But ask yourself: Would you know Mr. Right if he walked up to you today?

"I've yet to meet the man with whom I'd be willing to share my life." We've heard this lament time and time again from women of all ages and stages of life. If this phrase has come out of *your* mouth, we'll give you a very good reason as to why you're wrong: *you've got a cock-eyed view of the real Mr. Right.*

But seriously, don't blame yourself. Since birth, you've been spoon-fed some unattainable perceptions about love, lust, marriage, and commitment by the media, popular culture, and—ironically—by your family.

The Nine Mr. Right Archetypes

If you think your Mr. Right is your dream guy, you're correct. And that's just the problem: he's not a real person, but some mash-up of ideal traits gleaned from various societal stereotypes and leavened with warm fuzzies from your childhood.

To put it all into perspective, take a quick walk down memory lane. We've chronicled nine of the most celebrated Mr. Right archetypes. And we'd be willing to guess that, at some point in your life, you've fallen in love with at least a few good men who fit these descriptions!

He Said, She Said

Is attraction a state of mind? Apparently so. And in regard to women, they use all of theirs when falling in love. According to researchers at the University of Baleares in Palma de Mallorca, Spain, men process their attraction with the right side of their brains, which is visually stimulated. Women, on the other hand, use their whole brain to do the job, which is why they are better able to verbalize their appreciation for the men in their lives.

Archetype No. 1: "Father Knows Best"

(Ages 0–5 and maybe forever) He was your very first love, and you were his little princess. When he came home, you ran into his arms, smothered him with kisses, and felt his heart beat against your chest. He made you feel safe and sound—and best yet, loved unconditionally.

Why this is typecasting: invariably, our idols have clay feet. As you grew up, you gained some perspective on your parents and certainly realized they also had flaws, fears, and vulnerabilities. Whether he was a workaholic or Mr. Mom, the good cop or the disciplinarian, life with father meant living in his world and following his rules. But you're a big girl now, and it's time for you to think for yourself—even if that means breaking some of his rules in order to follow your dreams (and your heart).

Who you need to be looking for now: a man who doesn't want to control you but sees you as his equal. Yes, he thinks you're special. But he lets you make your own decisions, and he respects the ones you make. The best-case scenario is that you're making them together.

Archetype No. 2: "Prince Charming"

(Ages 6–8) Almost every fairy tale ends with a princess getting rescued by a knight in shining armor or getting whisked away to his magic kingdom. In your mind, *you* were that princess.

Why this is typecasting: we're guessing that, by age eight or so, you wised up to the fact that no handsome, smiling prince was going to sweep you up onto his trusty steed so that the two of you could go riding off into the sunset. And yet … deep down inside, you still hold on to the belief that "someday your prince will come."

Well, get over it. That's not going to happen. *And that's okay.* Smart women learn to fight their own battles. Besides, wicked witches, dragons, and evil stepmothers are *so* last millennium.

Who you need to be looking for now: a man who isn't a two-dimensional caricature. He will have some losses as well as some wins. He'll have both bad and good experiences. There will be a depth of his character, born of experiences that have tested his mettle.

 **He's a Keeper if …**

… his sense of adventure matches your own. A man who can keep up with you will be a partner for life.

Archetype No. 3: Harry Potter

(Ages 8–12) He's cute, sweet, and a stand-up kind of guy. You've grown up with him—and you've always had a crush on him. Why? Because he's too virtuous to even think of trying to get to first base.

Why this is typecasting: sure, he's a Mr. Right—if you're a 'tween. But eventually, you outgrew him (we hope). Besides, this boy may be a hero, but (broad hint) *he's still not that into you.* It's great that he's focused on a cause—but at this stage, that cause isn't going to be you.

Who you need to be looking for now: someone whose raging hormones have calmed down—at least enough to recognize that you're the right woman for him. If he still wants to be your hero, well, that's certainly all right.

Archetype No. 4: Justin Timberlake (or the Boy Band Boyz)

(Ages 12–19) He's a heartthrob-cute pin-up boy who makes all the right moves—on stage. Off it, he'd much prefer to be one of the boys. If you try to change him, you'll get kicked to the curb. Face it: at this stage of life, his priority isn't you.

Why this is typecasting: wait a few years, and he's the bad boy your mother warned you about. And between his entourage tagging along and all the girls throwing themselves at him, he has no incentive to settle down with his Ms. Right.

Who you need to be looking for now: a man, not a boy. If he prefers to hang with his posse as opposed to you, he's not mature enough for the kind of relationship you need and want—and deserve!

Archetype No. 5: Mr. Darcy

(Ages 13–15 ... or maybe 45?) As with most bookish heroes, he's wealthy, handsome, and mysterious. And because he is a product of Jane Austen's rich imagination, he's always the gentleman—even while other men act like cads. If this is love, bring it on!

Why this is typecasting: most guys you'll meet at that age don't have the manners or the life experience to deal with moral dilemmas. And if he insists on wearing a cravat, he's probably playing for the other team.

Who you need to be looking for now: a man who is not afraid to show his emotions—particularly his love and appreciation for you.

Archetype No. 6: Mr. Tolson (from *The Great Debaters*)

(Ages 15–21) Teachers and coaches can be the best mentors a girl can have, always pushing you to be your very best. If they are constant

idealists, you are taught to dream big, too. No wonder it's so easy to have a crush on him ...

Why this is typecasting: sure, he's older and wiser. But he's also smart enough to know that you're too immature for him. You have to wise up to the obvious: he's there to inspire but certainly not to encourage your advances.

Who you need to be looking for now: a guy who cheers you on to reach your goals and encourages you to do your best.

Dating 911

Be secure with who you are and with what you want in a man. The better you know yourself and what makes you happy, the better you'll know what kind of man will suit your needs and desires.

Archetype No. 7: Ross, Chandler, and Joey

(Ages 19–30) These *Friends* next door are cool enough to hang with and goofy enough to be friends without benefits (initially, anyway ...).

Why this is typecasting: eventually, these friends *want* those benefits. But not all guy pals can—or want to— transition into boyfriends. And if it doesn't work out, who moves out?

Who you need to be looking for now: a guy who can be more than a friend: a lover, a husband, a soul mate, and a life partner.

Archetype No. 8: McSteamy

(Ages 25 and older) He's smart and sexy. He's also a player—and never for keeps. He's the perennial Peter Pan: in other words, he'll never grow into the man you want him to be.

Why this is typecasting: fun for a booty call? Sure. Mr. Right material? Hardly! He's more like Mr. Right Now. And if you try to "change" him, you'll be wasting time that could be better spent looking for the real Mr. Right.

Who you need to be looking for now: a man who won't always be looking over your shoulder for his next conquest.

Archetype No. 9: McDreamy

(Ages 25 and older) He's got everything going for him: good looks, a great job ... and he flirts with you. Finally, a guy who's perfect! At least, it seems that way at first ...

Why this is typecasting: unfortunately, he's got baggage. Now you have to decide whether it's worth hanging in there to see whether he'll dump it. Then again, he may dump *you*.

Who you need to be looking for now: a guy who is willing to work on his issues for you.

Dating 911

Don't be a critic. You don't need to tell your date what's wrong with his clothes, his job, his home, his family, or his friends. In fact, that says more about what's wrong with *you* than him: you're too judgmental. And yes, you'll need to work on that, if you want to be emotionally open to Mr. Right. Even if you don't see this guy as your Mr. Right, do you see him as a potential friend? Then treat him as such. In other words, be gracious until the evening is over.

Myth Busters

You shouldn't be surprised to learn that there are a variety of myths that have developed about the identity of this seemingly elusive Mr. Right. Here are five of the most prevalent ones, accompanied by some truths and goals that allow you to do some much needed myth busting as an important first step in finding your very own Mr. Right.

Myth No. 1: "He Will Be Perfect in Every Way"

Truth: you're not perfect. And no one else is, either.

Your goal: seeking a mate who embodies admirable traits is one thing, but holding on to unattainably high expectations is another. If you want to have a realistic relationship, you have to be willing to compromise.

Myth No. 2: "He Will Have to Work Hard to Win My Attention"

Truth: according to a recent Naumann Research poll, close to two thirds of both men and women believe in love at first sight. Of these, a little more than half experienced this phenomenon first hand—and three quarters of them are still married.

Your goal: an initial attraction is *always* needed to get the ball rolling. But the true test of love happens over time and demonstrates itself in random acts of love. You, too, will have to work hard if the relationship is to have a chance to survive and thrive.

Myth No. 3: "He Will Always Be Romantic"

Truth: most men are not, by their nature, romantic creatures. Yes, they fall in love and are capable of loving someone—but *romance* is a learned trait. In fact, in a recent study quoted in *Men's Health* magazine, only 58 percent of men consider themselves romantic compared to 72 percent of women. When asked about their attitudes toward Valentine's Day, the average male response was, "I can take it or leave it." The second most popular answer was, "It's for her, not for me."

Your goal: find a guy who loves you instinctively and wholeheartedly. Then, teach him *how* to express his love romantically. If you take your time and are willing to show considerable patience, both of you will enjoy these love lessons.

 He's a Keeper if …

… he doesn't talk over you. Allowing you to get a word in edgewise isn't just common courtesy, it's also a sign of respect—and you deserve it.

Myth No. 4: "He Will Always Do the Right Thing"

Truth: that's great in theory. But will you always agree on what is "right"? And if he only sees ethics and mores in black and white, would you really want to marry a man who is incapable of compromise or who can't appreciate the viewpoint of others?

Your goal: to meet a man with a strong sense of self, purpose, and ethics—but one who is also willing to see the other side of every issue, *especially yours.*

Myth No. 5: "We Will Never Fight"

Truth: couples who never fight may be holding back from being honest, too. Eventually, however, this forced "honesty" wears thin on one or both partners. If you can't openly express your feelings to the one you love most, you may not love him forever.

Your goal: seek a mate who will be open and honest with you about his needs, wants, and desires and who will respectfully allow you the same courtesy.

He Said, She Said

In an okCupid.com survey of 10,000 women, it was redheads—not blondes or brunettes—who are the most sexually adventurous. They don't mind posing for photos in the buff or getting involved in three-ways.

The Importance of Personal Growth

The big lesson here is that time does not stand still, and neither do our perceptions of ourselves and others. If you're growing emotionally, your ideals are constantly changing as well. More specifically, you're becoming more discerning as to your needs and desires and are honing in on traits that will either turn you off or turn you on.

This change in attitude is a mix of several things, including:

- ◆ Your life experience and how greatly you have (or haven't) grown
- ◆ The number and variety of people who make up your social circle
- ◆ Your previous relationships with men

The Least You Need to Know

◆ Don't pass up your opportunity to meet Mr. Right because he doesn't live up to your original ideal of "Prince Charming."

◆ Find a guy who loves you instinctively. If need be, with your patience and guidance, in time you'll teach him how to express that love.

◆ Don't be held captive by some idealist set of myths as to what your Mr. Right should or should not do or be. Instead, judge the men who come into your life on their individual merits.

◆ Mr. Right won't be perfect, but then again neither are you. Remember, lasting relationships are built on the art of compromise.

◆ Your expectations of an ideal partner will evolve as you mature and partake in more life experiences. One thing should stay constant: your desire for passion and respect.

Chapter 2

Sabotage, Sins, and Virtues

In This Chapter

- ◆ How you work against your own best interests—and why
- ◆ The seven most common dating sins
- ◆ The seven virtues that make successful dates

When dating was new to you, maybe you fell in love at the drop of a hat—and got your heart broken easily, too. With time, maturity, and experience, however, you learned to take the process in stride. You now anticipate more hits than misses, and that may have left you feeling a bit jaded.

And when you're jaded in love, when you've given up on finding your soul mate, when you've convinced yourself you don't deserve a happy relationship, or have resigned yourself to the fact your Mr. Right doesn't exist, it's official: you are your own worst enemy.

The Many Ways You Sabotage Your Chances for Love

Do you find that hard to believe? Well, your past actions speak louder than any words we could say:

◆ You've refused to go out with a guy because he didn't fit your perfect picture of Mr. Right.

He Said, She Said

While 83 percent of 1,020 adults surveyed in a 2000 Vagisil Women's Health Center poll find sex very or somewhat important in a relationship, 90 percent of respondents age 35 to 49 insist work demands affect sexual relationships.

◆ You've dropped a boyfriend over some insignificant slight (you didn't like his laugh or thought he was "too serious" or "had a weird sense of humor").

◆ You've left a relationship because it was easier than discussing your feelings with that partner.

◆ You've judged a guy based on his looks although you thought he had a nice personality.

◆ You dropped a nice guy because he didn't make enough money.

◆ You have a pattern of picking fights with your significant others for no reason until they walk out on you.

◆ You do something you know will upset him—then regret it when it's too late.

◆ You've flirted with other guys in front of your boyfriend.

◆ You'll pick him apart in front of other people.

◆ You're always playing "hard to get." And why not? Seriously, you've yet to meet a man who's worth your time.

◆ You never show him any real affection.

◆ You make fun of him or tease him in bed.

◆ When he asks, you refuse to meet his family or friends.

- You don't want him to meet your friends or family either.

- Although you've been emotionally intimate and are now in an exclusive relationship, you refuse to be sexually intimate as well.

- He'd prefer to stay "friends with benefits," and you reluctantly go along with that—when you could be with someone willing to commit emotionally to you.

- You would prefer to stay "friends with benefits"—you refuse to get emotionally intimate with him.

- You'd prefer to stay with Mr. Wrong instead of continuing your quest to find Mr. Right.

Does any of this sound familiar? If so, then you've committed some pretty egregious crimes against your own happiness. It's time to find out why.

He's a Keeper if ...

... he knows when to stop joking. That he should have a great sense of humor is a given, but your Mr. Right will also know when a joke has gone too far. It's not funny if it hurts.

The Seven Deadly Sins of Dating

You can start by examining the seven most common dating sins: you know—those acts of transgression against your own personal happiness.

"But why would I knowingly hold myself back from finding my own Mr. Right?" you may wonder. Because, for some subliminal reason, you don't feel you deserve him in your life.

Dating should be fun. It should be a personal growth process. And most of all, it should teach you to discern which traits in a man make you happy. If the experience is less than heavenly, it's because you're committing at least one of these sins.

Sin No. 1, Pride: It Goeth Before the Guy

You're too good for him. Well, have you noticed that you feel that way about a lot of guys? If so, you may be wrong—which means you may be missing out on some pretty great company.

Your fall from grace is due to: a false sense of your own self-worth. If you were always Mommy or Daddy's little princess, you may not realize that they instilled in you the idea that no man will ever be good enough for you.

Redemption comes when you: look, listen, and ask questions. No one is asking you to lower your standards. But if you refuse to see beyond a mediocre first impression or judge someone only on his looks, in time you'll find yourself with fewer options—or you may be so desperate that you'll settle for all the wrong reasons.

Instead, approach each prospective date as a friend, first and foremost. Observe how he treats others. Is that how you'd hope he'd treat you? Listen to his opinions and to the tone he uses with others he respects and those he doesn't. Then, assess his attention to your ideas. If he cares about your opinions, he's certainly someone you should keep around.

Draw him out as well. Never be shy about questioning your new friend about his likes, perceptions, dreams, desires, and feelings. The more you know about him, the better idea you'll have as to whether or not he's right for you.

Sin No. 2, Sloth: Ignorance Is *Not* Bliss

If you're too lazy to get out and meet new people or you've gone ahead and settled for Mr. Wrong, you *will* miss your Mr. Right.

Your fall from grace is due to: complacency, which comes from a lack of self-esteem or perhaps an innate shyness. Change can be scary, and that's why many people shy away from it. But if you can get over this fear factor, the release will be exhilarating.

Redemption comes when you: recognize you deserve a great man in your life—and you act accordingly. That said, the first thing you must change is your attitude. If you believe you deserve a happy relationship, you'll make it a goal—one that takes precedence over any other activity that keeps you "too busy" to look for love.

In time, your determination will affect how you act toward others, including all the possible Mr. Rights within your universe. And if you're smart, it will expand the scope of your universe, too. It's time you looked for love in all the *right* places!

Sin No. 3, Wrath: Let Go of the Angry Young Girl!

Are you thinking that you've been there and done that? We get it: love hurts. But all men aren't alike. Anger over the past won't change your future. Action will.

Your fall from grace is due to: pain from another relationship. Even if it wasn't a guy who broke your heart—but, say, a parent, or another loved one—that hurt now affects how you view every subsequent relationship, amorous or not. Trust is one of the most important components of any relationship. If you've lost your ability to trust, you've lost your capacity to love.

Redemption comes when you: move beyond the pain that you're holding onto, because it's holding you back from seeing the goodness, honesty, and uniqueness in others. Does this mean therapy? More than likely, yes. But if you are ever going to move on from the emotional barrier you've built around your heart, first you have to open it in order to identify that original source of pain.

Dating 911

Don't be afraid to show your date your personality. Feel free to talk about your hobbies, your travels, and the issues that get your attention.

Sin No. 4, Envy: Serene, Not Pea Green

If you're always presuming the grass is greener anywhere but where you're currently standing, it's going to cost you: either a current boyfriend who gets kicked to the curb as you jump the fence for more verdant pastures, or some gal pal who will soon tire of your catty remarks about her luck with love.

Your fall from grace is due to: your inability to count your blessings. If you're never satisfied with what you've accomplished or with your relationships, you have to ask yourself why this is the case. Perhaps, deep down inside, you're afraid that you don't deserve your success. Or perhaps you feel it's fleeting, and you've braced yourself to do without—which is why you don't appreciate what you now have and why you'll never be happy if you can't change this very important facet of your personality.

Redemption comes when you: are serene, not pea green, at the joy and success of others. If you covet your friends' relationships, careers, possessions, or lives, you're taking your focus away from the steps necessary to accomplish what you need (which, by the way, may not be the same things at all).

Sin No. 5, Lust: Sex Siren or One-Night Stand?

Sex is a beautiful, memorable act of intimacy. Your heightened sensuality works like an aphrodisiac: men flock to women who are in touch with their sexual power.

But sex stops being special when it means nothing to you, let alone the men with whom you share your bed. At the very least, it's a waste of time and energy—and at the very most, a shameful memory.

Your fall from grace is due to: a diminished sense of self-worth. Somewhere along the line, you quit seeing your body as something priceless. That includes your heart. If you don't respect yourself, how can you expect others to do so? You're allowing those who don't—or can't—to take advantage of you, whether that's for an hour or for a lifetime.

Redemption comes when you: reconnect with your emotional center, which for whatever reason has become desensitized to the joy of sex and has dissolved your self-respect. Doing so is perhaps one of the most difficult tasks you will ever undertake. It will involve some deep soul searching. Should you follow through, you'll be in the right emotional state to recognize your Mr. Right when you see him. And if Mr. Right recognizes you first, he may be your salvation.

Sin No. 6, Gluttony: Give a Little, Get a Lot

If you ask too much of your loved ones, eventually they push back (or leave). The compulsion to test the boundaries of your relationship may actually leave it irretrievably broken.

Your fall from grace is due to: your inability to appreciate what you have. You feel you don't deserve it—and so one way or another, you're going to ruin it. This unconscious sabotage could also come from a previous trust issue. Even if some other guy did you wrong, you don't have to take it out on a potential Mr. Right.

Redemption comes when you: quit pushing your boyfriend's buttons for all the wrong reasons. Having him jump through hoops doesn't give you the proof you're looking for: that he loves you. If you're still in search mode, don't be so quick to turn off to some guy who has you in his sights. Give him a chance to woo you. And if there's some chemistry, don't be so quick to find fault or jump ship. Life tests us in so many ways. You don't have to create your own road hazards on the highway to happiness.

> **Dating 911**
>
> Don't be a diva! Putting on airs, boasting, and dropping names is more of a turn-off than a turn-on. The best way to impress him: be gracious.

Sin No. 7, Greed: Love Him, Not His Bank Account

He may have all the money in the world, toys galore, and several homes. But if he treats you like just another possession, you may find yourself replaced by someone who is more desirable because she's less attainable.

Your fall from grace is due to: your inability to see beyond his bank statement. Seriously, if he's wealthy and also a wonderful guy, that won't matter in the least. On the other hand, if a guy's a creep, that's truly the worst reason to stick it out. No woman should denigrate herself, put up with an abusive relationship, or allow herself to be treated like a doormat just because doing so gives her an allowance that affords her the latest designer clothes or gets her out of punching a clock. You'll pay another way: with emotional wear and tear. And you'll be working harder as you try to keep him happy and interested.

He Said, She Said

Sexiness wears thin after awhile and beauty fades, but to be married to a man who makes you laugh every day, ah, now that's a real treat.

—Joanne Woodward, actress, and wife of Paul Newman

Redemption comes when you: forget that old saying, "It's just as easy to marry a rich man as it is a poor one." That doesn't take into account those qualities that make a man a keeper: his ability to love, trust, commit, respect, and live his life desiring you.

Dating's Seven Virtues

Redemption comes in righting those wrongs. After the second, third, or fourth relationship blooper, "Oops ... I did it again" just isn't cute anymore.

All of us can make the right choices in our relationships—especially by remembering these seven virtues of dating.

Virtue No. 1: Make Prudent Choices

Take your time. Be discerning. Listen to what your date is saying. Better yet, judge him by his actions, not just by what he says.

Virtue No. 2: You Deserve Respect

If he doesn't respect you, he's not the right guy for you. Move on.

Virtue No. 3: Don't Jump into Bed!

It's a big mistake, because sexual intimacy should come after shared emotional intimacy and not the other way around. Otherwise, you're likely to get hurt—particularly if you're hoping he's into you for a reason other than your knowledge of the *Kama Sutra*.

Virtue No. 4: Have the Courage of Your Convictions

If something doesn't feel right in your relationship, don't push it. If you don't share the same virtues, it won't last. Eventually, you'll resent the fact that you've settled for less.

Virtue No. 5: Have Faith in Your Choice

As in all things in life, you'll be second-guessing yourself as to whether or not you're with the right person. If you need a litmus test, here's a good one: "When he's around, I'm happy, I feel good about myself, and I feel great about us."

He's a Keeper if ...

... he knows how to fight fairly. A man who argues by playing passive-aggressive head games or who puts you on the defensive by blaming you is not the guy you want. Pick a man who fights fairly, and when rough spots come along, you'll come to a mutually acceptable consensus in a loving manner.

Virtue No. 6: Hope Means Happiness

If you have a negative dating attitude, it will present itself to every man in some form. And he'll react to it in a way that makes sense for him: he'll run in the opposite direction.

Virtue No. 7: Charity: It Begins with You

First and foremost, address your own needs. Blind dates are fine, but don't feel obligated to go out with someone out of guilt, obligation, or because someone else feels you and he make a good match. Go—but only if you truly feel you may establish a connection.

The Least You Need to Know

◆ If you look hard for a reason to dump a guy, you'll always find one. Don't sabotage yourself. Instead, consider your needs and whether he meets them—or whether he's working hard to do so.

◆ You've committed dating sins in past relationships, and that's okay. Don't beat yourself up over it. Instead, set your sights forward and stay focused.

◆ When it comes to finding your soul mate, you *must* be virtuous. No matter what other achievements you'll have, choosing the soul mate with whom you'll spend the rest of your life is the most important decision you'll make. Don't take it lightly!

Chapter 3

What's Your Dating Personality?

In This Chapter

- ◆ Signals you send to a potential mate
- ◆ The many possible dating personalities: which is the real you?
- ◆ Why "the girl next door" is personality plus

You've seen it in your girlfriends. And trust us, they've seen it in you, too: that change in your personality when some gorgeous guy comes into the room.

It's not exactly a Doctor Jekyll and Mr. Hyde kind of moment but more like *Seinfeld*'s Elaine when an eligible doctor walks into the room. Your eyes light up. Your lips curl into a coy smile. There is a change in your stance and in the way you hold your hands and what you do with them—which may include something that catches his attention: perhaps a toss of your head or calling out an acknowledgement of someone else across the room. There is a sugar-sweet lilt in the tone of your voice. Even what you say has been strategically thought through.

For a woman in mating mode, it's totally instinctual to put your best foot forward (among other things; even your breasts jut out, right?). In fact, it's expected. But one thing you may not be aware of is that unconsciously, your dating personality sends both overt and subliminal signals to your potential mates.

The Five Most Prevalent Dating Personalities

Some signals may be appealing to him at first but not necessarily in the long run. Some may signal the wrong guy into your life or grate on the nerves of the right one.

Here are some of the most prevalent dating personalities, their appeal, and their pitfalls.

The Mommy

You are a take-charge woman in all facets of your life. So it's only natural that you take the dominant role while dating, too. This includes taking it upon yourself to initiate contact—maybe even making the first call (and subsequent ones)—to keep the ball rolling during the relationship's entre act.

Why this role: you don't trust that you have something to offer in a relationship, so instead you try to accommodate him by doing *everything*. If you make it easy on him, the decision by him to stick around should be easy too, right?

The appeal to him: you're a dream come true for the Power Rangers who don't mind being waited on hand and foot and to boys who are clueless about even the simplest aspects of a functional relationship (let alone a functional life). Both of these types of men want someone to look after them, and an over-accommodating girlfriend is the perfect person.

The pitfalls for you: where is the give-and-take, the quid-pro-quo, and the joint consensus between two people in sync that balances out every relationship? If you keep doing it all, he'll never step up to the plate when you need a little coddling. Besides, who wants to date their mother?

Long-term consensus: that depends. If he never wants to grow up, it's a pretty sweet deal for him. However, if you're looking for a partner as opposed to a child, you'll soon get tired of playing Mommy Dearest.

He Said, She Said

Sound—as opposed to silence—is preferred during sex, at least according to a 2008 study conducted by Sexual and Relationship Therapy. In fact, men find hearing sounds the third most arousing of the five senses, after sight and touch. On the other hand, women rank it fourth in importance.

The Diva

You are used to being the center of attention. You insist on having a large circle of friends around for every occasion. You don't persuade or cajole; you demand—and you always get your way. Of course, no one dares to cross your path. And you make no bones about it: you're high maintenance.

Why this role: you're like an M&M: despite your hard-core demeanor, you have a soft, vulnerable center. Your attitude is your first line of defense. Your loyal and enthralled entourage is your second. Your philosophy is that if, despite your princess act, he hangs in there for the long run, he'll be duly rewarded—and it's worth the wait.

The appeal to him: two types of guys will be attracted to you. Power Rangers (you know, those self-assured men) certainly aren't afraid to share the spotlight. In fact, they're attracted to your high profile because it complements their own. The second type of man is the Acolyte. He wants to bask in the rays of your glory in the hope that it will jump-start his own rep—even if that means carrying your purse.

The pitfalls for you: eventually, the Power Ranger may see green—particularly if your popularity eclipses his own. Also, he won't take kindly to your "me, me, me" mentality—specifically because it diverges too often with his own self interests.

As for the Acolyte, if you don't get tired of him because you prefer a guy who's more than a yes man, eventually he will resent his submissive role in your life. And when he lashes out, it will hurt. Of course, you'll dump him right then and there.

Sadly, most other guys will be too intimidated by you. If they can't—or won't—get close enough, how will they know the real you?

Long-term consensus: relationships are a joint venture. If you can't allow anyone else to share the spotlight in your life, you'll always be a solo act. Power Rangers are a great match because they share the same reasons for the M&M act. This is a guy with whom you'd proudly partner on a lifetime of duets. But that takes mutual respect and appreciation.

> **He's a Keeper if ...**
>
> ... he has no issues with your past. Any concerns he has about the life you led before you met him can be answered with the love and respect you've shown him since the day you met. If your deep dark secret doesn't bother him now, it never will.

The Desperate Bridesmaid

You don't even have to be at a wedding to act like a woman whose number one worry is that she'll never walk down the aisle with her very own Mr. Right. Your desperation is palpable; your vulnerability downright scary. Despite your great looks and wonderful personality, the fact that you're trying so hard to make an impression means you can only do one thing: *make the wrong one.*

Why this role: this fear can come from many sources. A loss in your life—say, a father or a boyfriend—may have convinced you that you'll never want to feel that kind of hurt in your life ever again. Or, you may have learned it at your mother's knees: was she afraid of living without a man and put up with a man, any man, rather than live without one? Did she scare you into believing that survival was not possible without a man in the house? If so, she did you a great disservice. Both men and women need to learn how to stand on their own two feet first. Your strength and self-reliance attract others to you.

The appeal to him: some men view a woman's desperate attempts to have and to hold onto them as an opportunity for easy sex without obligations. They promise anything and deliver whatever they feel they can get away with in the relationship. No matter their indiscretions, you'll always forgive them because you're holding onto the hope that they'll appreciate you, eventually (as if!).

The pitfalls for you: if you're afraid of losing him, he will always have the upper hand in your relationship. Eventually, he'll dump you for a newer, more challenging conquest—and your heart will be broken yet again.

Long-term consensus: if you haven't figured it out already, this is one personality you can—and *must*—do without. It comes out because of all your relationship insecurities. As Cher said to Nicolas Cage in the movie *Moonstruck:* "Snap out of it." *Now.*

The Party Girl

You're the life of the party and the first to break barriers to be the girl gone wild. It's your way of garnering everyone's attention—of showing that you're the cool one. You're so full of surprises that you've earned the reputation, "The party hasn't really started until she …"

Why this role: the clown is the saddest person in the room, but covers up her emotional turmoil with the loudest laugh. The one thing the Party Girl is afraid of is a disappearing act: if you aren't seen and heard, you don't exist. In your mind, loud means proud. Unfortunately, others—including potential Mr. Rights—might read this as "desperate."

The appeal to him: your lack of inhibition encourages others to let down their guard—including him. You're daring, witty, and wickedly funny. When you're in party mode, you're also naughty … so what's not to like?

 Dating 911

Learn to censor yourself. While on dates, you don't need to say everything that pops into your head—especially if it might be hurtful to the man across from you.

The pitfalls for you: unfortunately, when the party's over, it's over between the two of you, too.

Why? No guy wants to be known as the boyfriend with the girl who flashes the other guests and whose idea of trendy headgear is a lampshade. That's okay. Look at it this way: will he look so great to you the next morning when you sober up?

Long-term consensus: overkill, in any sense of the word, is a turnoff—all the more reason to tame that compulsion you have to stand out in a crowd. If you really want to attract Prince Charming, you're going to have to dress like a princess and act like a queen—which, deep down inside, is your natural state of grace, anyway.

The Girl Friday

You're the most efficient person in the office, and everyone knows it, especially your Mr. Right co-worker, who is the best reason to show up at work. You're the first to arrive and the last to leave. You know where all the bodies are buried, but you also know how to keep your mouth shut. You're indispensible, and he can't live without you—which is exactly how you like it. So why doesn't he realize it already and ask you to marry him?

Why this role: while your personal life is messy, your professional accomplishments are tidy and impressive, which is why you've allowed the office to take precedence over your personal life.

The appeal to him: he doesn't have to think. He has you to do that for him. Also, he has you to cover for him—to tell him what others think and do whenever he's out of the office. You're his "office wife." Unfortunately, he doesn't plan on giving you that promotion and title change you desire anytime soon.

He Said, She Said

Intimate relationships are more common in the workplace than you'd suspect. In fact, a 2009 Vault, Inc., workplace survey shows that at least 58 percent of people feel that "romance is a fringe benefit of their job."

The pitfalls for you: your efficiency is admirable, but it's not a turn-on. In fact, if you don't allow him to see the woman beneath the suit, he won't have any incentive to date her.

Long-term consensus: you need to move your relationship with him out of the office. If he sees you in a different light (candlelight, for example), he may gain a different perspective on your entire relationship.

Personality Plus: The Girl Next Door

Your appeal has less to do with proximity than attitude: you give everyone you meet a smile and a kind word every time you meet. With you, gracious is as gracious does. Your kindness is genuine, and you've got a laugh that invites others to join in. Yes, you flirt, but you're always adorable, never crude. All of this attracts men to your side. While they're comfortable as your friend, they'd prefer to have you as a girlfriend.

We now come to the one personality that will get you what you want: The Girl Next Door.

Why does Mr. Right fall for her? She is always sweet and kind to everyone in her life. She has a large set of friends (including him) who love being around her and always feel comfortable in her presence. They are very protective of her, although they are proud to introduce others to her as well. She always seems interested in what others have to say and answers in ways that offer encouragement and admiration.

Can she be you? Yes, of course!

Why this role: who says it's role playing? It *is* the true you. What he sees is what he gets—and this is exactly what he wants. What? You say the person described here is too good to be true—too good to be *you?* Don't sell yourself short. If you believe it, you can *be* it.

The appeal to him: whether he admits it to himself or not, The Girl Next Door is every man's ideal. Why? Your honesty is refreshing. Your great karma is a turn-on. You're the girl he's been looking for all his life. It's his turn to convince you that he's your Mr. Right. And guess what? *Every other guy in the room feels exactly the same way.*

The pitfalls for you: the fact that you're being honest and forthright doesn't mean that every man you meet will match your openness. There will always be those guys who will try to take advantage of your kindness. With so many men, there is too little time to let the Mr. Wrongs keep you from the Mr. Right you deserve.

Long-term consensus: be yourself. Don't lie, fudge, or pretend. Be true to yourself, too. Go for what you want. If that man across the room attracts you, let him know. Take the time to introduce yourself, find out who he is, discover whether you have similar interests—and, most importantly, whether the attraction is mutual. Learning about each other won't happen overnight but over a lifetime. The moment he crosses your path is the first moment of the rest of your lives together.

The Least You Need to Know

◆ Every inflection—be it your tone, your words, even the toss of your head—sends a signal to a potential mate. Be very aware of what messages you give, and you'll get the right messages in return.

◆ Your innate dating personality may attract him initially and may appeal to some men but may be wrong for a long-term relationship with your Mr. Right.

◆ He has an ideal, too. Believe it or not, it's The Girl Next Door. And that very girl lives within *you*. Let her out, and he'll be at your side—perhaps for a lifetime.

Chapter 4

Dropping Your Emotional Baggage

In This Chapter

- ◆ How your Critical Emotional Mass weighs you down
- ◆ How much baggage are you carrying? A weight test
- ◆ Six must-have traits that all happy women share

Everyone comes with some emotional baggage that holds us back from reaching our true potential and from attracting the right people into our lives—which in turn helps us live the life that will give us the greatest joy.

The goal of this chapter is simple: to help you toss off a few of the weightier issues that may be slowing you down on your journey toward finding Mr. Right.

Assessing Your Critical Emotional Mass

Each of us carries some emotional baggage: psychological issues that hold us back from recognizing what or who can make us happy. This is especially true when it comes to our primary relation-ship: if you can't see around the issues you fear most, you may not see your soul mate when he's right in front of you.

Detailed in this chapter are a few of the most common of these emo-tional bags. So that you can better understand the heavy toll they take on your happiness, we've "weighted" each of them. At the end of this section, add up the emotional poundage. And if you're smart, you'll shove them out of the way. If you can get rid of all of them, you will have achieved what we call "Critical Emotional Mass," or CEM. If you haven't figured it out already, an ideal CEM is zero.

Of course, everyone has some fears and anxieties. So yes, your score will be higher than you'd hope. But don't let that worry you. Recogni-tion is half the battle, and the other half is shedding as much of your baggage as possible—which gets you closer to finding your Mr. Right.

Bag No. 1: Negative Attitude (CEM: 20 pounds)

You've already given up on any dreams you have: for looking your best, feeling your best, and presenting your best face to the outside world—particularly to any possible Mr. Rights. You don't believe your attitude is evident to others? *You are so wrong.* They see the negativity in your eyes and in the slump of your shoulders. They can hear it in your voice.

In fact, here are a few phrases to lose from your vocabulary:

- ◆ "I won't …"
- ◆ "I can't …"
- ◆ "I'd never …"
- ◆ "That won't ever happen for me …"
- ◆ "I'm not that lucky …"

Now, flip these thoughts around and here's what happens:

- ◆ "I will …"
- ◆ "I can …"
- ◆ "Someday I might …"

- "That hasn't happened yet, but you never know what tomorrow might bring ..."

- "Wow! I can't believe my luck ..."

If Mr. Right heard *those* phrases coming out of your mouth, he'd be enticed, enthralled, and encouraged to check you out. Maybe he'd even ask whether he could join you—for an hour, for the evening, or maybe even for the rest of your life. Why? Because you sound like you're up for some wonderful adventure. *And so is he.*

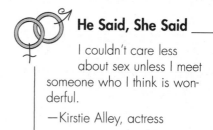

He Said, She Said

I couldn't care less about sex unless I meet someone who I think is wonderful.

—Kirstie Alley, actress

Bag No. 2: Transference (CEM: 5 pounds)

You've had a few bad experiences with some odious Mr. Wrongs. Needless to say, you're gun-shy—which is why some totally innocuous remark from a potential Mr. Right brings back a flood of memories (nightmares, really) of your life with He Who You Wish You Could Forget Forever. Who can blame you? The last thing you want is to go through those experiences again!

Well, guess what? You won't. This is assured by one simple fact: your dead-set determination to stay away from guys who will hurt you.

Now, here's the hard part: you have to learn to trust your instincts that, this time around, you've made a better choice.

To help you realize that he's not Mr. Wrong's evil twin, ask yourself these four questions before you walk away from this new relationship:

- Is his behavior a pattern of action or just an anomaly?

- Is he aware of any of your previous issues with Mr. Wrong?

- Have you had a heart-to-heart with him as to which actions of his concern you?

- If so, does he continue on the same path?

Unless you can answer no to all of these, you owe him—and yourself—another shot at love.

Granted, he'll have his own issues. And yes, they *will* come up in your relationship. The great news is that unlike Mr. Wrong, you and he will learn to discuss and work through them.

Bag No. 3: Sense of Inadequacy (CEM: 10 pounds)

No matter how hard you wish to change your single status, if you don't feel you deserve Mr. Right, he won't either.

He Said, She Said

According to *Human Nature* magazine, while 80 percent of men feel comfortable with one-night stands, only 54 percent of women do. Those who don't like them say it's because the experience makes them "feel used."

So *why* do you feel this way? We're guessing it has something to do with something someone said about you, perhaps over and over again. If it was someone you loved and respected—say, a parent, another adult relative, or maybe a former love—it hurt.

Worse yet, somewhere along the line you began to believe it yourself … although deep in your heart, you knew it wasn't true.

Well, now it's time you told yourself something more in line with the truth: you deserve to find your own Mr. Right. Say it now, loudly and proudly.

Bag No. 4: Comparisons (CEM: 5 pounds)

When a woman compares a possible mate to the other male role models in her life, and these men are her ideals for Mr. Right, she loses focus of her true goal: to find a man—maybe not so perfect, but certainly loving and respectful—with whom to share her life. Psychiatrist Carl Jung called this the "Electra Complex."

It's great that you have a strong adoration for your father. But if you must always have your father's approval before making any decision, then you're not as emotionally mature as you presume. And you certainly don't ever want your daddy issues to get in the way of finding your Mr. Right.

It's your parents' role to teach you core values when you're a child. After you've grown into an adult, however, their role in your life changes. No longer should they make decisions for you; rather, they should counsel you when you ask and support the decisions you make for yourself. If you still allow them to do your thinking for you, you'll never find Mr. Right. You'll end up with a man who you hope will please your parents—but odds are he won't be the right man for you.

He's a Keeper if ...

... your girlfriends love him. Your pals are your support system and the best vetting system you have. If he passes with flying colors, he has no one left to please but you.

Another consideration is that if, for any reason, your father doesn't accept the man who makes you happy, will you drop this potential Mr. Right for that reason alone? You shouldn't. Again, you have a right to lead your own life and to make your own mistakes—even as they pertain to your quest to find Mr. Right.

Bag No. 5: Fear of Loneliness (CEM: 20 pounds)

Your biggest fear is dying alone. Your second greatest fear is living a lonely life. Where does this come from? More than likely it was the loneliness you witnessed in others close to you. Or maybe you had a parent who dreaded it—out loud—and made it scarier to you than any imaginary Boogie Man.

Now, as an adult, you feverishly network—even going so far as putting up with "frenemies" who don't deserve your respect, let alone all the time you waste on them.

He Said, She Said

According to the *American Heritage Dictionary*, a "frenemy" is a person who is ostensibly friendly with someone, but is actually antagonistic or competitive.

In fact, because you hate being alone, you do your best to get invited everywhere—parties, openings, receptions, and weddings—even the outings of little-known acquaintances. When there are no private events, you begin to look for public events. At these events, you do your best to be the belle of the ball and to talk to everyone. But your frantic antics chase others away—especially men who wonder why you're acting so desperate. The guys who hang in there do so because it's so easy to take advantage of you. And sadly, you let them. When will you learn that they don't truly respect you?

The Emotional Weight Test

Here's the true test that you're determined to dump your emotional baggage. It's quite simple: just answer "true" or "false" to the following 21 questions. The answer key reveals which of the five emotional bags—negative attitude, transference, sense of inadequacy, comparisons, and fear of loneliness—you may still be hauling around. The answers will be revealed at the end of the test. Good luck!

1. You don't take compliments well.

2. You dump, as opposed to allowing yourself to get dumped.

3. It's easy to find fault with your boyfriends.

4. He enjoys rough sex, and you don't—but you go along with it anyway.

5. He's specific on what he likes you to wear—and you don't dare deviate.

6. In your opinion, no man can resist temptation.

7. You grin and bear it when your man makes fun of you in public.

8. Despite having caught your boyfriend in several lies, you hang in there.

9. You refuse to allow him to move in with you although you spend so much time together.

10. You tell yourself and others that you will never get married.

11. Your parents never approve of your boyfriends, so you dump them (the boyfriends, that is).

12. Although his flirting with other women hurts, you bite your tongue.

13. Although none of your friends like him, you feel lucky to have him by your side.

14. You have resolved that in the future, you'll die alone.

15. You never get your way in bed.

16. You believe that every guy hides something from his past.

17. No man will ever mean more to you than your father.

18. Sometimes, without cause, a guy can turn you off with a simple look or phrase.

19. You truly believe that you'll live the rest of your life without falling in love.

20. You've fallen in love often, and each time it was a man with whom you would have married—if only he would have asked.

21. No man will ever be good enough for you.

Answer Key:

If you answered "false" to all of these, congratulations! You have no unnecessary baggage. So why haven't you snagged Mr. Right yet?

If you answered "true" to any of these questions, you're carrying some emotional baggage. In fact:

> The following "true" responses indicate a *negative attitude*. Add 20 pounds for each "true": 10, 14, 16, 19, 21

> The following "true" responses indicate a tendency toward *transference*. Add 5 pounds for each "true": 2, 6, 9, 18

> The following "true" responses indicate a *sense of inadequacy*. Add 10 pounds for each "true": 1, 4, 7, 13

> The following "true" responses indicate unnecessary *comparisons*. Add 5 pounds for each "true": 3, 11, 17

> The following "true" responses indicate inexplicable *fear of loneliness*. Add 15 pounds for each "true": 5, 8, 12, 15, 20

If you answered "true" to just one question in one or more categories, you have now identified the reason for this baggage. It really is time to drop it and move on.

He Said, She Said

According to a 2005 survey from the Archives of Sexual Behavior, on average men rank attractiveness higher on their list of desired traits than women, whereas women rank honesty, humor, kindness, and dependability as more important traits.

If you answered "true" to two or three questions in one or more categories—or if you scored a Critical Emotional Mass of 20 pounds of baggage or more—take it as a warning: emotionally you are holding yourself back from finding a lasting and loving relationship.

If you answered "true" to all of the questions in any one category, your chance of finding a soul mate will increase if you make up your mind, right now, to lose this unwanted baggage.

Six Must-Have Traits of Every Happy Woman

If you're truly going to be successful in your endeavor to find a wonderful, passionate relationship, you'll need the right mindset—one that believes you deserve the happy, healthy relationship you so earnestly want in your life. Let's take a look at six must-have traits that happy women share.

Trait No. 1: Faith

She never gave up on her dream of sharing her life with a soul mate. Granted, she may have altered her fantasy to some extent. Or maybe life did, and she rolled with the punches. In any event, she always believed there was a Mr. Right out there for her. And so should *you*.

Trait No. 2: Tenacity

She never quit looking for him—whether she was in a locale that was familiar or one that was not; when she was out alone and surrounded by strangers or hanging with friends; or whether she was online or at work. And if he wasn't going to come knocking at her door, she was going to go out there and find him. Like everything else she ever wanted in life, she made finding her Mr. Right a goal, and went after it as such: she assessed her needs, worked hard on her weaknesses, played to her strengths, and put herself in the places and circumstances that allowed her to be near the kind of men she hoped to attract.

She understood that you have to do more than believe: you have to be in the game.

Trait No. 3: An Open Disposition

She smiled. She made eye contact. She said "Hello" back. She held up her own end of the conversation. And she wasn't afraid to give him her telephone number—then ask for his in return.

Trait No. 4: A Sound Notion of What She Wants

She didn't try to force men to be her ideal. Instead, she sought out men whose interests aligned with her own. She dated men who she found engaging and comfortable in their skins, and who recognized and appreciated what she brought to the relationship.

He's a Keeper if ...

... you can be silent with him. You should not have to entertain him constantly or put up with his constant chatter. In relationships, silence can truly be golden. When you can read each other's moods and minds, you're really a couple.

Trait No. 5: Strong Sense of Self

Her confidence shoos away any doubts she has about herself, and reinforces her resolve to hold firm to finding a mate with the traits she expects and respects in a man.

Because she has strong core values, of course it's expected that the man she chooses has a similar code of ethics. At the same time, they don't agree on everything (maybe he's from a red state and she's blue, or maybe he's a White Sox fan while she bleeds Red Sox through and through). Why does it work? Because the things that count most in a relationship are proven by deeds, not by words.

Trait No. 6: The Ability to Trust

There are two sides to every story—including his. That's why, even if something went awry, she gave him the benefit of the doubt. Her trust was well placed based on all the other must-have traits that went before it. Yours will be, too—as long as you remember to give the relationship time to prove itself.

The Least You Need to Know

- ◆ No matter what emotional baggage weighs you down, you can drop the extra pounds if you are willing to recognize them first and put forth the effort to address these emotional weaknesses.

- ◆ Don't ever presume that your doubts aren't sabotaging your relationships, because they are. It's up to you to keep them in check so that they don't spoil a perfectly wonderful relationship.

- ◆ Women who succeed at finding love have certain personality traits, such as faith in their ability to attract their Mr. Right and a sound notion of what they want in a mate. They also have an open disposition, a strong sense of self, and the ability to trust.

5

Criteria List Versus Wish List

In This Chapter

- ◆ Knowing what to look for: your criteria list
- ◆ What happens when your expectations are too high
- ◆ Why you react to emotions instead of assessing your needs
- ◆ How to make a list that works for you
- ◆ Mr. Right: if you see him, he will come

Every woman has a right to a wonderful relationship. But not every woman will have the luck of finding a man worthy of her. Your own journey may be an indication of the twists and turns of fate—of poor choices or bad timing.

Even more sadly, should you happen to find Mr. Right, you may not recognize him when you see him.

If you've looked longingly at those who enjoy loving relationships, you've probably also wondered: "How did she get so lucky? What does she have that I don't? Why her and not me?"

Quite simply, your lucky friend had a list ...

The Right List Versus the Wrong List

Certainly it wasn't a wish list, because wish lists reflect impulsive emotions based on whims or some unachievable great expectations.

No ... what got her in the arms of her Mr. Right was a well-thought-out criteria list, made up of some must-have traits she actively sought in the men who caught her eye—men who met a defined need of her own.

And that's what your criteria list will have, too.

But first things first: before you recognize what you should have on your list, you need to know the things that absolutely can't be on there.

He's a Keeper if ...

... he takes an interest in the things that interest you. Whether it's a chick flick, sushi, country music, or your favorite charity, if he goes out of his way to try something that's important to you, his open mind should win him some major points.

Great Expectations Lead to a Bleak House

What's wrong with the following description? "My perfect guy has blue eyes, will work as a lawyer, will have gone to an Ivy League school, and will drive a Lexus."

Well, for starters, while the wisher's criteria mentions a man's looks, job, and status, it doesn't stop to consider his emotional demeanor. And that's asking for trouble in the fullness of a shared life.

Like a heroine in any Dickensian novel, she begins the relationship with great expectations. He's handsome, well bred, and a pillar of society with a good name and presumed wealth—and yet, she really doesn't know much about his character.

In other words, she's interested in him for all the wrong reasons.

That said, when the situation proves him to be a detached, heartless cad and not the hero she imagined, their love moves from a dream cottage into a bleak house.

So how do you keep from making the wrong choice for all the wrong reasons? You don't let unfounded emotions dictate your actions. Instead, you assess your true needs.

 **He Said, She Said**

In a survey conducted between 1993 and 2000 by California State University/Sacramento, a full third of the 1,300 randomly selected adults claim they would reunite with their first loves if they could.

Defining Needs Versus Reacting to Emotions

Wishing for a great relationship is one thing, but recognizing it is something totally different. If you allow your emotions to choose the criteria for your mate, you'll end up with someone who will satisfy you in the short term but who may not be right for you in the long run. The same can be said for his feelings for you. If he chooses you to scratch an emotional itch—say, his ego—he may not feel the same about you after you've scratched it.

So how will you know whether you're reacting to an emotion such as fear, anger, or hurt as opposed to defining a need? The big hint: emotional reactions are impulsive, whereas a defined need is based on true consideration.

Here are some examples.

Emotional reaction: he must make lots of money.

Why you feel this way: you've been taught by your parents that money is a priority, or you've lived without good cash flow and you've convinced yourself that you'd rather be with *any* guy who has it—as opposed to a great one whose wallet is as empty as your own.

Why it shouldn't define the relationship: just because a man is good at making money doesn't mean that he is a great or kind person or that he shares his good fortune with his loved ones.

Defined need: he must take his responsibilities seriously.

How you've reached this decision: you're also adamant about reaching your goals, and you seek a mate who understands and appreciates that.

Why it works in the long run: if both of you are of like minds in this regard, you'll work in tandem to create a financially secure and emotionally sound life together.

Emotional reaction: he must enjoy a particular type of music, be into a particular hobby, or be a fan of a particular team.

Why you feel this way: you feel these things define you and therefore should define him as well.

Why it shouldn't define the relationship: one particular factor or interest should never be the sole consideration for this very important life decision. Interests are easily cultivated or changed, and differing interests aren't what defines his character. Finding a loving and devoted mate is far more important.

Defined need: he must have the same moral and ethical outlook as me.

How you've reached this decision: you've dated your fair share of selfish creeps regardless of their particular interests. You've made up your mind that the right guy for you won't lie, cheat, steal, or be cruel to others.

Why it works in the long run: in love, you must focus on the big picture.

Dating 911

If you want to be treated like a lady, act like one. If he wanted to be out with the boys, he wouldn't be there with you—so keep the belching as a novelty trick for your gal pals.

Emotional reaction: he has to be able to say, "I love you."

Why you feel this way: your past experience was with men who could never commit, let alone respond, "I love you" when you honor him with that term of endearment, or even demonstrate it with random acts of passion.

Why it shouldn't define the relationship: love is demonstrated in many ways that go beyond the phrase, "I love you," let alone flowers and candy hearts. Men learn the language of romance over time. That's why his true actions speak louder than his words.

Defined need: he must be passionate about us.

How you've reached this decision: you've been in too many relationships where a man's feelings about you were half-hearted. He said few words and wasn't passionate in the least.

Why it works in the long run: to have a chance at a lifetime of love, you must be involved with someone who is as vested in that concept as you—and shows it with kisses, cuddling, hugging, hand-holding, and caresses (as well as sex).

Emotional reaction: the sex has got to be great.

Why you feel this way: past lovers have left you dissatisfied. They've been more into pleasing themselves, or the sex was the only thing you had in common—but he was gone shortly after.

Why it shouldn't define the relationship: yes, sex is a very important component of love, but there is more to love than sex. There is also passion and desire, which are demonstrated both in and out of bed.

Defined need: he must find me sexy.

How you've reached this decision: it takes two to have great sex. If he's turned on by you, it'll show in the bedroom.

Why it works in the long run: a man who desires you will always be *in* love with you as well as *love* you.

He's a Keeper if ...

... he likes you as well as loves you. If you plan on growing old together, friendship is important in a relationship. To say that the man you love is your best friend is the highest compliment you can pay him (even more than "he's the best lover I ever had").

Making Your List, Checking It Twice

It's time to make your criteria list. Here's how you get started:

1. Take a piece of paper and a pencil. (You'll need an eraser, so skip the pen.)

2. You have needs. It's time for you to define them. Your needs may or may not include the following:

    ◆ He has a great sense of humor.

    ◆ He likes kids.

    ◆ He doesn't care how much I make.

    ◆ He loves to travel.

    ◆ He feels comfortable around my parents.

    ◆ He likes my friends.

    ◆ He volunteers for something.

    Why are these needs? Because they define a person's character as opposed to his looks, material possessions, or his position in life—all of which can change over time. Character, on the other hand, is a constant.

    So how long should your list be? If you don't have at least 10 important criteria on your list, it's unlikely that you'll ever find your Mr. Right. That said, if you have more than 20, you'll need to pare it down some.

3. Whatever number of items on your final list, your next step is to put them in order of priority. Only you know what character facets of your potential Mr. Right are the most important to you. Start by using the sample items we gave you. As an example, a sense of humor may rank below his ability to get along with your folks—just like his enjoyment of travel may be higher on your scale than his openness for volunteering. Of course, if you're afraid to fly but spend every Thanksgiving at a soup kitchen, the reverse may be true.

The goal is, quite simply, to have a very clear definition of the man you're looking for. You'll be attracted to men who meet none, some, or all of the criteria on your list. The best choice for you will be the one who comes closest to it. And guess what? You'll be his first choice, too.

4. When you're done, put your list in a drawer and forget about it … at least, for a week. When that week is over, pull it out again and reread it. Do its individual points still resonate with you? Would you shuffle any items around? If so, make those changes. And then put the list away again in a safe place. Trust that you'll remember it—maybe not verbatim, but certainly enough to recognize a few right Mr. Rights when they cross your path.

It's okay to revise your list periodically. You'll find that the experiences you have either reinforce your resolve to follow the list, or give you reason to modify it. Being open to change will bring you closer to your Mr. Right.

Dating 911

Men like smart women who know what's happening in the world. In fact, a 2005 Current Population Survey showed that women with graduate degrees who are unmarried at age 30 have a 75 percent chance of marrying their Mr. Rights by age 40, compared to the 66 percent chance of those women with lesser or no degrees. So go on … impress him!

Mr. Right Visualization Exercise

If you've gotten this far, you're serious in your intent to find your soul mate. Well … don't stop now! Trust us—he's a lot closer than you probably think.

In fact, with your five senses, you should try your hardest to *visualize* your Mr. Right. *He is very, very real.* In truly passionate relationships, every part of you feels alive. All of your senses are on, 24/7. The chemistry that is taking place between the two of you is very real and palpable—as is the love.

So yes, you can sense the taste of his lips and the scent of his neck. Write down what it's like: a musky aftershave or sweet sweat? Is it like fine wine or a warm summer night? Don't laugh. If he's real to you, you'll be real to him, too—when the time is right.

He's a Keeper if ...

... he's willing to talk out his issues. You'll always be frustrated if you choose a man who holds his feelings in or disappears because he can't express them—or worse yet, that he isn't ready to work on this most important communication issue. Talking in a relationship is important!

You still have three more senses to manifest: what he sounds like; what he feels like when your hands roam over his shoulders, his face, his hair, and then the rest of his body; and what he looks like.

Do yourself a favor: leave his looks for last. Whereas it may turn out that he looks exactly as you envisioned, looks are invariably deceiving. Besides, you can't see a soul—you can only sense its presence.

The Least You Need to Know

◆ Be it consciously or subconsciously, every woman who has claimed her Mr. Right once envisioned the criteria most important to her happiness in a relationship.

◆ Forget any wish list based on emotional whims! Your own list will be made up of the kinds of character traits your Mr. Right should embody in order to meet your defined needs.

◆ Don't get sidetracked with a man's looks, job, or status. These variables have nothing to do with his character and can change with time. Only his character is a constant.

◆ Your criteria list should include about 10 to 14 character traits that meet your needs. Prioritize them. The more of them he meets, the more certain you can be that he's right for you.

◆ Use your senses to manifest your Mr. Right. If he's real to you, you'll be real to him, too.

Part 2

How to Tell Mr. Wrong from Mr. Right

Most of us have experienced the joy of a successful relationship and the inevitable pain when a relationship that we thought was a winner turns into a loser.

Thinking that you're with Mr. Right—only to find out that he's really Mr. Wrong—is one of love's cruelest twists of fate.

In this part, you learn a number of ways to identify the telltale signs that you're on the right path but in the company of the wrong guy. Even more importantly, you learn how to identify the unmistakable traits of great mates.

Chapter 6

Mr. Wrong Archetypes

In This Chapter

- ◆ All the wrong guys you'll ever meet
- ◆ Resetting your "Guy-Dar" for a direct hit
- ◆ How to tell whether he has Male Pattern Badness

Now that you've made your criteria list in Chapter 5, the next step on your journey toward finding Mr. Right is establishing internal radar—call it "Guy-Dar"—that warns you if the guy you're attracted to isn't right for you. After all, the last thing you need is a broken heart.

The Usual Suspects

Here are the most common Mr. Wrong archetypes. All of these commit some degree of Male Pattern Badness. You may not have run into some of these, but they are out there. Here's how you'll recognize them.

The Dude

How you'll recognize him: he's the guy who comes on slowly—or, more than likely, lets you come on to *him*. He doesn't need to flirt because he exudes a *joie de vivre* that draws people (yes, women) to him like moths to a flame. He lives life to the fullest: he has been many places and has had many interesting experiences and quite a few wild and crazy adventures. He has tried it all. And yes, that means he has quite a few vices, too.

> ### He's a Keeper if ...
>
> ... he's considerate of your feelings. As past experience has shown you, not all men realize when they've crossed a line. A man who can read your nuances and respect them is one who loves you.

What you'll like about him: he's a free soul. He's easy-going and doesn't let anything get his goat. He knows how to lighten up a tense situation. He's the calm in the center of the storm. He has many friends—and, needless to say, many ex-girlfriends (some with whom he has also stayed friendly). He's a great lover ... perhaps one of the best you'll ever have.

Why you'll fall for him: he's the free spirit you always hoped you'd be. But because you have a real life with real responsibilities, it's just not a good match. You need a mature man—and that just isn't the Dude.

How he'll break your heart: he'll tell you how special you are to him and how much you mean to him, but he'll never commit. You'll want him all to yourself—then discover that you're sharing him with other women. When you get upset and jealous, he'll laugh at you or get annoyed that your attitude is such a downer. How can you plan a future with a guy who casts his fate to the wind and who doesn't want any obligations— let alone a wife?

The Player

How you'll recognize him: suave and sophisticated, he looks, acts, and dresses like he knows he's a winner. He's always in the power seat in any situation. He's a diva: things have to be perfect, in their place, as ordered by him. Don't make him angry, and certainly don't cross him or there will be hell to pay. He's got the best car, the best shoes, drinks the best wine, and always has the best seat in the house. He has an entourage that dotes on him, laughs at his jokes, and assures him that he's special.

What you'll like about him: he'll treat you like a princess: ply you with a flurry of roses and gifts, call you every hour on the hour, and come on like gangbusters. When you're at his side, you'll always feel special—and you are, because he only goes out with women who he deems worthy.

Why you'll fall for him: he is the closest thing to a second daddy that you'll ever have. And because you were always daddy's little girl, it strikes you as a very safe place to be—until you realize that he's *not* your daddy, nor does he want to be. He doesn't even want to commit to you in the long run. Unlike Daddy, he can't be there when you need him most.

How he'll break your heart: in time, he'll get restless. So many women, so little time—and he's a conqueror who needs constant conquests. When he drops you, it'll be quick and without an explanation. He'll just disappear. But it won't be *his* fault, according to him. After all, you couldn't keep up with him. You became boring, bitchy … a real drag. But it was fun while it lasted, right babe? (Yeah … until you ran into him and his new "arm charm.")

> **He Said, She Said**
>
> According to a 2006 survey by the Association for Behavioral and Cognitive Therapies, the lifetime rate of infidelity for men older than 60 is 28 percent, compared to 15 percent of women the same age—which is up from 5 percent in 1991.

The FWB ("Friend with Benefits")

How you'll recognize him: it'll be lust at first sight. The minute your eyes lock, there will be an electric current that flows between the two of you. Forget small talk. It's a full-court flirt. There will be nothing at all subtle about the innuendos flying between you. He'll undress you with his eyes—and you'll love every moment of it. When he says, "Can I give you a ride home?", you'll answer, "I thought you'd never ask."

What you'll like about him: the sex. He's sensual and knows how to hit all your hot buttons. Nothing is quick, although most of it is down and dirty. He won't ask a lot of questions, and that's okay. Your mind is too busy thinking up naughty ways in which to please him. You'll never get enough of him. He's your lost weekend (or two, or three, or perennial ...).

Why you'll fall for him: the sex. But when you dig down deeper to find the person, you'll come up empty. You want a full, well-rounded relationship, but you're not going to have it with him.

How he'll break your heart: wham, bam, thank you ma'am—he's in and out of there. There's no post-coital cuddling for this man. Seriously—he barely wants to know your name.

Even if the relationship rolls on for a few months or so, and even if he agrees to stay the night, he won't make himself comfortable in your home and will rush out the door as soon as you'll let him. (By the way, have you ever seen his place? Or does he insist on always meeting you at yours? Major red flag! See the next Mr. Wrong archetype, The Other Woman's Guy.) As for going out on a real date, forget about it! If you even hint around about it, he's out of there! The bottom line: he'll never, ever commit. To him, it's all about fun and games. The minute you presume anything else, the fun ends.

Dating 911

Don't have sex too early. Wait until you get to know each other. It will mean more to you both—*particularly* if he's your Mr. Right.

The Other Woman's Guy

How you'll recognize him: he's by himself; there's no posse to trip him up. He knows all the trendy watering holes because they're the best pick-up joints ... a great place to try out all his best pick-up lines. He scans the room, but when he sees you, he acts as if he has found the love of his life and moves in fast. He exudes charisma, but he comes off as vulnerable and totally self-deprecating: the joke is on him, and he doesn't mind because he's just so honored to be with you.

What you'll like about him: he's witty and charming. He mesmerizes you as he looks deep into your eyes, and yes, you truly believe he feels your pain. When he's got you in his sights, he comes on strong and gets right to the point: he has been looking for a woman like you all his life. And yeah, despite your best judgment that all of this is happening too fast, you actually believe him.

Why you'll fall for him: he comes on so strong, and he has to—because he's on a very short leash with the legitimate woman in his life. But this will not be long-lived—unless, in a moment of candor, he comes clean and you're stupid enough to agree to be his covert Other Woman. You're not *that* desperate, are you?

How he'll break your heart: it will become obvious real fast (to your friends, if not to you) that something just isn't right about him. Maybe it's the fact that he only wants to meet you at your place and that he deflects your very direct questions about his life with jokes, questions about you, or half-truths that come out when he slips up. Then comes the day that you find out he has a long-time girlfriend (or worse yet, he's married). Now, everything falls into place (except for all the broken pieces of your heart). *That* will take a long time to heal.

> **He Said, She Said**
>
> All love shifts and changes. I don't know if you can be wholeheartedly in love all the time.
>
> —Julie Andrews, actress and singer

The Liar

How you'll recognize him: he makes himself the biggest guy in the room. He has an answer to everything, and he wants everyone to know it. He's a yes man, a can-do guy, Johnny-on-the-spot, and the Answer Man. He exudes confidence—and yet, something's just not right (although you can't exactly put your finger on it).

What you'll like about him: he'll make you feel as if you're the only woman in the world. He'll insist on taking charge of everything in your life: your dates, your troubles at work, your issues with your family and friends, and even your finances. You'll love his coddling so much that you'll just lean back and let him take over all those nagging little details that slow you down. He lives to be indispensible.

Why you'll fall for him: you'll want to believe all of his sweet talk because he tells lies so convincingly. You're bored, lonely, and ready for a man to sweep you off your feet and take control of your life. Well guess what? *He's just not the right guy.*

How he'll break your heart: you'll discover that practically everything that has come out of his mouth has been a lie—that he isn't who he claimed to be. In fact, he hasn't done anything he said he'd do on your behalf—except maybe create rifts between you and your family and friends (who, in all probability, have not trusted him since day one).

The Company Man

How you'll recognize him: he's the guy with the tie that is loosened the moment he walks into the room. Others come up to him and slap him on the back. The assistants find any excuse to say something to him and to bat their eyes at him. The boss seeks out his opinion. Yep, he's a winner alright!

What you'll like about him: he's a hard worker, respected by his peers, looks great in a suit, and exudes the kind of confidence that turns you on. You've actually seen him in action in the boardroom or on a sales call—not to mention after hours, when he celebrates his latest triumph at the office's local watering hole.

Why you'll fall for him: he's the consummate salesman. So of course the very moment he has made up his mind that he wants to win you over, he'll approach that endeavor like a new account: seeking you out, making you feel important, wooing you to the hilt, breaking down all your arguments and defenses, and then coming in for the close.

How he'll break your heart: he's married—to his job. And because it is his one and only identity, you'll never come first no matter how hard you try. Late nights at the office will be a given. Forgotten dates will be par for the course. His boss and his clients will always come first. He'll be out of town when you need him most. This isn't a relationship; it's a convenient booty call. Instead, give yourself a promotion to a full-time boyfriend.

The Little Boy

How you'll recognize him: he'll be the sweet, stumbling, stuttering, helpless guy in the room (think Hugh Grant in *Four Weddings and a Funeral*). He seems vulnerable but not completely helpless—just needy enough to win the sympathies of some of the more caring women in the room, including you. And because he is intelligent and so totally nonthreatening, you easily get sucked in.

What you'll like about him: he'll win you over by the way in which he hangs on your every word and when he actually enjoys your strong mothering instincts. In fact, he allows you to take care of him, to coddle him, and to tell him what to do and when.

Why you'll fall for him: he makes you feel as if you are the most important person in his life. You'll presume that he can't live without you, which makes him even more precious to you: no man ever needed you as badly. And like a little boy, he brings you trifles to show his appreciation. How sweet!

How he'll break your heart: no matter how immature he is, he still thinks of himself as a man—so eventually he'll resent the fact that you interfere in every aspect of his life. But like a child, he'd rather pout or run away than face you with the news that he's fallen out of love with you (and in love with someone else, who's just as willing to baby him as you were).

 Dating 911

Take an interest in what he's talking about. Let him talk. Ask questions, and let him answer. If you show you're interested in what he has to say, he'll reciprocate.

The Tortured Soul

How you'll recognize him: he's a loner. He may not want to be bothered, but he knows how to make an entrance—which means he's certainly scrutinized by others in the room. He's the mad genius at school, the creative prodigy at work, that guy in the coffee shop who has a sense of mission about him—although he slouches in his chair and stares off into space.

What you'll like about him: his independence and the fact that he's not afraid to speak his mind, particularly at any injustice he witnesses. He believes deeply, and it shows in his actions as well as through his words. He'll put up a fight until he's the last man standing.

Why you'll fall for him: when he catches a glimpse of you, he's mesmerized. Needless to say, you can't keep your eyes off him. He talks in a very low voice, which makes you lean in even closer. When he touches you hesitantly, gently, a volt of electricity runs through you. He doesn't know the power he holds over you—or does he?

How he'll break your heart: he's moody, which always keeps you off balance. When he's angry, he's cold and distant. He will blame you for his poor decisions—including his addictions, which he doesn't even try to break. And when he plays his little blame game, his words will cut you like a knife. If you dare to disagree with him, you're a traitor and he'll treat you as one. You'll be exiled from his life for good, with no reprieve. Is he worth all this attention?

The Guy Who Thinks He's Too Good for You

How you'll recognize him: he's the best-dressed guy in the room. He holds his head up high. When he deems it necessary to speak, he'll drop a name or recall some impressive fact, locale, or event. Everyone wants to know him, to impress him, and to be his friend. Of course, all the women consider him a catch, and why not? He's the full package: pedigree, status, and confidence.

What you'll like about him: he comes across as magnanimous, gracious, and witty. He's smart and charming. He's not afraid to demonstrate his intelligence or stand his ground on the issues he feels are important. He's considered a stand-up kind of guy. He thinks highly of his family, and they are the ballast in his life. (And you know your mom would certainly be impressed!)

Why you'll fall for him: he will have chosen you over every other woman who was there vying for his attention. It's pure passion, and you know that because he can't keep his hands off you. That's fine with you. He's a gentleman out of the bedroom and an animal in it.

How he'll break your heart: he's obligated to marry someone who his family approves—and sorry, that's not you. He'll let you down easy unless you throw a fit, and then he'll turn his back on you for being an annoyance, for showing such poor taste, and for acting so "common." Your actions just proved him right. Call it a lose-lose situation.

The Uncharming Prince

How you'll recognize him: he's your ideal, your perfect guy, and the man of your dreams. No matter who he really is, this is what you'll see when you look at him. Now, if his actions match his looks, you're home free, right?

What you'll like about him: he's just too good to be true. He's there when you least expect him, but your cute meeting plays out like the fateful encounter that you always dreamed about. He says all the right things, and you must be, too, because he's hanging on your every word. Things couldn't go much better.

Why you'll fall for him: he, too, feels the electricity between you and is immediately at your side, trying to sweep you off your feet. He makes it obvious to everyone that you're worthy of his attentions—and because you live up to his ideal, he crowns you as his princess.

How he'll break your heart: didn't we say it was too good to be true? Didn't we tell you that no one is perfect? He proves it by falling off his white horse in the most unimaginable way possible: by being a frog rather than a prince.

He's a Keeper if ...

... he can show affection in public. A man who can easily kiss you or hold your hand in public proves he is comfortable with others recognizing your relationship.

Avoiding Male Pattern Badness

We aren't suggesting it's easy. We gave you 10 Mr. Wrong archetypes, and in your life you may have already encountered 2 or 3. In truth, as you can imagine, there are many more than that.

The best way to steer clear of these men is to look for these three "genetic" markers common to all Male Pattern Badness:

- Marker No. 1: he addresses his needs first before ever thinking of yours.

- Marker No. 2: he's inconsistent in his words and deeds, creating what you come to consider a trust deficit.

- Marker No. 3: when confronted with his inconsistencies, he doesn't care or makes excuses as to why it shouldn't matter to you.

The Least You Need to Know

- You'll meet many men in your life. All of them will have one or two great personality traits. But those traits may not make them great boyfriends, let alone great husbands.

- Don't be afraid to ask questions. Jump off his anecdotal tales with a few roundabout queries to which you already know the answers. That way, if he's lying, you can say goodbye and walk away.

- Watch for the classic markers of Male Pattern Badness. They're a sure sign that you're skating on thin ice.

Chapter 7

Telltale Signs That He's Mr. Wrong

In This Chapter

- ◆ Why it's not smart to be stupid about men

- ◆ Red flags that say, "Keep walking …"

- ◆ Don't be in denial about your Mr. Wrong

Tall, dark, and handsome. Broad-chested and deep-voiced. A full head of hair and a set of six-pack abs. All of these are features that invariably make a man attractive … on the outside, at least. As with the fairer sex, however, beauty is only skin deep. It's what's *inside* his head and his heart that truly counts.

Now that you're looking for your Mr. Right, don't just consider his body but also how his mind works: whether the idiosyncrasies of his personality mesh with your own and whether his character lives up to your expectations.

Ignorance Is *Not* Bliss

Before you buy a car, you scope out the models that appeal to you. Then, you do your research on its features, its gas mileage, and its performance record. And certainly, you take it for a test drive in order to make sure you like the ride.

So yes, you should also be "test driving" potential Mr. Rights. But first, you have to do your research. That means:

♦ **Lots of dating with a variety of men.** The more times up to bat, the more home runs you'll hit. The bottom line is that you have to get in the game.

♦ **Recognizing lemons.** You know, men who aren't worthy of your time and effort. The following section gives you some great clues that he is all wrong for you.

♦ **Assessing your dates based on your criteria list.** By keeping your criteria list (see Chapter 5) in mind, you'll end up with the Maserati of men: well-tuned to your needs and ready, willing, and able to give you the high performance you deserve.

> **He's a Keeper if ...**
>
> ... he likes to cuddle. A man who uses any excuse to jump out of bed immediately after lovemaking may not be capable of opening up emotionally—despite whatever great lovemaking you've experienced together. Sorry, but he's just not the full package.

Red Flags

If you want an honest, committed relationship, don't just listen to what comes out of your date's mouth. More important to you is how he treats you and the others in his life.

With that in mind, here are some red flags that indicate his baggage and how it's weighing down his life. Because you don't want to spend your life doing all the heavy lifting for him, keep these red-flag warnings close at hand.

You'll note that there is a red flag for every week of the year. While it would be tempting to memorize just one a week, keep in mind that doing so might mean waiting an *entire year* before realizing you're with Mr. Wrong.

That said, don't waste another minute. Take a look at this list. It's not in order of priority. They are *all* important:

- He drinks too much.
- He does drugs.
- He's married.
- Though he's fiscally fit and they are healthy, he still lives with his parents.
- He's always borrowing money from you, but never pays it back.
- He's obsessed with porn. In fact, he needs it to be intimate with you.
- He never remembers dates that are important to you.
- He hits you during sex, and can be physically aggressive out of the bedroom as well.
- He blames you for all the bad things that happen to him.
- You've consistently caught him lying to you.
- He has two or more ex-wives and he's younger than 40.
- He says he loves you but he isn't "in love" with you.
- He doesn't approve of your friends.
- He doesn't like your kids.
- He insists that you convert to his religion or he won't marry you.
- He always finds fault with how you look.
- Your friends don't like him.
- He refuses to meet your family and friends.
- He resents that you make more money than him.
- He plays too many mind games.

- He is still involved with his ex.

- He doesn't make your emotional or physical needs a priority.

- He has credit issues and doesn't care to resolve them.

- He angers easily, and too often.

- He refuses to deviate from set routines.

- No matter how hard you try, there is no sexual chemistry between you.

- He's a serial dater: he has a reputation of wooing them, loving them, and leaving them, without any reasons or farewells.

- He blatantly checks out other women in front of you.

He Said, She Said

Women, do you want to be around guys who put emotional pleasure before physical pleasure? Then stay in the United States. That's right! According to a 2007 survey discussed in the Archives of Sexual Behavior, emotional satisfaction rates high for 77 percent of American men as opposed to 69 percent of German men, 60 percent of French men, and 65 percent of South Americans.

- He puts work above everything else—especially you.

- He spends his money as quickly as he makes it and on frivolous things.

- He is obsessed with sex—with *and* without you.

- He won't introduce you to his family or friends.

- He has held on to pictures of his ex.

- He doesn't like to be around kids.

- He runs away from responsibility.

- He doesn't satisfy you sexually.

- He never compliments you.

- He is physically or verbally abusive.

- He always lets you down.

- He spends more on the upkeep of his car than on you.

- He makes fun of you in front of others.

- He prefers that you dress in a way that makes you uncomfortable.

- He lies to you about seeing other women.

- He wants you to have a boob job.

- He resents your closeness with your family.

- He has too many bad habits.

He's a Keeper if ...

> ... he apologizes when he knows he has acted unfairly. If he is mature enough to realize he didn't treat you with the respect you deserve and he's a big enough person to say he's sorry, then he is the kind of guy that deserves your forgiveness, so honor him with it.

Denial Wastes Time and Emotion

Let's say you think you've found the perfect guy, but he does have an issue (or two, or three) that appears on this red flag list. Or maybe he doesn't align exactly with your very own criteria list. Because you've spent practically your entire life looking for the right guy, you are so sorely tempted to put aside your concerns and just settle. Nobody's perfect, right?

That's true. Everyone has personality flaws. But remember this: you worked hard in creating a criteria list that is prioritized with the most important characteristics you seek in a man. If he doesn't match up to the first three or four, by your own accounting you won't be happy in that relationship.

 Dating 911

Don't talk about your ex on your date! No guy wants to hear your relationship history. And whatever you do, don't tell them how great the sex was with someone else!

So stick to your list. As for any red flags you find, if he can't or won't work through his issues, they will always stand between you. *You need to realize this.* You will have wasted time that would have been better spent finding—and enjoying—your real Mr. Right.

The Least You Need to Know

- ◆ Though physical attraction is what first catches your eye, it is how he thinks and acts, both toward you and others, that will prove he's truly your Mr. Right.

- ◆ Finding the right man is like finding the right car: you need to research, test drive, and avoid the lemons.

- ◆ There are numerous red flags that indicate he's carrying too much baggage for an honest, open relationship. If you don't take them to heart, you'll waste your time, energy, and emotions on too many Mr. Wrongs.

Chapter **8**

Timing Truly Is Everything

In This Chapter

◆ Finding the right guy, but the timing is off

◆ Why sticking it out with the wrong man is a mistake

◆ Revisiting a missed opportunity

It was as if you and that potential Mr. Right were on two ocean liners on some indigo sea, passing in the dead of night. If only, somehow, you could have reached out and touched each other! If only he could have pulled you on board with him and you could have sailed off into the night together.

Well, for one reason or another, it just didn't happen.

Perhaps you didn't realize he was right for you until it was too late for you to do something about it. Or perhaps you were right there, trying everything you could to get his attention, but he was preoccupied with some other issues (or some other woman).

Sounds like a scene from your favorite television show, right? Let's look at some scenarios.

Right Guy, Wrong Time

As we mentioned in Chapter 1, we take a lot of our relationship cues from popular culture. But our lives aren't soap operas or sitcoms. So that you'll do the right thing with your soul mate when you actually find him, read through the following scenarios, then consider the difference these fate-twisting script changes can make.

Scenario No. 1: Going from Coworker to Significant Other

Getting into character: you feel that you've found your soul mate across a crowded bull pen of workplace cubicles. You ask around about who is the cute guy in sales (or in accounting, or human resources, or whatever), only to learn that he's been asking about you, too. Every so often you meet in the break room and exchange small talk, inside jokes, and gossip, and sometimes you IM each other when you're bored with your day-to-day routines. But because you're involved with your current Mr. Wrong (and are in denial about it), you've convinced yourself that you're anything other than "just friends"—until it's too late.

> **Dating 911**
>
> Everyone has a secret or two that they may want to keep to themselves. But a man who insists on keeping every facet of his past from you is hiding something important, and that's not a good start to a relationship. If he won't open up, move on.

Going off script: if your friendship is something that puts a smile on your face every time you see him (and does for him as well), if you dread working on the days when you know he's going to be out of the office, and if your feelings about this guy are as strong as you think they are, it's time to speak up. Invite him out for a drink after work. Let him know what you're thinking. The worst he can say is that he's flattered but wants to keep things just friends. The best scenario is that he feels the same way you do. Then, you have the makings of a perfect merger.

Scenario No. 2: Moving from Friend to Lover

Getting into character: he's the goofy guy from next door or someone you've known all your life: sweet, funny, cute, and there whenever you need a shoulder to cry on. He has seen the guys you've dated and laughed with you at all those Mr. Wrongs. You've been there, too, when the women in his life have left him high and dry. You have what you assume is a crush on him, but you deny that it can go any further because it would break your heart to lose him, based on the fear that nothing will ever be the same between you. So what are you supposed to do now—watch some other girl lasso his heart and walk down the aisle with him? No way!

Going off script: it's time to take things into your own hands. Look fabulous whenever you see him—even if it's just in the laundry room. Invite him over to watch ESPN and eat Chinese food. Flirt with him. Go to the neighborhood pub with him. Oh yeah, and did we say flirt with him? He'll get the hint: you're willing to be more than just a friend.

He Said, She Said

In a 2008 University of Aberdeen study of sexual attraction based on facial features, those facing the viewer directly were judged more attractive than faces with distracted gazes. This effect was particularly pronounced if the face was smiling.

Scenario No. 3: Infidelity

Getting into character: warp speed some 15 years into the future, when some guy is fondly reminiscing with his two children about his relationship with their mom—*and it's not you.* Unfortunately, he loved you but dropped you—because you slept with his best friend. True, his pal broke the "Bro Code," and so rightly he deserved to be banished from your true love's posse. But you broke the "Girlfriend Code," and he's now "The One Who Got Away Because of Your Stupidity."

Going off script: there is no time machine, so you can't go back and undo what happened. You can, however, beg his forgiveness. And if he will take you back, you can suggest joint counseling so that any unresolved anger he has over what happened will be discussed, openly and honestly, so that the two of you can move on in your relationship together. If, however, he sticks to his decision to banish you from his life, you'll have to live with that—and learn the lesson that trust is the one cornerstone of any relationship that can't be broken.

In fact, if you have doubts as to why you're in the relationship, it's better to take a break from it and revisit it after you've thought it through than to kill the relationship with some irreparable act or lie.

Scenario No. 4: Abandonment Issues

Getting into character: he's dreamy, all right. But he has major baggage—say, an ex-wife who wants him back. But he'll do anything to make it work with you, so why do you keep pushing him away? True, you have abandonment issues: one parent was a workaholic or left when you were young. But why are you gun shy when happiness is staring you in the face? Life is too short!

Going off script: this is one truth we'll repeat again and again: no relationship is perfect. Recognizing this fact, you have one mandate: do what you can to put your fears and anxieties of failure and abandonment aside as well as any thoughts that you aren't worthy of the happiness that could be yours if you'd just stop being ambivalent about him. Yes, you deserve happiness with the right man—the man who is willing to work on a great union with you.

> **He's a Keeper if …**
>
> … he honors your emotional borders. A man who knows when to back off when you aren't ready to talk is someone who respects your feelings and deserves your appreciation.

Scenario No. 5: Traumatic Event

Getting into character: what's more important, your job or your relationship? If you feel neglected by your significant other, should you find solace in the arms of another? Do you fight to get noticed, or let some other woman get the man of your dreams?

Going off script: even if a relationship starts on the right foot, a traumatic event can tear it apart. If one partner blames the other for the cause or effect of a catastrophic event, it will take time to rebuild the trust that was once there—and that will take counseling.

Wrong Guy, Right Time

You're working and living at your personal best. But something is missing: someone to share all your successes and accomplishments. As you look around, you realize that while your friends and family applaud you, they aren't there with you to savor your victories when the lights are out. You want what others have: happiness in the arms of a committed partner!

Well, you certainly won't have that if you're with the wrong guy.

We've already given you a list of red flags in Chapter 7 that indicate why he won't make you happy. If you're still sitting on the fence because you'd like to believe that a mediocre relationship is better than no relationship at all, we're hoping these 10 reasons will change your mind:

- If you're hanging in there with the wrong guy, you'll never find the right guy.

- Your life won't be truly happy if you're always conceding to his wishes.

- His inability to agree with you on major life decisions, such as whether or not to have kids or where you want to live, means you'll never live the life you dreamed you'd have.

- He could be holding you back from your true potential in more ways than you know.

- Besides your own happiness, your Mr. Wrong may be trampling on the well-being of those who love you and realize your dilemma.

- The farther you go down the wrong path, the more difficult it is to get back to the journey you should be sharing with your true soul mate.

◆ If, for whatever reason, he decides to leave you instead of the other way around, you'll blame yourself for not seeing it coming and for wasting all that time.

◆ Although on some level you know he's Mr. Wrong, you cheat on him and feel guilty afterward. Now you're in the wrong relationship with the wrong guy and feeling guilty as well! This is going nowhere but downhill. It's time to develop an exit strategy and follow through.

> **Dating 911**
>
> Arrive on time. Doing so shows him that you have respect for his time. Otherwise, he has every right to be disappointed and dump you for someone who looks at her watch every now and then.

◆ You're never going to be able to give the best to a relationship that you don't believe in.

◆ Life is too short for silly, stubborn, or fear-driven mistakes—especially when it comes to love.

Reconnecting with a Missed Opportunity

If for any reason you feel that you and your Mr. Right have been separated by a few missteps, by all means get back into his life! Here are five examples as to why you should quit futzing around and go for it.

You're separated by a city/state/ocean.

Solution: make him your vacation destination.

Call ahead to catch up. Find out how life is treating him. Tell him you want him to be your tour guide. Absence has made the heart grow fonder, and romance blooms away from home (yours). With you back in his life—even for a few days—he'll remember all the things he loved about you in the first place. And while you're there, check out the want ads for a job that puts you back inside his orbit.

You broke up over some silly argument.

Solution: send up a signal that indicates you want to smoke a peace pipe.

There are thousands of great relationships that break off before they have a chance to develop—all because of some stupid disagreement. You probably don't even remember what you fought over. And at this point, who cares who was right or wrong?

The spark was there once and is probably still there, so pick up the phone and give him a call. It's possible he feels like you: that the blow-up wasn't worth losing your friendship over. And who knows? You may be very surprised by what develops from there.

He broke your heart when he left you for another woman—then realized his mistake. But by then it was too late and you'd moved on.

Solution: granted, the fact that he regrets that you were the one who got away and now wants to reconnect doesn't alleviate the hurt from when he kicked you to the curb. Still, if you are now ready to let bygones be bygones, ask for what you need to do so, with grace: a heartfelt apology.

Invite him out for a drink. Look fabulous. Be the scintillating wit he remembers. At the same time, don't be afraid to ask for what you need. If he mans up, graciously assure him that there are no hard feelings and both of you can begin again with a clean slate.

You and your high school sweetheart went your separate ways.

Solution: now that you're both single again, attend your reunion.

If you're thinking, "Is he worth pursuing now?", you'll never know unless you show up. In fact, call or e-mail him that you plan on doing so and that you hope he'll save you a dance or two. That's one way to keep it casual, but it also ensures that he'll come stag.

By all means, check this guy out. But be forewarned: if you're searching for the boy you once knew, you'll miss the man he is today. If he has become the kind of man who meets the criteria you've learned to set for a potential Mr. Right, follow your instincts and stay by his side. If he has developed into Mr. Wrong, have some punch, share a few laughs, and tell him that you'll catch up with him again at your next reunion.

He was an office colleague you enjoyed and trusted but let slip through your fingers because you were already involved with someone else.

Solution: now you're free, find an excuse to intercept him at his new work assignment. Timing is like a roll of the dice: sometimes it goes your way and sometimes it doesn't, so go out and make your own luck. Get into his space and in front of his face. You know how to let him know that you're now available and interested. See whether he follows your lead.

Dating 911

Don't string along a Mr. Wrong. Just because you don't have anyone else at the moment is no reason to leave the poor guy hanging. If the chemistry isn't there, cut your losses and move on.

The Least You Need to Know

◆ Make your own happy ending. Even if the timing is off, if the man is right, you can and should do your best to make it work.

◆ Fear of loneliness is no reason to stay with a Mr. Wrong, as opposed to being available and actively seeking your Mr. Right.

◆ When it comes to missed opportunities with a potential Mr. Right, never say never. If you put your head to it, you can always find a reason to get back into his life.

Part 3

Finding Your Mr. Right

Now that you've gotten stronger by "eating your relationship vegetables," you're ready to move on to the main course: finding that one guy who is going to share with you the relationship you have always deserved and worked so hard to achieve.

It's time to discuss not only the 99 best places to meet your Mr. Right and how to best catch his eye but also what you can do to make sure that your new Mr. Right stays as interested in you as you are in him.

Chapter 9

Traits of Great Mates

In This Chapter

- ◆ The four cornerstones of a healthy relationship
- ◆ Other important traits of great mates
- ◆ Moving beyond your mistakes

Ideally, the man who will attract you most will be the embodiment of the characteristics that ensure an emotionally happy relationship for both of you.

Will you know him when you meet him? That depends. To ensure that you know who you should be looking for, you first have to identify those traits that mean the most to you—and we help you do just that in this chapter.

Spotting Your Mr. Right

Realistically, while he won't have all the qualities you need, hopefully he'll have some of the most important ones. You're now thinking, "How will I know whether he's the real deal?"

You'll know by how he treats you and others; his actions in everyday situations are the best test for assessing his ability to make you happy in the long term.

To give you a head start, we've listed our Top Ten Great Mate Traits. The first four are, in our minds, the most important. The others are the icing on the cake. If he also embodies these additional traits, then you have yourself a champ. We'll leave it to you to prioritize which of those additional traits mean the most to you.

Trait No. 1: Honesty

Why it's important: of all the traits listed here, this is the one no relationship can do without. Because honesty gauges your ability to trust your partner, it is the first of the four cornerstones on which the foundation of your mutual commitment is built.

> **He's a Keeper if ...**
>
> ... he likes your body just the way it is. No man should make you alter your physical appearance to suit his desires. If he insists that you physically change something, take the hint: he doesn't want you ... he wants someone else.

Maybe you've been in a relationship or two with a guy who you didn't completely trust? Possibly he hid his actions from you then lied—even when you unwittingly questioned him. Only when he was directly confronted with proof did he confess—usually with some heartfelt excuse as to why he did it in the first place or why he felt he couldn't confide in the one person he supposedly loved and trusted the most: *you.*

Of course, that only reinforced your belief that he couldn't be trusted. Possibly it affected your view of the other men who followed.

And you know what? *That's okay*—if you temper your instinct to project his horrid actions on all the other men who walk into your life. When you paint all men with the same brush, you greatly hurt your chances of finding and keeping a happy and healthy relationship. No doubt he wasn't an anomaly; but more importantly, he was a lesson well learned.

How you'll know he has it: because you will rarely (if ever) catch him in a lie. And when describing him, his friends will use terms such as, "a straight-up guy," "true blue," or "a man of his word." Speaking of friends, he seems to have a lot of them. That's because they too appreciate this very characteristic of his personality.

We know what you're thinking: "Do little white lies count, or is it just the whoppers I should be concerned about?"

We'll answer with a question of our own: Why is the lie—no matter how tiny—needed in the first place? Unless it involves a surprise birthday party for you, there shouldn't be any reason for him to keep the truth from you. And the same goes for you.

No one is asking that he or you take a nightly polygraph test. And the fact that he wanted to stay and watch the last quarter of the football game with his buddies, and in truth he wasn't delayed by "heavy traffic," is not cause for hiring a special prosecutor!

But telling the truth about consequential matters goes to the heart of a quality relationship. All of his (and your) prior missteps are old news. You're moving into this new life together: with honesty and candor. And that alone is priceless.

Dating 911

Remember to say "thank you." Hey, you learned it when you were three. It's as important now as it was then. Nothing is more of a turn-off than someone taking your generosity for granted.

Trait No. 2: Respect

Why it's important: this is the second of the four cornerstone traits needed in every happy relationship. If he doesn't respect your needs, your opinions, your dreams, or your desires, you'll only be filled with doubts as to your own abilities—at least, as long as you're together. (And frankly, if you have any self-respect, that won't be very long.) Considering how hard you've worked for what you have in life, of course you'd expect the person at your side to demonstrate his appreciation of what you've accomplished.

How you'll know he has it: he's the first one you call with good news. That makes lots of sense, because he's also the first one to give you a nod of the head, a thumbs-up, or a cheer when he hears your great news. He's always excited for you, and he enjoys listening to your plans and your dreams. He lets you unload your concerns, never shrugging you off or laughing at you. He's the best cheerleader on your team. He asks your opinion on some issues in his life and takes your words to heart.

Trait No. 3: Romantic Passion

Why it's important: every woman wants to be in love. And just as importantly, every woman needs to know she's loved, too. Passion is the feeling he has for the love you share. Romance is the random acts of appreciation that demonstrate his love for you. We're combining these two traits because they are intertwined in their cause and effect on your lives together.

How you'll know he has it: that look of anticipation that lights up his eyes when you enter the room makes your heart sing. The gentle brush of his hand on your arm sends an exciting tingle through you. When he caresses your ear with his lips as he whispers, "I love you," you can't help but answer with a gentle kiss. If he leaves you sweet notes (in cards, e-mails, or written on a steamy bathroom mirror), you long to be with him right then and there. He remembers all the special occasions and anniversaries you've shared. He makes dates and keeps them. He treats you like a lady, both in public and in private. He showers you with unexpected surprises, be they flowers or small tokens from his heart. Doing all of this, some of this, or even just one of these things speaks volumes about his love for you.

And that's the point: he loves you, and he's not afraid to show it.

Dating 911

Give him some breathing room. If your potential Mr. Right is not giving you the okay to move into his personal space, respect that. You may want the relationship to become physical, but he may not be there yet.

If you have a man in mind, but you've noticed that he embodies none of these traits, don't make excuses as to why he could be your Mr. Right. Bottom line: he isn't. You may not want to believe that, but if you hang in there, in time you'll find this out the hard way. Why waste precious time on an obvious Mr. Wrong, when you should be looking for Mr. Right?

Trait No. 4: Commitment

Why it's important: you'll meet men who will love you. Some will profess to be *in love* with you. But if he isn't willing to commit to sharing his life with you, *he isn't your Mr. Right.*

You've had boyfriends. And as you grew older, the comfort level you achieved with one or more of these men led you both into exclusivity but not necessarily into a commitment to move the relationship to a permanent union.

Well, that's what commitment is all about.

Without that very necessary fourth cornerstone of commitment, your relationship topples back down into that dusty dating road. No amount of passion or romance can heal your heart when, with the honesty you've come to know and appreciate, he tells you, "Sorry, I just can't commit to spending the rest of my life with you."

And just forget about trust. Knowing he can't commit to you, you now wonder whether there is someone else out there who will win that all-important commitment from him.

How you'll know he has it: he's at your side in good times and bad. He shares his worldly possessions with you. He asks you to marry him and looks forward to that day. After your wedding, he treats you as his partner and his soul mate.

> **He Said, She Said**
>
> I believe that two people are connected at the heart, and it doesn't matter what you do, or who you are or where you live; there are no boundaries or barriers if two people are destined to be together.
>
> —Julia Roberts, actress

Trait No. 5: Compassion

Why it's important: a guy who is selfish and inconsiderate is not worth your time or effort, no matter what his other (and hopefully more admirable) qualities. On the other hand, his lack of compassion can be a sign that he is greatly in need of a woman's guiding touch. Even if he doesn't show it now, it's worth the cultivation if you're confident he can evolve, because a man who is compassionate is worth his weight in gold.

How you'll know he has it: he's interested in his surroundings. He doesn't stick to his posse but instead makes it a point to work the room and to engage everyone around him, whether he knows them or not. He gives to charities. He volunteers his time. He palms a dollar to the homeless guy sitting on the curb. He has a wide-open heart, which is why you love him.

Trait No. 6: Humor

Why it's important: any man who isn't able to smile (not smirk) isn't going to be a comfort to you when you need it most. It proves his optimism in the face of adversity. It shows that he doesn't take himself too seriously. His ability to see the irony of any situation—even a bad one—allows you to put things into perspective as you filter your own anxieties. All of these are reasons why you should never underrate a sense of humor as a great mate trait.

How you'll know he has it: others light up when he enters the room. You see it in his smile. You hear it in his voice. His tone is upbeat, yes; but beyond that, there isn't any snarky malice. His laughter celebrates; it isn't cruel or malicious.

Trait No. 7: Sociability

Why it's important: if he's a loner but you're the life of the party, you'll be miserable keeping him company in his cabin in the woods. If he hates crowds but you're a social butterfly, eventually you'll resent him for keeping you in a cocoon, no matter how posh it is. If he prefers ordering in to eating out, one day you'll just run away with the delivery boy.

How you'll know he has it: he has a wide circle of friends. He knows how to throw great parties (even if the only thing on the menu is beer and pretzels). He knows how to be a good guest. (Yes, he brings a bottle of wine, flowers for the hostess, and writes thank-you notes afterward.) And he knows when the party is over (and when you want to take him home ...).

Trait No. 8: Patience

Why it's important: you should take all the time you need to deliberate on the most important decisions that affect your life. That said, the last thing you want—make that *need*—is a man who wants to rush you into some impetuous conclusion that you may regret later. And you certainly don't want to live with the consequences of his shoot-from-the-hip mistakes.

How you'll know he has it: it's not always "his way or the highway." He doesn't cajole you into his way of thinking all the time but instead lets you come to your own conclusions. He gives you the space you need to make up your own mind. And if you take a misstep, he doesn't rub your nose in it by saying, "I told you so."

 **He's a Keeper if ...**

... he knows how to forgive and forget. Ali MacGraw said it best in the movie *Love Story:* "Love never means having to say you're sorry ..." What she forgot to add was, "... again. And again. And again." If he's into holding a grudge, he's just not into you.

Trait No. 9: Control over His Emotions

Why it's important: a man who has a short fuse makes all those around him anxious and nervous. Why should you be afraid to speak your mind? If you're afraid that he'll take out his anger on you, then you've chosen someone who can cripple you emotionally. That's the last thing you need. Life is too short to have to tiptoe around your partner.

How you'll know he has it: if the two of you have a difference of opinion, he doesn't explode, curse, hit the wall, or slam his fist (God forbid, into your face). A man with self-control will go silent, ask for a time-out, and go walk around the block to cool off. By the time he gets back, he will have thought through a better way to position his point-of-view—or, at the very least, he'll be willing to come to a mutually agreed-upon consensus.

Trait No. 10: A Passion for Life

Why it's important: the French call it *joie de vivre*. And it can make a big difference in your shared enjoyment of life. It's great to be a steady and faithful guy who loves his job and his family and embodies all the other nine traits. At the same time, life can be so much tastier with a little spice on top. That comes from being with a guy who says, "Let's hit the road this weekend," or, "Let's go to a concert," or a million other things that can add spice to your life.

You can have a great guy, but if he comes home every night after work and says, "I'm exhausted," life's not going to be a barrel of laughs.

How you'll know he has it: that's easy: he's always up to something, and he's always suggesting some new interest, passion, or curiosity. As the expression goes, "We all go around just once in life. But only some of us are wise enough to live life to the fullest."

Fool You Twice, Shame on You

You now know what traits your Mr. Right should embody. When you think back on some of the men you've dated, probably you'll recall a few guys who had at least a few of those traits. But you aren't with them now because at least one (if not more) of them was missing.

Well, now you have no excuse to accept anything less than those four (and hopefully more) of these Ten Great Mate Traits in your next Mr. Right. It will take time to assess whether he is indeed blessed with some or most of these traits. Please do *not* be tempted to settle for less or to overlook the warning signs if a cornerstone trait is missing.

No one wants to take a boat with a hole in the bottom out on the lake. Get into the wrong relationship, and you will see it quickly sink. It has probably happened to you before, so just say "No" and don't let it happen again!

> **He Said, She Said**
>
> According to a 2007 survey of 600 singles conducted by Engage.com, 68 percent of respondents claimed to be interested in falling in love and getting married within the next five years.

The Least You Need to Know

◆ Great relationships take place with men who have at least these four cornerstone traits: honesty, respect, romantic passion, and commitment.

◆ If you're lucky, your Mr. Right will also have compassion for others, a great sense of humor, a strong drive for sociability, patience, a sense of control, and joy for life.

◆ Most of the men you're attracted to embody some of these traits. It's up to you to take the time to assess whether your possible Mr. Right has them. If you don't, you'll make a mistake that may cost you time and heartache—so don't rush the process!

Chapter 10

Ninety-Nine Places to Find Mr. Right

In This Chapter

- ◆ Oh, the places you'll go to find your soul mate!
- ◆ Why you need to get out there
- ◆ Making yourself more approachable

Putting yourself out there gives you more opportunities to find your Mr. Right—and for him to find you, too.

That said, we're going to give you a goal: go to at least one of these places each day. And yes, you can cheat and hit one of them more than once (although hopefully in a different locale).

Here's your motivation: it's very unlikely that Mr. Right is going to ring your doorbell and introduce himself. So don't wait for him to find you—get moving and get out there! Even if you don't find your Mr. Right, you'll be out doing things you enjoy—and doesn't that beat sitting around?

Where in the World Is Mr. Right?

At this very moment, your soul mate might be just a few blocks away. Here are 99 places he could be right now:

1. Sitting at a cozy bar inside a good restaurant.

2. Working at a fire station. (Tell him you want a few safety pamphlets!)

3. Breaking a sweat hoofing down a local jogging path.

4. Watching his nephew at a Little League game.

5. Doing research at your local library.

6. Shopping at a men's clothing sale. (If he asks, you're there buying a shirt for your brother.)

7. Arriving at the airport. (Take a good book and look like you're waiting for someone.)

Dating 911

Be adventurous. Even if your date has planned or wants to do something you don't think you would like to do, be positive and try it. You just might have fun.

8. Enjoying a jazz concert.

9. Waiting for a business appointment at a very busy, very elegant hotel lobby.

10. Sitting alone watching the surf hit the beach.

11. Having a quick bite at a down-home diner.

12. Inside city hall getting a building permit.

13. Applauding a pal at a public awards ceremony.

14. Doing laps at a community pool.

15. Enjoying a fast-moving game of tennis.

16. Helping at a park volunteer project. (The guys who show up at these generally have big hearts.)

17. Toasting your mutual friends' happiness at a wedding.

18. Cheering on his niece at a bat mitzvah.

19. Sipping a latté at a coffee shop that is not your usual hangout.

20. Getting out the rings around his collars at the Laundromat.

21. Trying to learn Italian in a continuing adult education class.

22. Checking out the new exhibit at your local museum.

23. Shoveling his fair share at the local gardening co-op.

24. Checking out the golf clubs at the country club's pro shop.

25. Trying to catch some rays on the deck of the good ship singles cruise.

26. Waiting in line at a book signing.

27. Reading his Sunday newspaper at your local park.

28. Going nuts for his team at a college football game.

29. Looking calm and breathing deeply at a yoga class.

30. Soaking up the scene at a busy theater opening night.

31. Putting his palette to the test at a wine tasting.

32. Swaying to the beat at a free outdoor concert.

33. Getting a rush watching the competition at a bicycle tour.

34. Reading the morning paper while on route on a ferry boat.

35. Reviewing items at the silent auction table of a charity ball.

36. Following the group on a historic walking tour.

37. Expanding his world view at a foreign film festival.

38. Playing a game of Frisbee on the local college campus.

39. Participating in a cooking demonstration.

40. Serving as the volunteer bartender at a party.

41. Waiting in line for a Shakespeare in the Park event.

42. Attending a friend's college graduation ceremony.

43. Shopping at a car dealership (and happy to share his opinion with you regarding good mileage).

44. Cheering for his team at a hockey, basketball, football, or baseball game (so many games, so little time!).

45. Pumping iron at the local gym.

46. Speaking to students as a volunteer docent at the local historical society.

47. Lost in the beauty of a symphony.

48. Shopping for seasonal produce at a farmer's market.

49. Browsing the shelves of a bookstore.

50. Heading up a steep hill with a local hiking club.

51. Working for any one of many local advocacy groups. (Here's a man involved in a cause hoping to expand his horizons.)

52. Checking out the honeydew melons at the grocery store.

53. Enjoying the fellowship of the weekly service at his place of worship.

54. Working the phones at campaign headquarters for his favorite candidate.

55. Putting price stickers on items at a local garage sale.

56. Walking the convention floor of an industry's trade association.

57. Participating at ComicCon. (Buyer beware!)

58. Laughing at a local comedy improv night.

59. Waiting behind you for a bag of popcorn at the neighborhood movie theater.

60. Checking out the latest gadgets at the Apple store (especially during the holidays).

61. Shooting a game of pool at a sports bar.

62. Picking strawberries at a pick-your-own market.

63. In the next lane at the bowling alley.

64. Looking for gold doubloons at a pirate festival. (Dress as a damsel in distress.)

65. Taking his chances at a casino.

66. Getting into a sweat at a morning spinning class.

67. Playing for your company's softball league.

68. Taking a scuba-diving class.

69. Shopping at a do-it-yourself store on a Saturday morning. (In fact, take a workshop there.)

70. Hanging out in the park playing a weekend game of chess.

71. Squeezing the trigger at the shooting range.

72. Feeling silly trying to line dance.

73. Playing golf with a couple of buddies. (Come as a single and get added to their threesome.)

74. Expanding his horizons in a photography class.

75. Participating in a self-help seminar.

76. Hooting and hollering at the rodeo.

77. Drinking a martini in a high-end hotel bar.

78. Listening to a guest speaker at a Rotary or Lions' Club meeting.

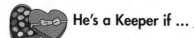

He's a Keeper if ...

... you feel as though he's your best friend. If you feel that comfortable with him, you're made for each other.

79. Looking for bargains at an art festival.

80. Getting off the Ferris wheel at the county fair.

81. Making a bid at an auction.

82. Working on improving his swing at a driving range.

83. Raising a hammer with Habitat for Humanity.

84. Serving sodas at the town picnic.

85. Taking a sailing class.

86. Helping out at a community pancake breakfast.

87. Sitting next to you all day in comedy driving school.

88. Eating a hotdog at a company picnic.

89. Enjoying a great rock concert.

90. Taking salsa lessons.

91. Admiring the chrome at a classic car show.

92. Watching a few of his favorite pros at a golf tournament.

93. Checking out some gear at your local sporting goods store.

94. On the sidelines at an adult soccer league game. (Rugby, cricket … it's all good.)

95. Taking a few swings at the batting cages.

96. Cheering along with the crowd at an air show.

> **He's a Keeper if …**
>
> … he always does what he says. A man who follows through on a promise proves that he's trustworthy. That speaks highly of his character.

97. Checking out the yachts at a marina or boat show.

98. Riding the rails (Observation cars aren't for scenery only.)

99. He's online, hoping that someone interesting is online, too (more about that in our next chapter).

What to Do Once You Get There

Walking into new places can be downright intimidating. You're wondering, "Do I stick it out? Do I look as if I belong? If I don't know what I'm doing, will I look stupid?"

Maybe you do. But guess what? Mr. Right will still be noticing you. He'll still be interested. And he'll still try to catch your eye.

When a male is interested in a female, it may flash across his mind, "What is she doing here?" A second later, his brain shifts gears and thinks, "I'm sure glad she's here!"

So when he does look your way, don't frown. Don't look nervous. Don't walk away, and don't feel as if you don't belong there. Instead, seek him out. Make eye contact. Smile wide. Go ahead and laugh. Send the message that you're willing to let him in on your secret—that you welcome him by your side. After all, that's why you're there, isn't it?

Three's Company

It takes nerve to get out of your comfort zone. It takes even more guts to mingle alone in some new venue—that is, without the physical support of your gal pals.

You may presume that there is safety in numbers, but consider how a gaggle of you and your friends—laughing and talking and totally engaged in each other—might look to a potential Mr. Right: in a word, intimidating. That said, don't be afraid to venture out alone. Even if you feel vulnerable doing so, to him you look more accessible than if you're with a group of friends. This puts you both one step closer to making contact, and perhaps changing the rest of your lives.

The Least You Need to Know

- Potential Mr. Rights are all around you. But if you stay home, you'll probably never meet him—so get out there!

- When you arrive, act as if you're happy to be there. He'll notice you immediately and make his move. And if he doesn't, you have a perfect excuse to talk to him: he can bring you up to speed on what's happening.

- Don't be too shy to go solo to new places and new ventures. Remember, the goal is to be accessible. You are more approachable without an entourage.

Chapter 11

You've Got Male! Hooking Him Online

In This Chapter

- ◆ The difference between dating services and social networks
- ◆ Making the most of your online profile
- ◆ Red flags in his online profile
- ◆ Why it's important to be honest online
- ◆ From virtual to reality: going offline with him

If you're serious about finding Mr. Right, you'll also have to get serious about online dating. Why? So many others are using it as a way to connect and communicate with their possible soul mates. In fact, according to a 2007 study by Mediamark Research, 2.5 million people participate in online dating in any given month—and 52 percent of these are men.

That's not to say the experience will be as easy as a click of a computer button. In no way does quantity translate into quality. And connecting with a potential Mr. Right at, say, Chemistry. com may not necessarily translate into face-to-face chemistry.

If you want to stand out so that your Mr. Right will somehow find you in this crowd, if you want to connect with a man whose relationship goals align with yours, you're going to have to learn the complexities of the Internet as a dating tool.

Dating Services Versus Social Networks

The many places to look for love online boggles the mind. According to the research firm Hitwise, there are over 1,400 online dating entities in the United States alone. So what's the difference between an online dating site and a social networking site? Knowing the answer to that question can save you time, effort, and money. More important, it can bring you closer to your prime objective: finding the best online venue (or two, or three) with a large enough pool of men—preferably in your town—who match up best with your criteria list (see Chapter 5).

He Said, She Said

According to a 2007 study by Comscore, 13 percent of all Americans who use a computer do so for online dating.

Dating Services

Yahoo! Personals. Match.com. Date.com. eHarmony. JDate. ChristianMingle. Amigo. Lavalife. Dreammates. Chemistry.com. OKCupid.com. There are thousands of online dating services serving some 40 million singles at any given point in time.

Sounds overwhelming, doesn't it? Not if you put it into perspective: online dating is just a personal marketing tool. It makes potential Mr. Rights aware of you and gives them a way to contact you.

But before the venues match you up with Mr. Right, you have to make a great match with the kind of online dating venue that will work best for you.

The subscriber fee, or number of members, should not be the only criteria from which you judge a dating service. You should also consider the kind of daters who are catered to by the site. For example, if you're looking for a long-term committed relationship, a site such as SeekingArrangement.com will certainly defeat that purpose, since it caters to daters for whom that goal is the furthest from their agendas. If you're Catholic, chances are you won't get a lot of action on JDate.com, which is a Jewish dating service. That said, your best bet is to compare their services as well as their fees.

Several dating services, such as DateHookup.com and MatchDoctor. com, are free. Keep in mind that the cheapest isn't always the worst—just as the most expensive isn't always the best.

Most dating services offer some type of online survey that, via some mathematical algorithm, quantifies your demographic information and your expressed needs and desires into a personal profile.

After that, how do they get you together? In the paid services, subscribers such as you and Mr. Right will peruse numerous profiles deemed great matches. He will read what you've written on your personal home page and scope out your photo or digital video clip. You'll do the same for his profile. If either person likes what they see, there are a variety of options for contact, including e-mail, instant messaging, online bulletin boards, and webcam chats.

Social Networking

Social networking sites are a bit different in that they allow members to:

♦ Join and build communities of both friends and strangers.

♦ Create groups within these communities.

♦ Blog.

♦ Upload photos.

♦ Send e-vites (online invitations) to others to join their private networks.

♦ Search community directories via categories for new and familiar faces.

♦ Text message other members who are online at the same time.

Some of the most extensive social networking sites include Facebook, MySpace, Friendster, Gather, Ning, and Eon. There are charges for some services, whereas in others building your community—or a

He Said, She Said

Before I met my husband, I'd never fallen in love. I'd stepped in it a few times.

—Rita Rudner, comedian

personal page or blog within a community—is free. These kinds of sites are a great way to network, find old friends, and make new ones—and of course, it's a more casual way of locating a Mr. Right in that you aren't specifically paying to get a date from the experience.

Composing Your Online Profile

All online dating and social networking venues allow you to build a homepage, which is where your online profile will live.

Creating a homepage can be a bit intimidating at first. If you're like most people, you haven't written an essay about yourself since high school, so don't let it bug you if you start out with a bad case of writer's block.

Fortunately, the online world is so populated with millions of profiles that you have a lot of examples of what other women have written about themselves. That should help get your creative juices flowing. Also, by doing a search using the keywords "online profile helper," dozens of ideas and practical options will appear.

Focus on the Positive

Once you do get started, keep the negatives in your profile to a minimum. If you have a "Don't be this" in your wish list of the kind of guy you're looking for, do your best to turn it into a positive by saying something such as, "Please be …" or, "I hope you are …." Here's an example of doing that successfully:

- **Negative approach:** "I am so tired of dating men who are not my intellectual equal. Please, no dopes!" Ouch, that's pretty intimidating. This leaves guys wondering, "Is it that the guy was a dope, or is she just a brainiac—or worse, a snob?"

◆ **Positive approach:** "Guys who are thoughtful and interested in a variety of topics and issues fascinate me. I appreciate a curious and open mind and the kinds of shared discussions that active minds can create."

Here's another consideration. If you say something like, "I want a guy who will always be honest, fair, and loyal to me," you're putting out the signal that you have been kicked to the curb one or more times. That might indeed be true, but it's not an example of leading with your best qualities. Imagine you were a product on a shelf at a store with 100 other products. The box you are in is marked, "Previously opened; partially damaged." Chances are you would move to the next item on the shelf. Remember, your goal is to attract Mr. Right, not chase him off. The emotional bumps and bruises that you've experienced in your relationship life are inevitably there and exist for practically every man and woman older than 18. But just like you want to lead with your best foot forward on a first date, you don't want to put a profile out there that basically shouts, "Damaged goods!"

Don't Ramble

You're looking for about 350 words—something a guy can read in about a minute. Writing useless openings such as, "I don't know what I should write here …" is wasting your time (and his).

After you've written your profile, read and reread what you've said. Any professional writer will tell you that they work and rework their essays to get them just the way they want.

Remember That Humor Is a Lovable Quality

No one is asking you to write the opening monologue for Jay Leno, but a little humor can go a long way toward saying, "I'm a normal human being, and while life has plenty of ups and downs, I'd rather laugh than cry."

Give Him a Sneak Peek of Your Life

Put out two or three things you would like Mr. Right to know about you. Do you love to dance, enjoy jazz, or speak three languages? Are you well traveled or totally into poetry? If there are certain aspects of life that you really enjoy and have special talents in, don't be shy to let the world know.

Engage Him

Mention a particular film you liked—perhaps a foreign film—and ask whether he likes foreign films as well. Or write, "West Point on Mount Tamalpais at sunset inspires me. Write me about your favorite sunset location." The idea is to encourage some online repartee and to try to get a better concept of whether the two of you share enough common interests to take it to the next step: a real-world meet and greet.

Be Confident, Not Arrogant

Confidence is an attractive quality to show any Mr. Right. But be careful not to turn your profile into a mini-bio of your lifetime accomplishments. It's fine to say, "I love to sing." But avoid saying, "All my friends want to know why I haven't gotten a recording contract." Your accomplishments will shine through in time, but let him make the compliments as opposed to you complimenting yourself.

What to Look for in His Online Profile

Succeeding in the challenging environment of online dating takes time and practice. A big part of that is getting your profile to present the real and wonderful you. Equally important is learning to sort through the winners and losers in the profiles of men who have caught your attention.

First, one obvious disclaimer: lots of online profiles contain fabrications, including photos, and what is written on personal profiles. So how can you tell whether a guy has written the truth?

Let's look at three red flags.

Bravado Is Great, but a Braggart Is Not

When you're looking for Mr. Right, take the time to read and reread his profile. And, if you begin to engage online, do the same thing. If he's full of himself, back off. You want to be with a guy who is interested in getting to know you, not in trying to impress you with all his accomplishments.

If It's Poorly Written, Move to Another

If his profile is riddled with typos and grammatical mistakes, or topped with a lousy headline and a mediocre photo, it's a sign that he has a half-hearted attitude about other things in his life, such as a possible future relationship with you. If he doesn't care how he puts himself out there to the world, he's probably not going to put a lot of time into impressing or pleasing you.

A Boy and His Toys Leaves Little Room for You

If his profile is filled with stories about his new car, new stereo system, new bass boat, and so on, that's a good indication that he's just as turned on (or perhaps more so) by his toys than he ever could be by the two of you. It's great that he has outside interests, but you want a guy who strikes a balance in his life between work, toys, hobbies, sports, and you. Learn to read between the lines. If there's little (if any) room for you among all his toys and hobbies, steer clear.

Corresponding Online

For all the technology that goes into making the Internet an everyday part of your life, corresponding with a potential Mr. Right by e-mail in certain ways is similar to the letters two potential mates exchanged centuries ago (only faster, of course). It still comes down to one person communicating with another.

Imagine that he was sitting across from you and saying some of the things that he has written. Does he sound like a cool guy who is fun to be with or more like a guy who is posturing to make up for his own insecurities? This often will reveal itself if you reread his words carefully.

If you have doubts, test him. Ask, "Did you really mean to say ...?" In the world of high-speed Internet, anyone can misstate themselves. But if he has made thoughtless comments—and when asked, repeats those same things—that's your sign to look for Mr. Right elsewhere.

Why Honesty Is Always the Best Policy

The need for honesty cuts both ways, not just in how you present yourself to potential partners but also in how they present themselves to you—and how you evaluate their profiles and responses.

A frequent lament that we've heard in conducting seminars for singles goes like this: "I'm over online dating! I just can't trust the guys that I meet online." While this frustration is understandable, you should not forget the simple fact that the number of happy couples who have met thanks to the Internet is growing by the thousands every month.

That's the equivalent of saying, "There are no interesting guys at the gym" and cancelling your membership when in truth Mr. Right might have joined the gym the day you quit. The twists and turns of fate are never ending. The day you give up online dating might be the day your Mr. Right posts his profile. So don't jump offline—just use the information and the resources we have suggested here to make your online experience closer to what you always hoped it would be.

An essential part of that is your intention to be honest. While you can't do anything about the honesty of others, you can follow your own code of conduct—and we think you'll be glad you did.

For example, just how recent is your photo? If it's 5 years and/or 20 pounds ago, it's time to replace it. Furthermore, how much of what you've written about yourself is who you are—and how much is how you would *like* to be?

Never forget that the ultimate purpose of these online meet-ups is to meet offline. In other words, the moment of truth is inevitable after a week, a month, or after whatever time you first spend chatting online. If you've invested time in the process, you should be invested in a successful outcome. If he's not going to recognize you from the photo you posted, that's a bad thing. If you told him you love sailing but in truth get seasick just at the thought, that's a bad thing as well.

At their core, successful relationships are built on a foundation of honesty. Putting your best foot forward in your online profile and your early dates is to be expected, but creating a fictional character for yourself is wasting your time and his.

He's a Keeper if ...

... children adore him. If he's comfortable around kids (and they feel that way about him, too), he's probably more than decent daddy material. That's good to know for the future, right?

Meeting in Person

The online dating pool is both wide and deep. You'll find all kinds of people in it. Some will be wonderful, sweet guys looking for their Ms. Right. Others may be creeps—or even abusers, rapists, and sociopaths, looking for their next victims.

No matter how comfortable you feel with a man online, you should always take safety precautions for your first face-to-face date, and up until you know him well. Here are some important safety tips:

- Always tell a friend or family member where you're going and when you expect to be back.

- Don't arrange for the man to pick you up at your place, or arrange to meet at his.

- Take your own transportation, both going to and returning home from the date. Sure, he can take you home—when you get to know him better.

- Always meet in a locale that has lots of people milling about, and never in a secluded place.

Dating 911

Don't give out your home address or phone number to anyone you don't know well. Your cell phone number is safer, since that can't be easily traced to a home address.

♦ Carry a fully charged cell phone with you. Ask a friend to check in with you in a couple of hours after your date. Call your friend a second time, when you're home safely.

If, after a couple of dates, you still haven't met any of his friends or family, find a reason to do so. Set up a meet-and-greet with your friends as well. Yes, you have good judgment, but it doesn't hurt to get a second opinion.

Because there is so much, shall we say, "fudging the facts" in the online world, we strongly recommend that your first meeting offline be a "coffee date." This is the social equivalent of when you agree to meet with someone at your place of work who wants to pitch you an idea or a product for your business. If you agree to the meeting, you put down the cautionary note that you have a busy schedule and therefore can only set aside 30 minutes. If you realize that this is something you're indeed interested in, you simply extend the meeting.

The coffee date gives you a 30-minute meet-and-greet option, and you can extend it to a walk in the park (or more) if you feel good about the guy you just met. On the other hand, if you agree to have dinner with the guy who looked and sounded like Matt Damon online and in person is a dead ringer for Elmer Fudd, you're pretty much stuck for two plus hours of biting your tongue and thinking, "No more online dating."

Great first dates happen as a result of online dating. It can happen to you, too, if you're fair to the guy you are about to meet and come into your reality date with an open mind. While that might seem obvious, what nearly all of us miss is that a negative attitude is far more transparent than we think. Previous online dating disappointments can shine right through us for all to see.

He Said, She Said

Always follow up your date with a thank you—either by phone or e-mail (especially if he paid).

So before you step from virtual to reality, take some time to perform an attitude adjustment. Focus on what some of your exchanges have been (perhaps you took some of them and saved them in a Word document). Follow up on a couple of those and use them as conversation starters.

For example, when he said that he really liked his job because of the people he works around or that he had a great trip to Italy last year, start your conversation there.

Most often when people first meet, those early awkward moments result from finding conversation starters. If you think about those online exchanges and you have a couple conversation starters ready to go, that first 10 minutes can turn from uncomfortable to natural and relaxed. Think of it as learning to ride a bike. The help you needed was in that first 10 minutes; after that, it all seemed to come together quite naturally. Now, we're not suggesting that it's all that easy, but getting things off to a good start can make a world of difference in putting your relationship on the right track.

The Least You Need to Know

- If you're serious about finding Mr. Right, consider online dating. We're not promising that you'll find him online, but he may be looking there for *you*—so that makes it one more place you should try.

- Try both online dating services and social networking communities. Whereas one allows you to assess your own needs and desires, the other gives you a place to showcase your interests and backgrounds in a creative manner.

- Put your best foot forward in your online profile, but keep it honest as well.

- If he's more interested in impressing you than knowing you better, he's not going to be that interested in you when you're dating.

- A first face-to-face date with a stranger requires certain security precautions. Arrange to meet in a public place, carry your cell phone, and have a friend check in with you after a couple of hours.

Chapter 12

The Art of the Flirt

In This Chapter

- ◆ Why flirting is important
- ◆ Obvious (and not so obvious) ways to get his attention
- ◆ Body language tips
- ◆ His pick-up lines, and how you play along
- ◆ Beyond flirting: moving to the next step

Birds do it, chimps do it, and of course we humans do it. But, flirting does not come naturally to all of us. You know immediately the women who relish this coy ploy because they approach it like a game—one they have no intention of losing. They suit up (think the highest heels, the tightest dress, the lowest-cut blouse, and the bra that gives them the most prominent breasts in the room) and put on their war paint with the intent of a Sioux warrior getting ready for battle. Lips are plumped, lashes are lengthened, and hair is expertly tousled for that perfect just-out-of-bed-but-I-wanna-go-back look. Despite the practiced mien that gives the impression of apathy, there is a sparkle in the eye that challenges any man who dares to catch her gaze. "I'm game," it implies. "Give me your best opening line."

If you're reading this chapter, it's because this is *so* not you.

That's okay; you have lots of company. The tips you pick up here will allow you to attract your Mr. Right with the right message: "I like you, too. Let's meet, and discover what we have in common."

Yes, You Need to Flirt

If you have any doubts whatsoever about needing this skill in your dating arsenal, get rid of them—fast. Yes, you need to flirt. It's the quickest way in which to widen your great date universe of men. Why? If they don't feel that you'll welcome them into your world, they will stay away. Put yourself in Mr. Right's loafers: why fight an uphill battle when there are other women out there who are more open to talking to him?

He Said, She Said

Smile! Of course, you'll attract men if you're quite a looker. But a 2007 study from the University of Aberdeen's Face Research Laboratory shows that the expression on your face is the biggest turn-on to him. It tells him you're approachable, whether you're cute or not.

Getting His Attention

In the Mr. Right Visualization Exercise in Chapter 5, you used your five senses in order to manifest your ideal Mr. Right. Now that you're actually standing within range of him, the last thing you need is to be tongue-tied.

That's why you need some finely tuned flirting skills.

First on your agenda is to get his attention. To do that effectively, you must learn how to entice each and every one of his senses—or, as we like to think of them, his singular sensations.

Singular Sensation No. 1: All Awareness Starts with What Men See

Envision what you want him to see the very first time he catches sight of you. Are you wearing makeup? (If not, go to the makeup counter at your local department store and ask for a makeover. With the purchase of some eyeliner and lipstick, you'll learn a few fresh tips that will have you looking like a million dollars.)

Are you dressed like you're on a date? If not, then how can he imagine you at his side? Are you in heels? Even low ones will flatter your legs. Oh yeah, and would it hurt to show a little cleavage? Not all the way to your navel—just enough to catch his wandering eyes.

Are you making eye contact with him? Is there a smile on your face? The answer to both those questions should be yes. Just those two physical acts alone signal him that you are open to what he has to say. Speaking of which …

Singular Sensation No. 2: It's What You Say and How You Say It

Talking softly entices him to lean in to hear you. Bringing your voice up from your diaphragm gives you a throatier, sexier tone. If you ever took an acting class, your teachers taught you to talk more slowly, choose your words carefully, and watch which words you emphasize. The same rules apply when you flirt: you want to move him emotionally and physically (to your side).

Go ahead and laugh. Just don't giggle. Subliminally, that tells him that you're immature. And by the way, don't say anything that is blatantly sexy. Wit, irony, and subtlety are far sexier.

He's a Keeper if …

… he's not afraid to show his sensitive side. A man who can listen, encourage, compliment, empathize, and cuddle proves that he loves you.

Singular Sensation No. 3: Subtlety Is One Way to Pass His Sniff Test

Perfume works—if you're not drenched in it. But men love the smell of scented soaps and shampoos on a woman. They are subtler than perfume and subliminally indicate your cleanliness (which is next to naughtiness as a plus factor).

Just as we said that a lower voice causes him to lean into you, the scent that attracts is subtle and draws him in closer, rather than powerful scents, which push him back.

Singular Sensation No. 4: You Can—and Should—Touch Him

Brush up against him gently. Casually touch his arm, shoulder, or chest with your hand. Squeeze his hand gently. All of these signal him that you are open to his touch, too.

Touching again is an area of subtlety. An aggressive touch such as grabbing his arm pushes him back, whereas a gentle touch draws him closer.

Singular Sensation No. 5: You Have Great Taste

If none of this brings him to your side, when you catch his gaze, gently lick your lips. If he finally takes the hint and a conversation strikes up, when you're ready to leave, give him a gentle kiss. That's the broadest hint you can give him about following up on your lead.

 Dating 911

Don't drink too much. Nobody likes a sloppy drunk, and no one wants to get into a car with one. This is one way to prove you're *not* his Ms. Right.

Best-Bet Body Language

There is more to body language than meets the eye. Here are 18 important moves you can make that signal to him, "Yes, I'm interested. Make your move!"

- Catch his eye, then drop your gaze down.

- Tousle or toss your hair.

- Put on lipstick.

- Put something in your mouth (small, like a piece of chocolate, a piece of fruit, or an appetizer).

- Turn your body toward him.

- Push your shoulders back. (As you can imagine, that thrusts your chest forward—which is *always* a good thing!)

- Leave your hands by your side. (Never cross your arms. This tells him that you are closed or at the very least, guarded.)

- Melt into him. (Leaning in closer tells him it's okay to do the same to you.)

- If you're sitting down, cross your legs and move your knees closer in to his.

- If you're sitting, you can also dangle one of your shoes from your toes.

- Stroke the stem or the rim of your glass.

- Listen intently to what he has to say. It shows you genuinely care about what he has to say.

- Nod slightly when he says something you like. (A shake of the head indicates you don't agree, as you well know. Well, guess what? He really, really wants to say all the right things, so yeah, those nods are very important!)

- If he says something funny, do laugh!

- Touch a fingertip to your lips. (As mentioned previously, anything going into your lips is fine with him!)

- If you say something softly, gently touch his ear and pull him closer. Your touch will send a chill up his spine.

- What's even bolder, touch the top of his leg about six inches above his knee.

- Brush the tip of your foot against his ankle. That will get his heart to skip a beat.

Practice in the mirror and think about each of these moves. As Shakespeare said, "All the world is a stage." In a sense, that is very true about the art of flirting. You need to think about how flirting enhances your attractiveness and own your moves.

Now, road test your new skills. Go with a friend and have her assess you. Remember: you walk before you run, so be patient with yourself. Practice makes perfect. It also makes dates.

> ### He's a Keeper if ...
>
> ... he's willing to share your traditions. A great guy is one who wants to know what makes you tick, who loves to hear your family stories, and who not only accepts your traditions but revels in them and makes them his own.

He Picks Up; You Play Along

Men who know how to flirt also know how to sound smart, funny, cocky, and cool. Everything coming out of his mouth, if he is indeed interested, is said to impress you. Of course, you already realize this. That said, there are hundreds of pick-up lines he can use. Hopefully your Mr. Right will say something that isn't too stupid or lame. (Then again, that's the first clue that he's probably just another Mr. Wrong.)

Should his opening line grab you, keep your comeback smart and sassy. Go for humor and a sign of wit.

You should prepare a few quick and interesting comebacks. We'll give you our take, but feel free to edit or embellish. The goal: make it your own. And never ever be afraid to show your intelligence!

Here are three opening lines we've heard recently. They fall in the show-off and lame categories, for sure. But if delivered off-handedly by a guy who exudes confidence, we could see how they might turn a pretty head or two. We prepared a comeback for each line that demonstrates a playfulness that might keep him on his toes.

He says: "Didn't we meet once in Paris?"

You answer (without batting an eye): "Could be. Do you stay at the Georges V?" This tells him you are well travelled and travel well.

Better yet, answer him in French. If he was asking in all seriousness, then he can probably converse in the language. Otherwise, it was a straight pick-up line, and you're calling his bluff in a playful way.

Then again, if you're now thinking, "But I've never stayed at the Georges V! I can't afford it!" or even, "I've never been to France" let alone, "I can't speak French to save my life!", then a safer line is, "Nope, but I've always wanted to go. Can I tag along on your next trip?" Asking playful questions leaves the ball in his court.

He says: "You're an actress, right?"

You answer: "No. But I know why you think I look familiar. I'm a super-model." (You'll probably leave him tongue-tied, but try hard to keep a straight face with that one. If you say it with a wicked smile on your face, he'll realize that you're volleying his serve with your backhand.)

He says: "Is this seat taken?" or, "Will you let me buy you a drink?" or, "Do you come here often, because I have a question ..."

You answer (in this order): "No. Feel free ...", "Sure ...", and "Ask away ...." With any of these, he's looking for a straightforward opening. Because you're interested, too, just give him enough rope to lasso your heart.

 Dating 911

Assess his long-term potential. If this guy does nothing for you, don't lead him on. It's not fair to him, and you're only fooling yourself. Doing so allows you to keep the friendship intact (if that's what you want).

He Moves ... He Scores!

He has finally popped the question: "Hey, what do you say we get out of here?" Of course he means, "Let's go back to your place" or his place.

And yeah, you'd love to ... but don't. You're looking for Mr. Right and not Mr. Right Now, remember? Instead, smile longingly and shake your head slowly. That says to him, "Tempting, sure ... but hey, I'm worth the wait."

If at that point he says, "Well, do you mind if I call you some time?", certainly give him your phone number. But do not ever sit by the phone! You're too busy. You've got to keep putting yourself out there, flirting with other possible Mr. Rights.

He Said, She Said

In a 2005 speed dating survey of 2,620 participants conducted by the University of Pennsylvania, more men were swayed by what they saw and heard in their partners: 49 percent, as opposed to 34 percent of women.

The worst thing that can happen is that only a few men prove that they really, truly are interested and call you back.

The best that can happen is that all your instincts were correct, and all of these potential Mr. Rights call you up for dates.

The more you date, the more you discern which man best matches your holy grail: your criteria list (see Chapter 5).

Now, get out there and flirt, flirt, flirt!

The Least You Need to Know

- Flirting is an important skill to have in your dating arsenal. The more you get out there and flirt, the more possible Mr. Rights will see you, feel attracted, and get the message from you that you're open to their advances.

- Even if you don't feel you're attractive, look the role and play the part. Remember, you're not cleaning out your fridge; you're trying to change your life. Dress for success, and enjoy the journey.

- Your body language sends a signal to him: "I'm approachable."

- Hopefully his first line will prove he was worth your efforts to entice him to your side. But remember: the fact that he's there says he is interested, so give him a fair shot.

- If several guys are attracted to you, go out with all of them. Dating is a numbers game, and there are many possible Mr. Rights for you. But you won't know who he is if you don't have any comparisons.

Chapter 13

In the Company of Men

In This Chapter

- ◆ Hanging out on Mars: a totally different world
- ◆ A quick survival guide for mixing with men
- ◆ Learning to speak his language

As a single woman looking for Mr. Right, your search is going to put you frequently in the company of men. So we thought it best to focus one chapter on how you can best navigate the red planet of Mars, making the positive impression you're hoping for while staying grounded in your Venusian sensibilities. Learning his language is crucial. Otherwise, what one of you says, and how the other interprets it, can lead to a miscommunication that sinks your relationship before it has a chance to set sail on the Sea of Happiness.

Language barriers do exist—but you'll give them a wide berth just by understanding this very important rule: never presume you understand what he means.

Welcome to Mars!

Since John Gray's groundbreaking book of the early 1990s, *Men Are from Mars, Women Are from Venus* (see the Resources appendix), stirred controversy by suggesting—contrary to popular thought at the time—that men and women actually think differently, the term "Men Are from Mars, Women Are from Venus" has come to symbolize the concept that men and women bring two distinctly different points of view to communicating about everything, from how to be a loving and supporting partner to good ways to spend their leisure time.

Here, we've created five encounters that women commonly have when involved with men. You've got the setting, the issue, and your best approach.

Mars Moment No. 1: The Tribe

The setting: you've been invited to a party where guys are watching a big game. It could be a big college bowl game, a basketball final, a World Series baseball game, or even the Super Bowl. Some guys came with girlfriends, whereas others came on their own. You're into the game and you're particularly into being with him, so you sit by his side and cheer on your favorite team.

The issue: you grew up in Boston and he grew up in Los Angeles. He's pulling for his hometown favorite, and you're pulling for yours.

Your best approach: don't get too amped up, because if your team wins, you may lose in the long run. Why? When several guys are in the same room watching a big game, they have this male bond that invisibly connects them. Subconsciously, they see you and any other woman in the room as being in their space. Your presence is fine as long as you don't make yourself the center of attention.

If they're all rooting for one team and you're rooting for the other, they will close ranks against you. It seems petty, but on Mars there is a strong sense of tribalism—and you are, after all, not a member of their tribe.

You may have brothers, but Mr. Right's friends are not your family. So keep it low key. If you have to pull for your own team, do it with a sense of humility. Don't copy the chest-beating mannerisms of the men around you. They don't see you as one of the guys, and you don't want them to.

He Said, She Said _____

Make suggestions for inexpensive dates. Let him know that every date doesn't have to be a budget buster. Suggest a less-expensive lunch instead of a high-priced dinner, discount movies, and picnics that you can prepare (and then astound him with your culinary skills). Better yet, take a cooking class together. It's a great way to see what kind of team you'll make (both in and outside the kitchen).

Mars Moment No. 2: His Old Flame

The setting: you and your new boyfriend are out at his favorite club, and a woman walks over and taps him on the shoulder. He gives her a smile, they exchange a couple words, she gives him a kiss on the cheek, she gives you a quick glance, and then she fades back into the crowd.

The issue: you're put off when you learn from him that "they dated a couple of years ago" and by the fact that he didn't introduce the two of you.

Your best approach: don't give too much thought to the fact that he didn't introduce you to his former flame for two important reasons. One, guys typically get brain freeze at a time like this, and just like Bambi in headlights, they have no idea what to do. Two, he's not offering any introductions because the last thing he wants is for two women who have known him intimately to become acquainted—or worse yet, friends—and begin analyzing him, both in and out of the bed-room.

You see the lack of an introduc-tion as a snub. He sees it as a matter of caution. One of the basic rules on Mars is: if it's not broken, don't fix it. He's happy with your relationship and is

He's a Keeper if ... _____

... he doesn't blatantly stare at other women. It's disrespectful to you, and it's proof that he'd rather be somewhere else (or perhaps with someone else).

hesitant to rock the boat. Therefore, your best approach is to smile right through the moment and let it roll off your back. He'll be relieved and impressed that you let him off so easily. Your stock will shoot way up in his view.

Mars Moment No. 3: His Old Pal

The setting: you've been dating regularly for a month, and he suggests a double date with his old pal from college and his new girlfriend.

The issue: his old pal's girlfriend is a little too loose with the booze, and she gets a little too friendly with your guy. It's an awkward moment for you, your boyfriend, and his pal—everyone but the other girl, who is too far gone to actually care. The bottom line is that the night's a disaster, and your guy just picked up a $200-plus tab for dinner (and drinks!).

Your best approach: while it's tempting to state the obvious, resist the temptation. He knows the evening was a disaster, and picking up the tab for the wreck doesn't help his mood at all.

So when you're finally alone (perhaps back in your car and heading back to your place or his), reach over and give him a kiss on the cheek and just say, "You're such a sweetheart." He'll be relieved beyond words that you didn't jump on him with something like, "What a jerk she was, and I don't know what your old pal sees in her." Or worse, "I hope we never have another evening like that!" All that accomplishes is to put him on the defensive, and it makes a really bad experience for him that much worse.

Dating 911

Express your views with respect. Yes, you have a right to your opinion. No, you don't have to bully him into agreeing with you, because he has a right to his own opinion as well. Learn how to agree to disagree.

By quietly recognizing his disappointment without verbalizing it and by showing affection and compassion, you've let him know that you're not someone who takes a bad situation and makes it worse. You know that the big picture is about the two of you, and in your heart that's what really matters.

Whenever a guy makes a suggestion about an evening, a double date, a ballgame, or a movie, he feels an overwhelming responsibility for the evening to go well. Sure, what happened was out of his control—but men tend to take on the role of the captain. When things go wrong, they go down with the ship—regardless of their role in the disaster. Your quiet support tells him that you want to cut him some slack even if he doesn't know how to do that.

Mars Moment No. 4: Your Office Party

The setting: you have invited Mr. Right to come to your office staff party, and Mr. Obnoxious, who always has something inappropriate to say, starts acting like a jerk (big surprise).

The issue: you were hoping your boyfriend would put him in his place, but he didn't do that. Now you're back at his place, and you raise the issue but he shrugs it off. You're put off by this, and he's frustrated because he's uncertain as to what you expected him to do.

Your best approach: in truth, you want a guy who recognizes that discretion is the better part of valor. Remember that when inviting him into your world, he's going to be cautious not to make any waves. Men in general are acutely aware of when they are on their turf and when they are not. Appreciate the fact that your guy is not a bull in a china shop. He recognizes boundaries, and he is going to hold back unless he has clear direction from you.

What you see as his not rising to the occasion, he sees as a demonstration of his ability to stay cool, calm, and collected. What you want to do is give him clear direction as to what you would like to see happen. Women expect men to act the way another woman would act, intuitively, and rise to your defense. But, in social interaction, men are generally not intuitive creatures. Tell him what you had hoped, thank him for his even-tempered manner, and move forward.

He Said, She Said

According to the 2008 Sun Media's Great Canadian Male Sex Survey involving 1,026 men, believe it or not, only 13 percent of respondents think they know when their partners are faking an orgasm—proof positive that there are lots of great actresses out there.

Mars Moment No. 5: The Forgotten Moment

The setting: it's the one-month anniversary of your first date, and you're expecting him to take note of this special occasion.

The issue: instead of making it a special evening, you go out for a pizza, a couple of beers, and then back to your place to watch a DVD. Before he has a chance to hit the play button, you let him have it—expressing your disappointment that he did not do something "special" tonight. He gets in a huff and takes off. He's ticked, you're in tears, and your special night has turned into a total bust.

Your best approach: not in all areas are men Neanderthals, but when it comes to "honoring special romantic occasions," some are pretty much back to being cave dwellers. Rather than fighting their evolutionary progress in this area, you're far better off accepting the fact that they suffer in general from a romance deficit.

Here's a better way to handle all such occasions. Drop a not-too-subtle hint. For example, "Can you believe this Friday night will be a month since our first date? We should really do something special, like going back and having dinner where we went that first night."

If you really want him to hear your message, tell him when you're wrapped together in a loving embrace.

Men have a lot of great qualities, but romance and sentimentality are not two that come naturally or easily to most men. So take him to school and show him the way. A man in love—and yes, in lust as well—will follow wherever you lead.

He Said, She Said

In a recent British study, 26 percent of participants admitted to having sex on the beach during a past holiday (and no, we're not talking about the cocktail with the same name). Of these frolickers, 36 percent were younger than 30 while another 19 percent were older than 40. Around 5 percent also admitted to getting caught in the act.

Tips on How to Mingle with Men

Let's start with two quick rules:

◆ **Don't be intimidated.** Martians, in spite of their bravado, are
typically more intimidated by Venusians than the other way
around.

◆ **You need to cultivate a sense of comfort with men.** The more
you can do so, the easier it will be for you to be open and relaxed
in their presence. Therefore, it is far more likely that the best of
you will come forward.

Having said that, here are some general rules of engagement that are
helpful to keep in mind:

◆ Because men and women think differently, never presume he will
react to a situation the way a gal pal would. Accept that reality,
and learn to live with it.

◆ Men take responsibility for most things that go wrong in a
relationship, even when they have no idea what that might be.
Although you're tempted to go silent, don't. Let him know your
point of view so that he stays engaged in those issues that are
important to you, rather than pulling back and retreating to lick
your wounds.

◆ On Mars, you only help when you're asked. Women offer their
help, but men in general need to be asked. If you want him to get
off the couch during the football game and help you carry a package down to the car, for example, you have to ask.

◆ Probably half of all men have difficulty initiating a conversation
with a woman to whom they are attracted. If you like the guy and
he's having a hard time getting his brain and tongue to work well
together, help him out with a few warm-up lines. He'll be ever so
grateful for the assist.

◆ Subtlety is a woman's greatest tool. The same guy who has trouble
spitting out a few words also doesn't want to feel put upon. If you
come on too strong, it is highly likely that you'll chase him away.

Therefore, keeping the conversation casual keeps him in his comfort zone. Suggest, but don't push. The male ego is like a cat. It loves to be stroked but can get its back up if cornered.

He's a Keeper if ...

... he makes up special occasions for the two of you. It is a testament of his thoughtful disposition, and the fact that he honors your company.

The Least You Need to Know

◆ Finding Mr. Right means playing in the sandbox with boys. They are unique creatures, and the more you understand how they see the world, the better your chances of success will be in finding and keeping a great guy.

◆ If romance is not your guy's strong suit, cultivate his sensitivities and over time he'll follow your lead.

◆ It's a big mistake to presume that men think like women. They don't, and the sooner you learn Martian speak and Martian ideas, the easier time you will have mingling with them.

Part 4

Is He Mr. Right?

There's a rush of excitement nearly every woman feels when she realizes that the guy she has been seeing might indeed be Mr. Right. At this point, the dynamic of the relationship turns and questions begin to arise. Is he a good friend but a lousy lover, or is he a good lover but a lousy friend? Ultimately, you want both and much more. If he's going to be the love of your life, you want to know that this man is worthy of a lifetime partnership.

Mr. Right and Mr. Right Now are two very different guys. Here, you find a guide that helps you distinguish between the two. As you move closer to a committed relationship, it's time to ask yourself: "Does this man love me, truly?" "Can I see myself spending the rest of my life with him?" Assessing your commitment at this stage will save you heartache later and ensure that you have found a man who is worthy of being your soul mate.

Is he really "the one"?

Chapter 14

First Date Don'ts and Do's

In This Chapter

- ◆ How to prepare emotionally for your date
- ◆ How to prepare physically for your date
- ◆ What to say and do on a first date …
- ◆ … and what *not* to say or do
- ◆ First date deal-breakers

If you've read the first two parts of this book, you can now recognize a Mr. Wrong from a mile away. Better yet, you also have all the skills that can put you within kissing distance of many possible Mr. Rights. And in fact, more than a few of these great guys are asking you out.

This leads you to another very crucial step: the first date. A first date has two possible outcomes. Either it leads to a second get-together that is just as enjoyable because both you and this particular Mr. Right candidate feel a mutual attraction in which you'll learn even more about him (and he about you); or you'll part ways, with one (or both) of you having no intention of having a second date.

The goal of this chapter is to ensure that any and every first date is the former as opposed to the latter. If that's the case, you'll have many opportunities to discover whether the men with whom you share a mutual attraction are Mr. Right-worthy.

Attitude Spot Check

There are a series of emotions that accompany your saying "yes" to that very first date: excitement, euphoria, shyness, and ... doubt as well.

All of these are expected. But what you don't want to do is allow any doubts to dissuade you from enjoying the experience and learning more about this man—who also wants to learn more about you.

The very first step in preparing for your date is to mentally prepare yourself for this very unique opportunity to make a new friendship: one that may lead to the happy, satisfying, committed relationship you've been seeking and know you deserve. In other words, you need an Attitude Spot Check.

So that you have the right attitude going forward, here are three very important things to remember before he knocks on your door:

◆ **Your primary goal is to make a new friend, not a new *boy-friend*.** All great relationships start with friendship. To alleviate any emotional pressure you feel to make more of this encounter than it should be at this stage of your burgeoning relationship, go into it with the idea of coming out with a new friend—and nothing more.

◆ **Be yourself.** He's there to learn about you and to spend time with you. Having said that, don't pretend to be someone you're not. If he asks you a question, answer it directly. Or, if you feel that the question is too personal to divulge on a first date, feel free to say so. A nice way of doing this with someone whom you hope remains interested is to say, "That's a great question—for our tenth date." And leave it at that.

He Said, She Said

Believe it or not, a man's biggest turn-on is his smell. In a 2007 study conducted at the University of Lausanne/Switzerland, almost a majority of 49 single women were attracted to those shirts worn by men whose scents were similar to men they'd previously dated. The reason: we are all genetically coded with a hundred "immune system genes"—also known as our major histocompatibility complex, or MHC. Your attraction to men with a substantially different MHC is part of your primal survival urge: to procreate, you seek a mate who is immunologically dissimilar. This ensures that the healthiest babies will be born. In other words, mutts are far stronger than purebreds.

◆ **You should have no expectations other than to enjoy yourself.** That means being yourself—you know, that person you are when you're with family and close friends. In fact, if you treat him like an old friend, he's sure to be flattered and live up to the honor. And who knows? In time, he may become just that in your life.

Date Mode Physical Prep

Hey, no one needs to tell you how to prepare for a date. Considering the number of dates you've had, by now you're a pro at that, right?

That's what *you* think.

Here's our Date Prep Laundry List. Our guess is that you'll find at least a couple items on it that you never considered, forgot, or skipped:

◆ Take a shower. You'll feel great, and it will show in your attitude. And since all men love great scents on women, use a scented moisturizer, or lightly spritz your favorite perfume.

◆ Wash your hair—then take time to style it so that it flatters you.

◆ Get your nails done.

◆ Dress sexy, but not slutty (if you're unsure about the difference, see the sidebar on the following page).

◆ Unless it's a casual date, wear heels. (Even short ones give your carriage a lift.)

◆ Wear makeup. (Don't think "kabuki." Think "barely there.")

◆ Wear a bra. Don't laugh! Again, it changes your shape—and that can go a long way toward changing your attitude, too. This time, though, think "WonderBra" as opposed to "barely there."

◆ Wear jewelry, but don't wear so much that he'll feel like he's your bodyguard.

Yes, all of this is important. By giving your appearance serious thought and by looking your best for this endeavor, you give yourself even more confidence to succeed in your goal of finding Mr. Right.

Dating 911

What you wear on a first date says a lot about your expectations. So that he gets the right message, don't wear clothes that are too tight, or that are see-through. Forego the plunging neckline, too. He already knows you have breasts, right? And don't wear a skirt that is so short that it leaves nothing to the imagination. The goal is to have him imagining spending the rest of his life with you—as opposed to thinking that he's (literally) seen all there is of you on this first date.

Okay, now that you look marvelous ...

What to Do When You Open the Door

Smile. Give him a big "Hi!" along with his name. Shake his hand, or if it's appropriate, give him a welcoming kiss.

Be gracious and invite him in. Take a minute to make small talk. ("Did you have trouble finding parking?" "Do you think I should take an umbrella?" "Was my place easy to find?")

As he answers, look him in the eye as you listen to his answer. And smile. Nod. Laugh. In other words, show that you're engaged.

Then, ask him to wait while you grab your shawl, coat, or purse. This gives him a minute to collect his thoughts and you a moment to check your smile in the mirror one more time.

Now breathe. You're ready to go!

First Date Don'ts

Here's the thing about first dates: *both of you are out of your comfort zone.* Think about it: you don't know whether anything you say will offend the other person. One of you may be going to a place you've never been before. One of you may be meeting new people for the first time.

Yep, there is a lot of potential for disaster. And any disasters may mean that this first date is also your last with this potential Mr. Right.

 Dating 911

How interesting are you to him? Know what's happening in the world, and be able to comment on current events.

To avoid misunderstandings, let's look at some First Date Don'ts.

Don't Play Hard to Get

The reason he invited you out in the first place was because he felt you were accessible and that the two of you had something in common. If, while on the date, you're too quiet, too coy, or too stand-offish, you'll be giving him the wrong signal: that you don't feel he merits this opportunity to get to know you better. In fact, if he feels you are toying with him or aren't interested in him, he may not bother to call back. Is that what you want? No, of course not! All the more reason to be the girl he asked out, not some frigid diva with an attitude.

Don't Take Him for Granted

He has invested his time and money to hang out with you. If you complain about the movie, the meal, the way he looks, or what he says, you're giving him a very cruel message: "Sorry, guy, I couldn't care less about the effort you've made on my behalf." Even if you aren't impressed, being ungracious says more about you than it does about him.

Don't Put Up with Behavior That Makes You Uncomfortable

Yes, you should be gracious. Saying thank you after your date, inviting him back for a cup of coffee or conversation, or even sending him a handwritten note that tells him that you had fun and look forward to seeing him again gets the point across that you enjoyed yourself.

That said, you aren't obligated to do more. No one has the right to make you feel guilty or to coerce or force you to do anything that doesn't make you feel in control. He has no right to make cruel or dirty comments, to kiss you against your will, or force you into having sex with him.

Always bring cash with you. That way, if for any reason things get creepy, you can excuse yourself from the room and immediately go outside and call a taxi, or a friend to pick you up.

Don't feel you have to go back to him. If you do, however, all you need to say is, "It was fun—until now. I've already called a friend to take me home. Enjoy the rest of your evening." And get out of there. That's all the explanation you need to give.

Don't Expect Too Much ...

If you have great expectations that he is, in fact, going to be your Mr. Right—that in no time at all the two of you will be discussing your futures together (setting the date for your wedding and planning the number of children you want)—you're setting yourself up for heartbreak.

Trust us on this. Otherwise, as you chatter on about all that *you* presume the two of you have in common and about "your lives together," he'll be inching his way slowly out the door—and will never look back.

Yes, there is such a thing as love at first sight. *But declaring to be in love with someone doesn't make it happen.* Remember, *he* also has to be in love with *you*. And even if he is, that still doesn't mean that he's your Mr. Right. Remember: this is only your first date, and hopefully the first of many. The proof of that comes over time and is demonstrated in what he does, *not what he says*.

... But Don't Expect Too Little, Either

If you go on the date with the mindset that (a) you don't deserve him, (b) he doesn't deserve you, or (c) you're just not going to have a good time, you're creating a self-fulfilling prophecy. Don't forget your primary objective: to have a fun time—and at the same time, assess his potential to be your Mr. Right. If you don't give him a chance to prove himself, you may be missing out on the chance of a lifetime.

Don't Presume That a Second Date Is a Given

The best-case scenario is that you've both had a great time. He was interesting and certainly seemed enthralled with what you had to say, too. And while he didn't come out and ask for a second date, he did ask how your week was shaping up.

Oh yeah, and when he kissed you at the door, he said, "I'll call you."

So of course he will ... right? Maybe he will, but maybe he won't. Men aim to please. They will say what they presume you want to hear at that moment. But will this person feel an obligation to follow up on a semi/ quasi/half-hearted attempt to leave you with a smile on your face (as opposed to broken-hearted or in tears?)

Dating 911

Don't take a phone call during your date unless it's an emergency. You shouldn't be chit-chatting with friends and family unless it's something serious that needs your attention. That's being disrespectful of his time.

Short answer: no.

If you leave the door open, there's a 50/50 chance he'll walk through it again sometime soon and set up a second date. If he doesn't call immediately, keep in mind that like you, sometimes real life gets in his way.

He may have a job that keeps him hopping. Or, he may have an attraction to you, and he is looking forward to following up on it as soon as possible—but he needs to disengage himself from some other relationship obligation first. And of course, you'd prefer that he do so before he rings your doorbell again.

And if he doesn't call? Chalk it up to the guy just trying to give you a polite kiss-off. For whatever reason, he isn't as attracted to you as he thought.

Don't Be Afraid to Initiate the Second Date

It took a lot of time and effort on your part—and his—to get you to that first date. Even if everything wasn't storybook perfect, the odds are good enough to allow you to presume that he's worth pursuing further.

So give it a week or two, then pick up the phone and call him. Be casual. Maybe invite him to a sports bar to watch a game with you and a bunch of friends. Or, follow up with a coffee date and some token that shows you got a glimpse of his personality in the short time you spent together: perhaps a book that reflects something you talked about, or even an article on a subject in which he expressed interest. The odds are good that he'll be flattered and say yes to your offer.

Even if he doesn't, you've made it clear that you are attracted to him, and you've left the door open for him to contact you in the future. But if he doesn't follow up, don't be hurt. Be pragmatic. If he's not that into you (in *that* way), isn't it better you know now than find out after you've spent more time with him? That time could have been better spent with your Mr. Right.

And if he didn't turn out to be Mr. Right, maybe you'll become good friends.

First Date Do's

You've taken time to both mentally and physically prep for this date. You're really into him, which is why you're walking out the door with a big smile on your face. Nothing can go wrong at this point, right?

That's what you think. You still have plenty of time to do or say something that you don't mean, that will hurt him, or that will turn him off.

But you don't have to. Here's how to keep your foot firmly in your new high heels (as opposed to in your mouth).

Do Be on Your Best Behavior

What turned him on about you in the first place was a combination of a lot of things: your grace under pressure, your humility, and your sense of humor. Don't feel you have to do anything bizarre to get his interest. Nothing wild and crazy—no Girl Gone Wild—is needed. *Don't rock the boat.* Keep doing what you're doing, and he'll stay interested.

Do Ask Questions

If every sentence that comes out of your mouth begins with "I," it's time you come up with some new talking points: preferably ones that end with a question mark. Asking questions gives him a chance to get a word in edgewise and to shine in front of you. Remember, he's trying to impress you as hard as you're trying to impress him.

That said, don't ask questions that are too personal. And certainly don't ask your questions in such a way that it sounds as if he's in a courtroom and will end up in jail if his answers are wrong. If he answers with a simple "Yes" or "No," it means you've touched a sore spot and he's taking the fifth. That's not a good sign for either of you. This isn't an inquisition; it's a date.

Do Listen to Him

Show interest in who he is and what he has to say. Listen to his words, his tone, and his inflections. He is a real person with a lot to offer. This is your time to find out what that is. Don't worry, he'll be asking you a few questions, too. And when he does …

Do Be Candid

Like you, he's on a fact-finding mission. He wants to get to know you—the *real* you. So give him the highlights. In other words, stay away from the low points. You're in a "No Whine" zone! As you two get to know each other better, there will be plenty of time for that. A relationship is like an onion. Peel it away slowly, a layer at a time, in order to savor the flavor.

If you get the urge to embellish, squelch it: *no little white lies.* Because when he finds out the truth (and if he sticks around, he will), he'll only think less of you, not more.

Do Flirt, but Only with Him

He loves it when you tease him. But he'll hate it if you bat your eyes at any other guy. So why do you feel the urge to flirt with other men in the room? It's not like you have to cover your bet that you have a ride home; you came with him, remember? That kind of behavior only shows insecurity on your part. You don't have to prove your sexual prowess to him. He invited you out because he's already well aware of it.

Do Give Him the Benefit of the Doubt

Look, he's just as nervous as you. He's afraid he'll put his foot in his mouth—and his shoe is a lot bigger. If he fumbles, laugh with him, not at him. If you have any concerns about anything he says, toss out a question that tests his response and his mettle. And keep in mind: it's not the word but the deed that matters.

 He Said, She Said

> We come to love not by finding the perfect person, but by learning to see an imperfect person perfectly.

—Angelina Jolie, actress

What to Do If Your First Date Goes Horribly Wrong

There are so many ways in which your first outing with a potential Mr. Right can sour you on him forever (or vice-versa). What sorts of incidents should be considered out-and-out deal-breakers?

Here's our Top 12 List:

- He says something cruel to you.

- He's mean to others (your friend, his friend, a waiter …).

- He bores you.

- He doesn't pick up the tab (if he invited you out, he should).

- He talks about his ex as if he's still in love with her.

- He talks about an ex (or more than one) as if what went wrong between them was all *her* fault. (A breakup takes *two*.)

- He's not ethical. He actually describes cheating people and goes on to explain why he felt that was justified.

- He does something—*anything*—that is crude or vulgar.

- He shows signs of bigotry or prejudice.

- He's married or in a serious relationship.

- You catch him in a lie.

- And of course, he insists on your doing something that makes you feel uncomfortable in any way, shape, or form.

The Least You Need to Know

- Don't start out with a negative attitude. You've said yes because you're attracted to him. Now is not the time to sabotage what could be a great first date!

- Take time to look your best. Otherwise, why should he take the time to consider you as his Ms. Right? And besides, you'll kick yourself if it turns out that you blew your one chance with your Mr. Right.

◆ Give him time to shine. Give him time to know you, too. Most importantly, give him the benefit of the doubt.

◆ Don't read his mind as to how the date went. The proof that it was a great date comes with his next phone call.

◆ As always, his actions speak louder than words. If he does anything that makes you think twice, listen to your gut. That's a good indicator he's not your Mr. Right.

Chapter 15

Crossing into His Comfort Zones

In This Chapter

♦ Why relationships derail

♦ When and how to give him his space

♦ His most common comfort zones

A brand-new relationship is a thing of beauty. And, as is often the case with all things beautiful and new, it can be very fragile as well. "Handle with care" is the guiding principle in the early days and weeks of this new situation for both of you.

But often, we make the mistake of trespassing into each other's comfort zone. So how can you ensure that you both will survive those early trials and tribulations that take place as you're learning how to best meet each other's needs and expectations?

A Good Thing Gone Wrong

Relationships often derail before they get too far down the track. There are times that this is a good thing, however—specifically, when this new relationship was not destined to go the distance. At other times, however, it is really unfortunate because the relationship had the right mix of qualities that could have—and should have—spelled success.

So how does this first (or perhaps second and third) date go spiraling off into the land of broken dreams? One common cause: crossing over into his comfort zones. Think of it as trespassing. The problem is that there are no posted signs to give you a clear indication that you have indeed done this.

The first important factor to recognize and accept is that men are, more often than not, creatures of habit. And while this is true of both men and women, as they get older, it is particularly true of men at almost any age.

He Said, She Said

If he wants to go to a football game, he goes. If I want to go to a fashion show, I go. We don't have to do everything together. But we like doing most things together.

—Joan Collins, actress

What does this mean to your relationship? Primarily, it means that you should be aware and sensitive to those things that he holds near and dear to his sense of self. That can be a number of different habits and interests, depending on the particular guy.

Here are four examples of how you can unknowingly cross over into his comfort zone and make a good thing go bad.

The Drop In

You and your new guy agree to go out to a Sunday afternoon movie. He says, "Meet me at my place at four and we'll go from there." That's fine, because it's a half-hour before the movie starts and his place is just two blocks from the theater. But you decide to surprise him and arrive earlier—say, three o'clock. He comes to the door, bleary-eyed from watching three hours of football, and he doesn't look as if he's ready to go anywhere—much less out on a date with you. He needs a shave. A shower wouldn't hurt, either. His place is pretty messy, the game is blaring on TV, there is an open can of beer on the coffee table, and there's another empty can next to that.

You do your best to ignore his sad condition and the squalor in his apartment. In your perkiest voice, you say, "It was such a pretty day I thought I'd surprise you and come a little early so we can go for a walk before the movie."

He pushes his hair back away from his eyes, blurts out a confused "Sure," then switches off the TV, grabs the mess from the coffee table, and hurries off to the kitchen. He comes back out, hurries off to the bathroom and says, "I'll just be a minute." He closes the bathroom door, you hear the shower start, you sit down with a satisfied glow and think, "He's a really nice guy."

In the meantime, he's in the shower—embarrassed that you caught him looking like a slob, unhappy that his place looks like a dump, ticked off that you made him miss the last 10 minutes of a really good football game, and nervously wondering if you're snooping around his place—about to stumble across his stash of X-rated videos (which is why he's out of the shower in record time).

Where things went wrong: there are lots of things that went wrong here, but for the sake of brevity, we'll stick to the most obvious. First, whether a guy lives in a 12-room McMansion or a studio apartment, he considers his home his castle—*and you just breached the castle without giving notice.* He wanted to roll down the drawbridge on his schedule, not on yours. Second, that little football game he was watching may be inconsequential to you, but it's a big deal to him: he *always* watches that team on a Sunday afternoon. It's a ritual he has come to enjoy. In other words, you just ran right over it and never noticed that you were trespassing on his comfort zone.

What you could have done differently: first and most obviously, call ahead. Second, if you do stumble in well ahead of time and find him obviously not in date mode, you could make a big deal out of the fact that you're sorry but that you just wanted to spend some time with him before the movie. Then, suggest that you leave and come back later or meet him at the coffee shop down the block in 30 minutes. There's a very good chance that he'll invite you in, but even if he doesn't, that's okay because his space (perhaps as you feel about your own) is his sanctuary. Think about how you would feel if the roles were reversed, and act accordingly.

Your Long-Term Plan

You've gone on two great dates, and so far from what you can see, as you tell a close gal pal, "What's not to like?" He's good looking, considerate, smart, and has a good sense of humor. "This might be the guy I've been looking for," you tell your friend with a warm sense of satisfaction.

Now you're out on your third date, and your potential Mr. Right mentions that his birthday is in January. You come up with the name of a great restaurant where you would like to take him to celebrate. You describe the place and everything you like about it. "That would make it a really special occasion," you tell him, and give him time to respond with enthusiasm.

Rather than enthusiasm, he seems distracted and somewhat uncomfortable by your suggestion. The rest of the evening has this uncomfortable, strained air that hangs over the rest of your date. Perhaps he's one of those guys who is sensitive about his birthday, you wonder silently.

There's a warm kiss goodnight, a promise to call midweek, and a vague plan to do something next weekend. But the call never comes, the plans are never made, and the relationship drifts into limbo. You're left wondering what happened. A few weeks later, your gal pal reports seeing your potential Mr. Right at a local bar with his arm around another woman—and the rest is history.

Where things went wrong: you never knew it, but you scared him away. It was sweet of you to offer to take him to dinner for his birthday. The problem was that his birthday is in January—and your third date was in July. Although you're feeling really good about the way your new relationship is going, making plans six months in advance tells the guy that you're planning a long-term relationship without getting his input on that decision.

As a general rule, guys are not great at making long-term plans. That's why men go through the grocery store with hand baskets while women are pushing carts. Men are challenged to come up with an idea of what to do for dinner in three hours. Three, four, or five days ahead is beyond their imagination.

There are a lot of ways to scare off a guy, but few are more effective than making plans six months out for a relationship that's three weeks old.

What you could have done differently: here's a completely different approach. Suppose you had said, "You know, a couple of years ago this guy I was dating took me to this great place for dinner on my birthday. Unfortunately, the dinner was the best part of the date. It would have been a lot more fun with you." Having said that, you give him a quick kiss and a sly smile.

When you put yourself out there to a guy in terms of making long-distance plans, you're making him feel that the decision that this relationship is going to be serious and lasting has already been made and there is no reason to consult him about that. Wrong—it takes two to tango, and even if he's not really leading the dance, it's unwise to let him think that.

He Said, She Said

What do your finances have to do with infatuation? Apparently more than you thought. In a recent poll conducted by Opinion Research Corp., 57 percent of respondents admit that worry about their love lives increase when their wallets are empty.

Playing Mom

He's so wonderful in so many ways, but let's face it: he needs more than a little help on the road toward perfection. For one thing, he has no idea how to dress for success. So what's wrong with taking him shopping to show him how? He's paying too much for his health insurance and too little attention to the upkeep and maintenance of his condo. Worse, he gets a cold and has no idea what to do to get better in a hurry. Going out without a jacket in chilly weather is not going to help, and not getting enough rest or vitamins is pretty silly as well.

You do so much, and where's your thanks? Instead, after two months of dating you get the old, "It's not you, it's me" routine. He says that you're wonderful, but he's just not ready to get that serious about a relationship and he thinks it would be a good idea if you both took a break and let things cool down. After all, you can still be friends.

Where things went wrong: guys are funny about being mothered. They may act at first as though they appreciate your help and concern. It's not uncommon for them to even lean on you and give you the idea that they want more mothering rather than less. In truth, however, more men want a partner who is their equal. They also value intimacy more than nurturing. Of course, you can find the exceptions to this rule, but in most cases men will move away when they feel the grip of their "new mom" closing in around them. In fact, there is no faster way to push past the boundaries of a man's comfort zone than to fall into the role of being his surrogate mom.

Most importantly is the fact that you don't want to assume this role. Sure it's fun to take him shopping: that is, if he's really cool with that. It's always great to have your own live Ken doll to dress. But in the big picture, you want to be his life partner and his lover. That's the relationship you've been looking for and the one you deserve.

What you could have done differently: while the guys who really want a surrogate mommy are few and far between, most men do like to be coddled in one fashion or another. This is particularly true if you are an affectionate, giving, and nurturing person by your nature. In that case, a man's natural inclination to be lazy will kick in. Whether it's picking up his dry cleaning or making him a hot dinner, he won't complain. A wiser approach is to be a giving girlfriend. On special occasions, buy him gifts that supplement his wardrobe. Or show him how much you appreciate him during moments of intimacy. In other words, accent the physical love, but minimize the emotional nurturing. We appreciate that it is your nature to "always be there," but in no time at all this form of open-ended support can become suffocating—and he'll resent your level of intrusion into every aspect of his life. You, on the other hand, will resent how much you're doing for the little thanks given

He's a Keeper if ...

... he respects your need for privacy.

in exchange—all the more reason to steer clear of these rocky shores. You'll be very glad you did.

His Annoying Friends

You've had a few great dates, and now it's time to meet his buds. Unfortunately, you're a bit disappointed. You were expecting something different—say, more maturity; more consideration; and more of any of the qualities you appreciate in your own friends and acquaintances, regardless of their sex. You are reminded of that old Gertrude Stein expression, "There is no there, there." You try to cover your feelings, but you don't do a very good job of it—and before long, he's on to the idea that "You think my friends are creeps!"

"It's not that," you explain, "it's just …" But try as you may, you just can't hide the fact that you're disappointed in his buddies.

Your next date has an entirely different feel to it. He's a little detached and cautious in a way you've never seen before. What seemed to be going so well for the past month is now going south, and it seems that neither of you can stop the slide. He pulls away, you're disappointed, and it seemed like the inevitable conclusion to a good thing gone bad.

Where things went wrong: you won't be the first woman (and certainly not the last) to meet the buds and think they're duds. Of course, it's disconcerting because you presumed this potential Mr. Right had friends whose traits mirrored the things you love the best about him. Now, having met this bunch of boobs, you're wondering, "Is there something I'm not seeing here?"

Not necessarily. While on occasion, women shed friends as they move through life, men often regress when it comes to their friendships. It's a tough one to explain, but it goes back to men having some very different ideas about how their lives function happily.

A man will hang with some guys for the simple reason that he has known them for many years. It might be 10 or 20 years after high school, but if he played with them on the same team, he is just as likely to keep the relationship going for years—despite the odd fact that this little bit of history is his only real connection with them. In fact, his social network may be made up of 1,000 silly little threads like this: the buddies from poker night, the guy with whom he goes fishing, and his workout pals from the gym. As a general rule, a man doesn't establish (although on some level he may wish he had) considerably deeper relationships with some of his buddies. This is why your Mr. Right may be much more sophisticated than most of his goofy friends.

None of this is truly a reflection on your guy, and you're wise not to judge a guy by his old golfing buddies. Now, if he hangs with a group of Brooklyn mobsters, yes, you should be concerned. But if his old high school teammate's idea of a good read is *Penthouse Forum* as opposed to Tolstoy's *Anna Karenina*, it's no cause for panic.

What you could have done differently: changing the outcome of this seeming disaster is simpler than you might think. His pals are part of his comfort zone. You simply don't need to go there. In fact, as in all cases, it's wise that you skip out. Whatever his pal ritual—poker nights, the occasional baseball game, fishing trips, and more—just give him a kiss on the cheek, tell him to enjoy himself, and let him go. It gives him space, and it gives you a breather to spend some time with your posse.

Dating 911

We've known many women who have caused great problems for a relationship—or stifled it altogether—just by not looking the other way when the brew crew showed up. If we're talking every now and then and not twice a week, just go along. It's okay that he has some pals with whom you'd rather not share a cabin for the weekend. He might feel the same way about some of your girlfriends. It's not worth derailing the relationship.

Warning Signs That You've Crossed Over into a Comfort Zone

So how exactly will you know when you've crossed the line with him? Steer clear of these six comfort zones filled with emotional land mines, and the two of you will be on the road toward happiness.

Zone No. 1: Letting Him Move at His Speed

If he becomes quiet and distant when you talk about future plans, take the hint and peddle back a little. When a relationship this good has not presented itself in a long time, of course your natural tendency is to get a little anxious. Monitor yourself and look for signs that you're doing that. For the first couple months of this new relationship, use this one simple rule: never suggest any event that is outside a four-week window. If he wants to make such a suggestion, that's great. But he'll back off in a hurry if he thinks that after a couple dates you're making long-term plans.

Zone No. 2: Allowing Him to Make His Own Decisions

He snaps back at you when you simply try to make a helpful sugges- tion. He's getting ticked because chances are you've made unsolicited "helpful" suggestions more than once. Storm warnings are up: don't go deeper into these waters. Women are accustomed to sharing their thoughts openly. For men, as a general rule, you will do well to share only when your input is sought. In a man's mind, unsolicited advice is one of the least-welcomed forms of communication.

Zone No. 3: Respecting His Opinion

His usually easy-going demeanor has abruptly turned abrasive. Why the sudden change? It could be that you're winning one too many argu- ments. He admires your intelligence and wit, but not always when it's aimed at *him*. If you're thinking, "I'm too fast for this guy," move on. If, on the other hand, you want to build a lasting relationship, let him win one every now and then.

Zone No. 4: Letting Him Be Himself

For the first few dates, he was pretty open about his hopes and dreams—perhaps even showing a bit of his vulnerable side by telling you some of his fears. But now, after a few weeks of knowing each other, he has become much more guarded. What's up? It could well be that you, not even realizing it, have been on a one-woman reform campaign.

From poking around in his closet, suggesting that he dump a couple of those old sweatshirts, making a change in hairstyle, to pushing him to ask his boss for that much-anticipated but unrealized salary hike, you can think of a lot of ways his life could be better. Great—but if you toss all these at him, he'll think he's just not good enough.

> **Dating 911**
>
> Have a plan or an idea of what you can do together. Arranging a date and then saying "Let's do whatever you want to do" shows a lack of imagination.

That said, beware of suggesting too many reforms too quickly. If you hope to knock a little of the Neanderthal out of your guy or turn your Frankenstein into a sophisticate, that *can* be accomplished in time. But if you're thinking it's a four-week turnaround, the only change he's making that quickly is ending your relationship. Despite the good intentions on your part, unfortunately you'll get the wrong results.

Zone No. 5: Acknowledging His Attempts to Get It Right

He was making all kinds of suggestions: places to eat, movies to see, and things to do. After a couple months, though, he's not doing that at all. Is he taking your relationship for granted?

Possibly. But a more likely reason for his new reticence may be your reaction to his ideas: rarely do you praise his suggestions. You don't have to pander to the guy, but would it kill you to say, "That was really fun" or, "What a great little place—thanks for suggesting it!"?

One way in which most men are forever little boys is in their reaction to praise. If a guy suggests a place for dinner and you say something like, "Wow this is a really great place," his happiness quotient doubles. It's as if he went back into the kitchen and made the risotto himself.

If he's like most guys, he may be worried that he won't be able to please you. Without any positive feedback on your part, he may assume his original negative instinct was correct—and he'll simply stop trying. Chances are, when he stops making suggestions, he's not overly comfortable with your relationship. He's simply discouraged. Try stepping up the praise and seeing whether he comes around once he believes again in his ability to get something right.

Zone No. 6: Encouraging and Appreciating His Sexual Performance

He has been sexually aggressive from the get-go. Now after just a couple weeks of intimacy, he seems much less likely to initiate sex. Why the sudden drop in interest? Something is clearly wrong here, because as a general rule when it comes to sex, men are the "little engine that could."

One common concern that women have in this situation is the simple fear, "He's just not that into me." More often than not, what's really going on is that he's thinking the opposite: "She doesn't seem sexually satisfied, and I'll never get it right." If you want to make a list of five insecurities that men have about how their partners perceive them, reasons one through four are their performance in bed. It starts with the thought, "What does she see in me?", and it goes downward from there.

No one is suggesting that you start faking an orgasm, but remember one simple rule: if sex is a symphony, a woman is the conductor. He might bring one impressive brass section to the orchestra, but he needs your subtle touch to realize the power of his contribution. Verbalize little and show a lot. In bed more than anywhere else, body language speaks volumes.

The Least You Need to Know

- ♦ When and how you cross into his comfort zone may make all the difference with whether this relationship succeeds.
- ♦ If you're too pushy, you may push him out the door.
- ♦ Not all areas of his life will be open to you, so live with that.
- ♦ One comfort zone you control is the bedroom.

Chapter 16

Friend or Lover?

In This Chapter

- ◆ Friendship issues that stand in the way of love
- ◆ The best of both worlds: a great friend and a great lover
- ◆ What to do if he's a wonderful lover but a lousy friend …
- ◆ … or a wonderful friend but a lousy lover

There are two possible areas of serious concern in every relationship: his ability to be a great friend and the skills that make him a satisfying lover. Whereas the ideal scenario is that your Mr. Right is all that and more, it's more likely than not that those aspects of your relationship *won't* be in sync.

You're absolutely right in your determination not to forget about intimacy just because he has quickly become a good friend—or to discount the importance of friendship in a long-term relationship because he's such an effective lover.

Which Issues Count—and Which Don't

Ideally, in this primary relationship, you and your Mr. Right are friends, first and foremost. That said, all friends have issues that make the relationship less than perfect. The great news is that most of these differences can be worked out—that is, if both parties take the time and effort to communicate their feelings and are willing to compromise.

So yes, you will have a few points of contention with the man in your life. But most of them should not be deal-breakers. These are simply petty annoyances and should be chalked up to, "It's who he is, and I can live with it … or make him aware of them and work with him to change them."

Issues such as his sloppiness or some annoying habit or two (it gets on your nerves when he calls you "dude" all the time, doesn't it?) fall under this category. In the following sections, we discuss 12 petty annoyances that may have you shuttering but aren't reasons to throw in the towel.

He Wakes Up Too Happy—or Too Grumpy

Why this shouldn't bug you: someone's morning mood is a temporary state.

How to keep this in perspective: if his morning mood is sweetness and light, let it rub off on you. Otherwise, ignore any negativity by leaving his proximity as quickly as possible. Or better yet, have morning sex. This will change his grumpy mood post haste.

He Makes Frequent—and Loud—Bodily Noises

Why this shouldn't bug you: obviously, this is a medical condition or a result of a diet that doesn't agree with his metabolism.

How to keep this in perspective: ask him to see a doctor. In the meantime, research foods that may make him gassy—and be sure to avoid them. And, as a final resort, ask him to show you some consideration: when he feels an imminent gas attack, he should go either outside or into the bathroom and let loose in there.

He Leaves the Toilet Seat Up

Why this shouldn't bug you: he forgot. Sometimes you forget things, too—like when you use his razor instead of your own on your legs.

How to keep this in perspective: remind him again and again. And leave a note on the inside of the lid.

He Won't Ask for Directions

Why this shouldn't bug you: it's very much a guy thing. Some men innately feel doing so indicates a weakness.

How to keep this in perspective: just because he won't ask doesn't mean you can't. Another solution: invest in one of the many affordable portable GPS systems around.

He Has a Cough/Sneeze/Nervous Laugh/Stutter

Why this shouldn't bug you: it may be a psychological symptom (stress) or a physiological issue (allergy or medical symptom).

How to keep this in perspective: making him aware that he has this habit is the first step toward helping him get over it. Whether he was aware of it or not, he now will acknowledge it and try to voluntarily control it. Gently suggest that he see a doctor to determine why he has fallen into this habit.

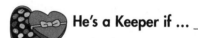

He's a Keeper if ...

... he doesn't comment on your weight (and even makes you feel beautiful if you gain a little).

He Won't Let You Drive

Why this shouldn't bug you: many men have control issues. And many men want to protect the women in their lives. Being in the driver's seat is a position men have taken since the invention of the wheel. In other words, it's in his genes.

How to keep this in perspective: if it's your ride, you have the right (and the insurance policy) to take the wheel. Then again, if it's his car, he gets the reins—and you should just quit fussing about it and enjoy the ride.

Now, if the car is in both of your names, you're free to bargain as to how and when you take turns. But be forewarned: when you get behind the wheel, he may drive you crazy with his gasps, backseat driving, or judgmental tongue clicks. Is it worth all that?

He Won't Help Around the House

Why this shouldn't bug you: he sees this as your domain. Okay, fair enough. Now you can explain to him how you see it as shared space.

How to keep this in perspective: to prove it, make up only your side of the bed. Then, give him his own domain: say, the yard or the garage, and certainly his bureau and closet. Don't forget to include any and all bathroom space he shares with you.

If he continues to make his domain a sty, hire a maid service and give him half the bill.

He Forgets Important Dates

Why this shouldn't bug you: he has a lot on his mind. Or, it has yet to sink in that he now has to be considerate of your priorities, too, just like you are considerate of his.

How to keep this in perspective: put it on a calendar that is hung where you both can see it (perhaps on the kitchen refrigerator). Send reminder e-mails or text-message him the morning of your date.

His Voice Gets on Your Nerves

Why this shouldn't bug you: we all have regional colloquialisms, such as accents, inflections, or twangs. And some of us have unique tones to our voices—perhaps high-pitched, breathy, or nasal in quality. These traits can be endearing or annoying.

How to keep this in perspective: in any regard, it makes him unique. And believe it or not, it's part of his charm. Granted, you may not think so now, but what comes to mind when you think of him is his voice—as well as his look, his smell, and his touch. You hear endearments in your ears, and they reverberate in your heart. So yes, eventually you'll grow to love his voice.

He Has a Few Obsessive/Compulsive Traits

Why this shouldn't bug you: granted, it is more extreme in some than others, but everyone exhibits some form of Obsessive Compulsive Disorder (OCD)—even you.

How to keep this in perspective: think about something you may do that drives him crazy, then come to an agreement with him in which you both commit to working on changing at least one annoying habit. However, if his OCD becomes severe or emotionally debilitating, ask him to seek help in addressing this very important issue.

He Unconsciously Picks His Nose

Why this shouldn't bug you: it's an involuntary act. Perhaps he has an irritation in his nostril, or maybe it's a nervous habit.

How to keep this in perspective: no one wants to be gross. That said, the first step is to make him aware of it. Then, suggest to him that you create a "signal" between you that makes him aware of the fact that he's doing it again. He'll appreciate your help—just as you'd appreciate his if this annoying habit were yours instead.

He's Not Good Looking

Why this shouldn't bug you: it's true that looks are fleeting. And sometimes it takes a few years for men to grow into their faces. (A perfect example is the actor Patrick Dempsey. He is more handsome now than he was at 20.)

How to keep this in perspective: don't judge him in a way in which you wouldn't want to be judged. Besides, his looks obviously weren't what attracted you to him in the first place. Remember: in relationships, actions speak louder than looks.

Dating 911

Don't spend the evening checking your BlackBerry. Playing with your cell phone is annoying and gives the impression you have more important things to do than to be there with him.

Again, none of these items are deal-breakers. However, any issues that keep him from being either a great friend or a caring lover will also eliminate him as your Mr. Right if he isn't willing to change.

Now, the moment of truth: is he both a concerned friend *and* a caring lover? There are only three possible answers to that question.

He's Both a Great Friend and a Great Lover

Obviously, the best of both worlds is a combination of these two traits: a caring companion who is solid, reliable, down to Earth, interesting to talk to, fun to be with, has bedroom eyes, and knows how to finish whenever he gets you started.

We're sure you'll agree that's quite a list. If you can honestly answer yes, congratulations! You've hit the jackpot. You have a wonderful guy, and you're going to do all you can to hold on to him. (Feel free to move on to Chapter 17.)

Of course, if he's lousy at both these functions, you shouldn't even be reading this chapter because you aren't in a relationship, per se; you're in the third circle of Girlfriend Hell. (To return to Life-As-You-Want-to-Know-It, reread Chapters 1 through 15.)

This leaves us with two areas of concern that must be addressed if your relationship is to thrive.

He Said, She Said

If you judge people, you have no time to love them.

—Mother Teresa, humanitarian

He's a Great Lover but a Lousy Friend

If there is only one point you take from this book, we hope it's what we wrote earlier in this chapter: first and foremost, your Mr. Right has to be your caring, concerned friend. In fact, this mandate takes precedence over his boudoir technique—no matter how phenomenal that may be.

Friendship is built on these shared traits:

- Trust
- Concern

- Loyalty

- Compassion

Can you honestly say that your Mr. Right exhibits all four? If you say yes, then he has the potential to be a good friend if he isn't already. Then again, if he does any of the following, he's not your friend—but you're his friend with benefits:

- Outside the bedroom, he's not very responsive to any of your needs.

- He leaves after lovemaking.

- He drops by unexpectedly—for booty calls only.

- He doesn't like to kiss you.

- He doesn't like to cuddle.

- He's reluctant to meet your friends or have you interact with his.

- He disappears on one of the few nights he agreed to take you out to dinner or to a movie—then, days later, reappears with a breezy (but not very convincing) reason for why he "forgot" to call.

- He's a lousy listener. Worse yet, he doesn't seem to be at all empathetic when you tell him that you had a rotten day at the office or that you just got treated shabbily by your best gal pal.

- Just when you feel closer to him emotionally, he pulls away.

- He makes you laugh in bed—but you cry when he leaves because you're lonely, and he just doesn't give a damn.

If you're fidgeting now, it's because he has shown one or more telltale signs that he's not truly your friend.

Yes, of course it hurts! In the bedroom, he's confident, responsive to your desires, and just plain sexy. You two are having so much fun that you've almost forgotten about the friendship part. After all, if a loyal friend is what you're missing, you can always get a dog, right?

Wrong.

Yes, we know: it would be a lot easier to have dumped this guy and moved on if he wasn't a 10 between the sheets. But it's time to face facts: you two are friends with benefits and no more.

So the obvious question becomes, "Can this skilled lover become your constant, consummate companion, too?" Yes—but that desire must be his, not yours. What do you do to get the ball rolling?

Make Your Feelings Known

At the right place and the right time (yes, it's okay if it happens in bed after another round of wonderful sex), make your feelings known in very clear terms—perhaps something like this: "I so enjoy you and our time together. I know you do, too. So I hope you agree with me that it's time to take it to the next level."

Hear Him Out on His Concerns, but Stick to Your Agenda

Pause to get his reaction. Obviously he likes things the way they've been and will be resistant to change: sort of like a four-year-old who has stayed home with Mommy all his life and doesn't like being left at preschool. You love him, so you will listen to his concerns. Smile. Nod. Then take your turn explaining to him what kind of relationship makes you happy: one in which the two of you enjoy each other beyond the bedroom. Hey, if he doesn't see it that way, you understand—and you hope he will, too: you need to move on. If he's not your Mr. Right, you want to move ahead with your life and find him.

He Said, She Said

Is marriage the end game? Not to 48 percent of women. According to a recent Chemistry.com survey of 737 people, they would be just as happy if they lived in a committed relationship but never got married.

He's a Great Friend but a Lousy Lover

After a month or so of dating, you've fully anticipated that by now the two of you would have moved beyond a few tentative kisses and warm embraces. But it has been nothing of the sort. From start to finish, he seemed uncomfortable and distracted. In other words, he's nothing like the guy you've gotten to know outside the bedroom.

Or, on the contrary, he was the proverbial bull in a china shop: not showing the slightest inclination to learn about your sexual needs. Instead, he was in an all-out rush to get to the finish line: *his* finish line, that is.

The bottom line is that he's a real disappointment in the bedroom.

Your guess is that (a) it was the wrong night, (b) he had one too many cocktails, or (c) there was a full moon—which is why your prince has turned into a frog.

You of course initiated a return attempt just to make certain ... and unfortunately, it turns out your first impression was right: this guy just does nothing for you sexually.

So where can you go from here (with him)? The good news is that he's trainable—and that's because he loves you and wants to please you. Even better news is that because he's such a good friend—your *best* friend—he'll be a great listener when you tell him what you need from him in bed. And because you *want* him to be good in bed, to satisfy all your intimate needs, here's what you say to him:

- ◆ You love him, but you also want to be *in lo*ve with him.

- ◆ That said, you want him to feel free to speak up about any concerns he has regarding being intimate with you.

- ◆ You'd also like to have sex more often.

- ◆ You want him to describe his most intimate fantasies, and you want to do the same with yours. Be specific. Describe positions you'd like to try, any role playing you'd consider, and other places outside the bedroom in which you'd like to make love.

- ◆ You want to play out these fantasies. Together, plan how you'll do that—the how, where, and when.

- ◆ Also tell him about more romantic things you'd like to do with him. How about a picnic? How about a walk at sunset on a beautiful beach? Consider, perhaps, a quaint town that the two of you can both discover. The goal is to make romantic memories together that you can both visualize during your lovemaking.

These requests may shock him. That's fine. Even better, they might just tantalize him—and perhaps rejuvenate his own efforts at making you happy in bed.

Even if your lovemaking isn't perfect, if you're both open to discussing your intimate needs and if he's willing to make the effort, then you're halfway there. Remember, practice makes perfect. But we get into that in our next chapter …

The Least You Need to Know

◆ You are friends first and foremost. But even friends have issues that come between them.

◆ Some issues are petty and worth putting into perspective.

◆ Some issues are more important, but even these most often can be worked out.

◆ If your Mr. Right is more of a lover than a friend, he may not be the right person for you in the long run.

◆ If your Mr. Right is a great friend but a not-so-adept lover, there is a possibility he can change—with a little help from you.

Chapter 17

GIB (Good in Bed)? Here's How You Know

In This Chapter

◆ When it's the wrong time to have sex

◆ How to assess his sexual prowess

◆ Setting a sensual mood

◆ What makes sex great: 16 turn-ons for you and him

◆ Why romance is important in a relationship

◆ The difference between sex and intimacy

By now, you and your Mr. Right have probably either had, or are moving toward, the decision to have sex. As we mentioned in Chapter 16, his being both a good friend and a good lover are the two keys to lasting commitment on your part. Of course, the same would be true for him: he wants the woman in his life to be someone he trusts and respects—and lusts after as well.

The Wrong Time to Have Sex

Is there a "right time" to have sex with Mr. Right? Because everyone reading this book is at a different age and stage of life, it's a lot easier to give you all the *wrong* times. Here are some examples of when you must undeniably, indisputably say *no* to sex:

◆ **It's your first date.** Sorry, but there is no circumstance in which a first date constitutes a "yes." Face it—it's totally slutty. Okay, we'll make one exception: you're both on the *Titanic*, and it's sinking. Yeah, okay, go for it.

◆ **He's drunk.** It's true what they say: the difference between a fox and a pig is a six pack.

◆ **You're drunk.** That old saying goes both ways.

◆ **Before, during, or after your office holiday party.** You may not get fired for it, but you certainly won't get a raise. All you'll get is a reputation.

◆ **Neither of you have contraception.** Just because you want to have sex doesn't mean you also want to have a baby. Find a method of contraception that works for you, or keep a box of condoms ready.

◆ **He wants it but you don't.** Love is a two-way street. Lovemaking takes two, too. It's a participatory activity. If the only reason why you're doing so is because (a) he begs you, (b) you feel sorry for him, or (c) he's willing to shower you with bling and take you places you could otherwise never afford, then you're really just not that into him. For whatever reason, you're compromising.

◆ **You just don't feel right about it.** We can't say it enough: timing is everything, particularly with regard to how you feel about him, or if you're one of the many who believes sex happens only after marriage. That said, if he hasn't proven that he's right for you, he certainly doesn't deserve you.

At the same time, don't hold off just because you feel obligated to do so based on some formality dealing with time, place, person, or custom. Only one person can live your life: *you*.

He Said, She Said

Kissing—and I mean, like, yummy, smacking kissing—is the most delicious, most beautiful and passionate thing that two people can do, bar none. Better than sex, hands down.

—Drew Barrymore, actress

Is He GIB? Take This Test

Your first time in bed with him is a lot like your first date (and we're hoping they don't happen the same day): exhilarating, scary, exciting ... and not at all what you expected.

That could be a good thing—or not. Was it as good for you as it was for him? That depends on the answers you give to this simple true/false quiz:

1. His kisses were gentle, then passionate.

2. He's into foreplay.

3. He didn't hard-sell his way into your bed. Instead, he sweet-talked you—between the jokes and the flirting.

4. He treated your body as if it were a treasure trove.

5. He followed your subliminal directions.

6. He took his time with you.

7. You had an orgasm.

8. He waited to climax with you.

9. You had a second orgasm.

10. He stayed and cuddled. Then, he asked when he could see you again.

If you answered "false" more than twice, he may not be the stud muffin you'd hoped your Mr. Right would and should be. But before you judge him on this one experience, consider the reasons why you may want to give him a chance to redeem himself:

- Because his not-so-stellar showing may be due to the fact that he may have been too excited or nervous at the thought of you agreeing to go to bed with him

- Because you really like him in every other way

- Because he too may have realized that he wasn't in top form and is ashamed to say so out loud (just in case you didn't notice, too)

All that being said, be a sport and give him a rematch. But before you do, you'll want to help him bring his best game.

Setting the Mood

Sensuality is a mind game. It's what you say to him and how he answers back. It's where you have sex and when. It's how you communicate with him: before, during, and after.

To ensure that sex with Mr. Right lives up to all your expectations (and his), go ahead and set the mood. Take time to consider:

- **Where this momentous occasion is to take place.** Will it be at your place or his? Are you considering a hotel or a bed-and-breakfast inn? Where it occurs will be part of a very important memory.

- **How you will look.** What will you be wearing? (Something sexy, for sure.) And your hair: will it flow but be easy to sweep off the nape of your neck so that he can kiss it? His mind's eye will want to remember every detail.

- **What you will say.** Certainly the majority of your remarks will be spontaneous. You'll go with the flow. But verbalizing through a thought you want to express isn't a bad idea. It doesn't have to be "heavy." In other words, whatever you want to say, keep it light, bright, and gay, such as, "Hey, what took us so long?"

- **Other mood enhancers.** Candles or soft lighting. Music. Soft, warm sheets and a little spritz of perfume. Let him know you've put some thought as to what this experience will feel like to both of you.

And if this is a rematch, hopefully the results will match your best laid plans.

"Just" Sex Versus *Great* Sex

When it comes to sex, all men are created equal; that is to say, they all come carrying the same equipment. But what separates the boys from the men is how they use whatever Mother Nature has given them.

There are many reasons why a man may leave the woman he loves less than satisfied between the sheets. For example:

♦ Maybe what he knows about sex comes only from what he's heard from other men or seen in movies, which is no sort of sex manual whatsoever—only a lot of grunting and groaning without a big passionate prelude.

♦ Perhaps he's too lazy or too shy to experiment.

♦ Maybe he has never asked women he has been intimate with (that includes you) what they wanted from him but just presumed that what he was giving was good enough.

♦ Maybe he's less experienced than you and therefore is somewhat intimidated by you in the sack.

In any regard, if he's going to stay in the coveted position of your Mr. Right, he needs a wake-up call *now*. Does he want to hear it? You better believe he does. No man wants to even consider the possibility that he's lousy in bed.

 Dating 911

Don't be negative or complain. Nobody likes a whiner—especially in the bedroom!

The Sweet 16: Sexual Turn-Ons for You and for Him

Essentially, orgasms happen when a spasm occurs in certain muscles located in either your clitoris or the Gräfenberg—your "G spot." His touch—that of his palms, his fingers, his tongue, and his penis—is the catalyst for this involuntary and ecstatic shiver.

As with an avalanche, your orgasm (and his) needs all the right conditions: not just time, place, and mood, but also how he touches you and the speed in which he does so determines whether you shake, rattle, then roll off the bed.

Needless to say, not everyone is a sexpert. Then again, the fun doesn't necessarily come from knowledge but from the process of discovery—which you'll take together. Experiment, because not all men or all women like the same thing. There is no time like the present to discover your sexual preferences.

A great place to start is with the following 16 sexual turn-ons for you and for him. Feel free to embellish and reinvent at will:

- *For you:* he grazes the back of your neck with his lips, then kisses the back of your ear. *For him:* you run your finger from his earlobe down his spine.

- *For you:* he stimulates the edges of your clitoris with his tongue. *For him:* you take his organ between your lips and massage his testicles at the same time.

- *For you:* on your back with your legs over his shoulders as he moves in a circular pattern. *For him:* you're on top and moving sensually up and down.

- *For you:* he stands behind you and enters your vagina that way. *For him:* he pins you against the wall and lifts you onto him.

- *For you:* he tears off your panties. *For him:* he holds your panties, and after sex, he gets to put them back on you.

- *For you:* a gentle spanking. *For him:* dirty talk. (Or vice-versa.)

- *For you:* doing it in a pool. *For him:* doing it in an elevator.

- *For you:* he finds your G spot using your dildo. *For him:* you tease the spot between his testicles and his anus with your dildo.

- *For you:* he massages your breasts, gently, with scented lotion. *For him:* you give him a hand job but let him explode inside of you.

- *For you:* he puts both his thumb and forefinger in your vagina at the same time, inching them in and out. *For him:* run a silk scarf over his testicles.

- *For you:* he blindfolds you. Then, he kisses every spot that causes you to tingle. *For him:* blindfold him. Then make him lie down on his back, then tease him with your tongue from his shoulders, down his spine, to the base of his back.

- *For you:* on top of him, backward: the "reverse cowgirl." *For him:* he loves watching you in this position, especially as you lift yourself up and down slowly on his penis.

- *For you:* he kisses you behind the knee and works his way up your leg. *For him:* you play with his nipples with your fingertips and your tongue.

- *For you:* long, leisurely kissing sessions. *For him:* he wants to feel your lips all over him—before they reach his penis.

- *For you:* roleplaying: "The Pole Dancer and the Big Spender." *For him:* roleplaying: he's the boss, and you're his new assistant who always loses her pencil under his desk.

- *For you:* in the shower. You love the way he kisses you under the massaging shower head. *For him:* in the bathtub. He loves the way you scrub him all over.

> **He Said, She Said**
>
> Does marriage mean the end of passion? Not according to a recent National Science Foundation's General Social Survey, which shows that married men and women actually have quite active sex lives, reporting sex with their spouses a little more than once a week.

Yes, Romance Is Important in Your Relationship

Men love sex. That's a given—at least in most cases. Women love sex, too. But what makes a woman *long* for sex is different from what turns on a man.

For the majority of men, visual stimulation is more important than mental stimulation: it's why the porn industry has been around for centuries. Also, men look at women in the abstract. A breast is a turn-on no matter how unattractive the face that sits just inches above it.

For most women, mental stimulation is the key ingredient. For her, sex is a puzzle ... a game. It isn't abstract but up close and personal. It's all about her—and all about the man with whom she wishes to share this experience.

If you ask a man what is considered sexy, he lists body parts: Butts. Boobs. Legs. Mouths. When you ask a woman the same question, you get a personality profile: "He's got to have a great sense of humor," she'll say. Or, "He's got to be adventurous. I don't want a man who can't tell me he loves me."

To men, women are flesh. To women, men are ideals. That's why romance is important to women. Romance is the way in which a woman gauges her lover's passion for her. It is also the litmus for her passion for him. After all, anyone can have sex. Sex means you're "in lust," not "in love." That's why sex with Mr. Right must have a romantic prelude in order to be better than your run-of-the-mill sex (which could turn your Mr. Right into Mr. Wrong).

But what if your Mr. Right isn't romantic? Is there a way to get him to up his game?

Yes, of course! Your Mr. Right wants to please the woman in his life. He wants you to enjoy your sexual encounters with him, not just endure them. So that you both are on the same page (or, more importantly, in the same mood at the same time), take time to discuss the things that get you there.

When to Have That Conversation

Have it as soon as possible, but pick the right time. In other words, don't just fling it on him while he's in the middle of watching the last few minutes of a tied Lakers game. You want his full attention, and you get that after you've shared an intimate moment or when he has declared how wonderful you two are together. That's your opening.

What to Say and How to Say It So He Hears You

Now, here's what you say: "I love you too, babe. And I love having sex with you. But do you know what would make it even better for me? I love it when …" Then you tell him the kinds of things that speak romance to you. Here's our short list. Feel free to add to it:

- ◆ "… you get in the tub with me."

- ◆ "… we light scented candles."

- ◆ "… you call me and talk dirty to me."

- ◆ "… you're standing there naked, except for your tie."

- ◆ "… you get me hot and bothered with some serious foreplay" (then describe what you mean).

- ◆ "… you start a fire, and then lay a blanket in front of it."

- ◆ "… you take me in the woods, just the two of us and a sleeping bag."

- ◆ "… you pick out a sexy negligee for me and I get to model it for you."

- ◆ "… you write me a love poem and read it out loud to me."

- ◆ "… you bring me chocolates, then feed them to me one by one."

 Dating 911

Pay attention to your appearance. Your date likes to feel you've made a special effort to look nice for the occasion.

Each of these random acts of romance has something in common. There is a physical aspect to it. You both have to use your senses. There is a visual, oral, or tactile component to it, and he initiates it. In other words, romance begins with him and ends with both of you.

Will he get the message? Of course—because he can visualize himself doing this. And best of all, he can just imagine the ecstatic and passionate look on your face.

Sex with Regard to Emotional Intimacy

Just because a couple has sex doesn't mean that they share emotional intimacy. What has taken place is *physical* intimacy. For emotional intimacy, you need:

♦ Two open hearts and minds

♦ The ability to say anything that is on your mind

♦ The ability to accept what has been divulged to you

♦ To know that tears are okay

♦ To know that there will be no regrets for what has been done or said

♦ The resolve to keep this bond between you just as it is now: clear and candid

The Least You Need to Know

♦ There is a wrong time to have sex.

♦ Be prepared that your first sexual experience with your Mr. Right will be a total wild card.

♦ The difference between just sex and great sex is the effort put into it and the ability to listen to your partner.

♦ Romance is important to you. Therefore, it is important to your sexual satisfaction—and concurrently, to your relationship.

♦ You have a right to ask for romance. Pick your time and your words carefully so that he understands its importance to both of you.

♦ Sex is the act of physical intimacy. Emotional intimacy takes two people opening their hearts and minds to each other.

Chapter 18

Mr. Right Versus Mr. Right Now

In This Chapter

- ◆ The seven stages that relationships go through
- ◆ Signs that he's committed to you
- ◆ Signs that he's feeling ambivalent
- ◆ Can you change him?

Yep, he's the one. No other guy makes your heart go pitter-patter. He's saying all the right things. And when it comes to any other man, you now wear blinders—even when some hottie comes into your peripheral vision.

And yes, you can envision spending the rest of your life with him. You trust him with your life and with your future.

But does he feel the same way about you?

The Seven Stages of a Relationship

Relationships must move through seven critical stages before they fully form. They are a lot like that game you might have played as a child, Chutes and Ladders. You'll move many steps forward, only to fall several steps back. If you want to win at the game of love, ideally you and your Mr. Right will move through these seven stages *together*. However, that does not always happen. If, say, you jump ahead before he has a chance to join you, any uncertainties he has are sure to come to the forefront. Even if you both skip a stage together—say, you become intimate before you've both emotionally committed—the relationship won't survive, unless you're both willing to go back through the stage or stages you missed. Otherwise, the issues that arise in these stages will have never been addressed, and may eventually pull you apart.

Stage 1: Attraction

You see each other from across the room. Your eyes lock; it's an instant attraction. It's physical. It's lust. It's his look, his smell, and his laugh. It's your fantasy—or close to it.

Stage 2: Seduction

He asks you out. You say yes. That date goes well—along with the next and the one after that. The dates are constant. He's there to please: dinners, movies, and romantic walks in the woods or on the beach. You are seriously falling for this guy!

The feeling seems mutual. The way he wants to protect and cherish you is so wonderful. He's your knight in shining armor, and he kisses like a dream. It's inevitable that you let him sweep you off your feet and carry you into your bedroom.

Stage 3: The Honeymoon Period

Wow. The first time you had sex with him was hot and passionate. You're into him, and he can't seem to get enough of you. If you were to rate his lovemaking on a scale of 1 to 10, you'd have to say it's an 11!

Not only that, but he wants more of you. You are more than an item. The two of you are inseparable. Your friends adore him, too.

 He's a Keeper if ...

... he helps out in the kitchen. He understands that keeping a nice home is a shared responsibility.

Stage 4: The Honeymoon's Over

Little by little, you notice the first kinks in his armor. Maybe, for the first time, you notice his teeth are crooked. Or you don't like his laugh. Or he has this nasty little habit of running out of money before payday. Or he's got a nasty ex-wife. Whatever the problem, you've got to ask yourself some hard questions:

- ◆ Are you willing to overlook his problems?
- ◆ Will you take the time to talk through your issues with him?
- ◆ Will he be open to listening?
- ◆ Can you come to some form of compromise?
- ◆ Is he worth you hanging in there?

If you can answer yes to all of these, then you're ready for the next stage.

Stage 5: Moving in Together—or Not

Unless you're moving in for all the right reasons, doing so will certainly test the mettle of your union. You remember all those little idiosyncrasies of his that drive you crazy? Well, now multiply them by 24/7: yep, 24 hours a day, 7 days a week. Add (a) his friends, (b) his hobbies, (c) his work frustrations, and (d) his laundry, and you have yourself a full-time boyfriend. Enjoy! And you will, because at first it may actually feel like a second honeymoon phase.

Stage 6: Learning/Growing/Compromising

This stage will either make you or break you as a couple. When living together, you learn practically everything about each other's strengths and weaknesses. If you didn't know he was, say, afraid of spiders before, you will now. Or that he hasn't talked to his father since he was 16. Or that he cheats on his expense reports. This is also the time of mergers and acquisitions: friends and furniture, for sure, and shared expenses and closet space, maybe. Some secrets will be learned. Some skeletons will leap out of closets. If what you see and hear only endears him more to you, than you're ready for the next stage.

Stage 7: Saying "I Do"

You have moved together through a series of stages, and now you're ready for him to pop the question. This isn't a "have the cow, so the milk is free" situation. And it's not necessarily a biological ticking-clock scenario. It's an "I want to spend the rest of my life with someone I love" situation.

And you presume that he does, too—but does he?

He Said, She Said _____

I think you have to marry for the right reasons, and marry the right person.

—Anne Bancroft, actress

The True Meaning of Commitment

Because relationships go through many stages—and each half of a couple goes through these stages at his or her individual pace—your feelings toward commitment to him may not align with his own views of where this union stands at this particular moment.

So how do you know whether he's as committed to being in a long-term, monogamous relationship as you are? Here are seven very important signs that he is indeed serious about you:

- **He suggests, but he doesn't push.** He sees you as his partner; that means he respects your opinion enough to allow you to prove your points, and he doesn't insist that he's always right.

- **He makes you laugh—for all the right reasons.** He never laughs at you but with you. And he's not afraid to laugh at himself. If either of you are laughing, it's for joy and not out of nervous discomfort.

- **He doesn't play games with your heart.** He doesn't leave you guessing as to where he stands on any issue, let alone how he feels about you. He's candid, not covert.

- **Your life values are in sync.** You're never second-guessing what he'll do in dire situations. He agrees with you on the *big* issues: those things that are important to you and to your familial sensibilities. Sometimes it's so scary because it's almost like he can read your mind, as if he's your twin.

- **He thinks "we," not "me."** You are always uppermost in his mind. For example, he never just wanders off. Out of courtesy, he mentions where he's going and calls when he's running late. If he's invited somewhere, then so are you. When he plans ahead (vacations, job offers, and holidays), it's a given that you are *always* part of the equation.

- **He makes sure that both your families are involved in your lives.** He takes the time to get to know your folks and really wants his parents to know (and like) you, too.

- **He doesn't just hint around that you're "the one."** He treats you like it, too. He is consistently loving in his manner toward you. You'll happily admit he treats you as if you're his queen. In fact, he acts as if it's a given that you'll be spending the rest of your lives together.

In most cases, your Mr. Right will have exhibited some of these signs, if not all of them. Then again, if none of these have set off your Mr. Right Richter Scale, you need to ask yourself: "Am I dating an Ambivalent Man?"

Traits of the Ambivalent Man

What was just described was an ideal relationship—one in which both of you is in love and committed to living your lives together. But not all unions end up happily ever after. Under the best of circumstances, the breakup is a mutual decision, and both work to keep the friendship. The worst-case scenario is that one of you leaves kicking and screaming.

He Said, She Said

According to a 2002 survey by eNation, 35 percent of Americans admit they've been through a breakup at least once in the past 10 years.

No, you don't want that to be him. Breaking hearts leads to guilt (yours) and heartache (his). And you certainly don't want to be the one who is kicked to the curb.

But guess what? That's bound to happen if the man with whom you've invested all this time and effort isn't who you think he is: Mr. Right. So what are the telltale signs that he's ambivalent as opposed to committed? Here are five that should put you on permanent alert.

He'll Never Be Able to Say "I Love You"

In Chapter 5, we discussed how a man's inability to say "I love you" is not as important as his ability to show you his love in many ways, both big and small. However, if his feelings toward you are uncertain, saying those three little words won't be your biggest problem.

A larger issue in your relationship is *why* he doesn't feel the need to perform some of those random acts that demonstrate his love—in ways that words can't even come close to doing.

Maybe it's because he just doesn't care. That said, maybe he can say "I love you"—but he just doesn't want to say it to you. Why? Doing so will give you the wrong idea: that he plans on sticking around, that he's committed to making the relationship work, or that he loves you.

He doesn't want to lie about it. At least *that* is something you can appreciate about him.

He'd Prefer to Stay "Friends with Benefits"

Things are great between you, especially in bed. And you two are also friends. But whenever you bring up the fact that you want to "take the relationship to the next level," it's as if he looks right through you. Maybe he cracks a joke or comes up with an excuse to change the topic. The bottom line is that he doesn't want to go there—at least, not now. (Or even worse, maybe he doesn't want to go there *with you*.)

So what's your game plan now—to hang in there until, by some miracle, he changes his mind? Fat chance. You see, he already knows how much you're willing to give because you've been giving it to him. But unfortunately, he's not willing to match it.

He Said, She Said

Mr. Right may be in the cubicle next to your own. According to Vault's 2009 Office Romance Survey, 58 percent see romance as a fringe benefit of their jobs.

He Doesn't Want to Meet Your Parents

He'll grudgingly hang with you and your friends, but he draws the line at meeting your family. Why? Because to him, that is tantamount to admitting that you guys are a *couple*. Because he doesn't believe it himself, why would he want to lead on two people—your parents—with whom he doesn't ever plan on spending Thanksgiving? He wants to enjoy his meal, not choke it down because your dad is eyeing him as if he's an ax murderer and your mother is already planning your wedding.

He's Immature

If a man can only think about women on a physical level and still eyes other women—with absolutely no guilt for doing so—he may not be mature enough to be in a relationship. Other signs of emotional immaturity are as follows:

♦ It seems as if he never listens to you, and certainly he forgets half the things you say to him.

- He has no interest in getting to know you beyond the bedroom.

- Sometimes he out-and-out bores you.

Well, then, it's time to face facts: you're more mature than he is about life and love.

You Can't Trust Him

If, for any reason, he has proven to be unworthy of your trust and your love, he probably has personal unresolved issues that keep him from feeling as if he deserves this from you. He realizes it, and now you have to, as well: he's just not right for you.

Can Ambivalence Change to Commitment?

Whether your Mr. Ambivalent can somehow change his stripes and view you as his one and only—and therefore become your Mr. Right—depends on certain factors that have to do with:

- **Timing.** As we pointed out in Chapter 8, timing truly is everything in a relationship. You'd done some extensive weeding before jumping into this union, which is why you were so sure, so positive that he was Mr. Right material. And more likely than not, your instincts are spot on. That said, this could be a perfect example of meeting the right guy, but for whatever his reason, it's just not the right time for him to get involved with you—or with anyone, for that matter.

- **His communication skills—and yours.** So why hasn't he been honest about his reasons for backing away before now? More than likely it's because he, like you, is having a wonderful time in your relationship. Still, that is no excuse for him to dodge the issue of commitment. Only until he can express his concerns can he truly be your Mr. Right.

- **His ability to keep issues from his past from coloring your future together.** Even without realizing it, most of us judge our new relationships by old experiences. He has put up a barrier to his true feelings about you because he's afraid of getting hurt again. Until he's able to consider his pain in the context in which it happened, he won't be able to move beyond it to a real relationship with you.

♦ **His vision of Ms. Right and whether you meet it.** We all have fantasies of how we'll live our lives and with whom. But when reality doesn't live up to our ideals, we weigh in our hearts whether or not we want to compromise. If he's not yet ready to have an equal partner—one with whom compromise is both important and necessary—you'll never be his Ms. Right, no matter how hard you try.

♦ **His true feelings for you.** Sometimes a man finds it easier to just "go with the flow." He may not want to rock the boat in his relationship because his comfort level is being met on the basest level: security. He's got a nice girl at his side, right? But that's just it: he doesn't see you as anything more than "nice." Will that remain enough for him? As he gains more confidence and as he matures emotionally, will he someday ask himself whether he "settled" before he was ready?

Of course, you don't want that. What you really want is to be loved, appreciated, respected, and admired for all you do and for what you bring to the relationship. Otherwise, it's *you* who is settling for less than you deserve.

There are times when we avoid the simple truth of a situation. No one would spend much time trying to put a square peg into a round hole, but we do that often in matters of love and relationships. In truth, every fiber of your soul will tell you when it's not working. Listen to your heart and move on with dignity. You deserve nothing less.

The Least You Need to Know

♦ Relationships have seven stages: attraction, seduction, the honeymoon period, the post-honeymoon period, the move in or move on stage, learning/growing/compromising, and saying "I do."

♦ The key to moving successfully from one relationship stage to the next is to do so without skipping stages.

◆ In many cases, the two partners who make up a couple may have different levels of commitment to the relationship. If so, the more committed partner must readjust his or her expectations if the relationship is to grow.

◆ For reasons out of your control, the man you love may not be ready for a commitment to you. Don't deceive yourself about these warning signs; they'll only come back to haunt you in time.

Chapter 19

Should You Settle for Less?

In This Chapter

- ◆ What it truly means to settle for less
- ◆ Talking to him about your expectations
- ◆ Ten tradeoffs you should make for your Mr. Right
- ◆ Ten deal-breakers that should end a relationship
- ◆ The many paths taken toward finding Mr. Right

Is there such a thing as "settling for less"? That very term sounds as if you're preparing yourself to be disappointed. And yet, in various ways and in every day of our lives, we do just that. Or, at least we perceive it as such—then, through circumstance, we discover that our relationship satisfies us in other ways we'd never even considered before.

Until you give someone a chance, you never know what they're capable of doing. In this chapter we talk about how, and when, that may be beneficial to you.

Defining "Less" as It Pertains to Your Relationship

A simple example of settling for less occurs when you get to the multiplex and the film you were planning to see is sold out, so you choose to see another film instead. Or when you find a pair of shoes in a style you like, and (yes!) they're in your size—but they're not the right color.

In both of these examples, did you settle for less? Yes, in a sense you did. Every day, and in a variety of ways, you're making compromises and sacrifices. Realizing that you're going to have to make certain compromises is a simple acceptance of living in the real world.

Now of course you're thinking, "My Mr. Right isn't a movie or a shoe! He's the one and only man with whom I plan on sharing my life."

He Said, She Said

Does his voice turn you on? According to research conducted in 2004 at the State University of New York at Albany, it does if he's a low-talker. It seems that research participants loved any trait in men that was testosterone-driven: yep, such as a deep voice.

And you're right. Then again, it's time you define what you mean by "less." For example, do you mean less than what your girlfriends or your family expects in your boyfriend, as opposed to your point of view? Do you mean less than what you expected when you first met? Or maybe less than your fantasy (circa age 19) of the perfect Mr. Right?

Remember, *no one else's criteria counts but yours.*

How High Is High? Talking It Through with Him

Define those expectations in honest and concrete terms. For example, what did you expect—and in what ways is he not meeting those expectations? If something about him does not appear to measure up to your hopes, what exactly is it that falls short?

Have you ever communicated these expectations to him? If not, then why not? Are you afraid that he won't be receptive?

Well, you'll never know if you don't get it out in the open. Here's how to broach that topic:

- ◆ **Pick your moment.** Don't have a discussion when either of you are in a down mood. Instead, discuss this when he is both open and receptive to hearing your concerns.

- ◆ **Be specific.** If you're going to have a meaningful exchange on this very important subject of living up to your expectations, there should be no room for uncertainty. What is it that you're expecting?

- ◆ **Be kind but direct.** Equally important can be the need to give examples. "I would feel better about our relationship if you did …" Tell him what you feel is missing, and give him a chance to respond, counter or agree, compromise, and adjust.

Many of us have the bad habit of coming too quickly to the conclusion that someone who is important in our lives is simply not receptive to hearing our concerns. Often, we're wrong about that. So before you presume anything about Mr. Right, talk to him and allow him to come up to the bar you've set. It may be the kick in the pants he needed. You might be very glad that you did.

Ten Tradeoffs You'll Be Happy You Made

What one person calls "settling for less" another may call "the art of compromise." In truth, successful long-term relationships are built on this skill.

To help you to do just that, here are a list of 10 tradeoffs you might make in order to build a successful relationship. That is followed by a list of what we call "deal-breakers," and here we give 10 examples as well of issues that you are simply not willing to deal with or that you would be wise to avoid.

He's a Keeper if ...

... he takes care of you when you're sick.

Of course, it is always possible that, as you've gotten to know him better, you now realize that your new Mr. Right falls somewhat short of your original expectations.

He's Not the Physical Type You Had Imagined

As you know, this runs the gamut from too short to too tall, too thin to too heavy, and all points in between. Whatever you imagined that he would look like, consider the fact that often the guys with the Hollywood good looks come with a lot of other baggage—be that a mama's boy, a little short on gray matter, or a little too long on ego. Most women want a man who will admire their beauty as opposed to admiring their own.

With some life experience under your belt, you'll be more inclined to conclude that there are many qualities you put above a chiseled jaw and dimpled checks. That's not settling for less; that's shifting your priorities.

He Makes Less Money Than You'd Like

In your fantasy universe, Mr. Right was going to make a healthy paycheck. Reality check: you've fallen in love with a guy who is not making a very good salary. At the same time, you're in awe of the fact that he teaches science to middle school students and that he is totally jazzed each time a kid looks into a microscope and sees a world he or she previously knew nothing about.

It turns out that your Mr. Right is funny, sweet, kind, and makes $48,000 a year—about $200,000 short of what you had hoped for. Are you settling for less or taking a different path? We think the latter. It's a choice that you might be very glad you made, even though you're going to have to keep that five-year-old Honda you've grown tired of and forget about that sexy new BMW.

The amount of money he makes isn't half as important as whether he's happy in his profession. Because if he's happy, the woman in his life will be happy, too—and that could be you.

As for an unemployed boyfriend: before you walk away from him, consider the issues that stand between him and a paycheck. If his jobless status is the result of his attitude toward work as opposed to any economic downturn, you won't be a happy camper footing his bills as well as yours. You deserve a man who wants to be your partner both emotionally and financially.

He's Older—or Younger—Than You'd Hoped

Your ideal guy might be just two years older than you, the same age, or a year or two younger. You never thought about a significant age difference. Now at 25, 35, or 45, you're in a happy relationship but concerned about the age difference.

True, it can be an issue. Then again, it might not be an issue at all.

It's not fair, but in many ways people don't age at the same rate. There are 35-year-old men in better physical condition than men 10 years their junior. Also, you might find that you like the higher level of maturity that a man older than you brings to your relationship. Like so many other aspects in the art of creating a more perfect union, this unplanned twist in your finding Mr. Right might turn out to be a blessing in disguise.

If you're a "puma" (a woman over 30) or a "cougar" (a woman over 50), who loves dating younger men, the same goes for you: do what makes you happy, even if it turns out to be a temporary fix. The men who are attracted to you are those who love what you have to offer: both in life and sexual experience. He doesn't expect you to look like you're 20. He just appreciates that you try to look your best for him.

At this stage of both your lives, you aren't interested in starting a family. You want a partner who shares your *joie de vivre*, both in and out of the bedroom.

 Dating 911

If the man you choose earns less money than you, he will certainly appreciate your generosity. However, if that is the sole basis for the relationship, eventually this may bother one or both of you.

Some women are willing to accept the role of "sugar mama." But for the one who can't, at some point she asks herself: "Is that all I am to him, an open wallet?" She'd be better off with a guy who's willing to step up and shoulder some of the responsibility. She wants a man who can't put aside his pride and allow her to shoulder the full financial burden of their love affair. He may be a younger man, or not. Hopefully she'll keep an open mind and not let his age get in her way.

He Has Less Hair Than You'd Like

It happens to the best of men. Most women, however, are able to see beyond hair loss and are able to focus not on what's on top of his skull but what is inside.

There are a lot of good reasons to bail on what is otherwise a good relationship, but a receding hairline is just not one of them. Just like those shoes that fit well but the color was not quite what you had in mind, the abundance (or lack) of hair is generally not an issue to get wigged out over. (Sorry, we just couldn't help that one.)

Everyone wants to look his or her best. In fact, he may have considered a hair transplant, but thought it might seem vain on his part. You can always broach the topic in such a way that it shows support for the idea. If so, do it without making him feel ugly or putting him on the defensive. Remember: the decision is his alone to make. What makes him a keeper is what's in his heart, not what's on his head.

He's Shyer Than You Had Hoped

Shyness is a double-edged sword. You may have imagined your guy as being more outgoing—perhaps even the life of the party. While a quiet man can be more than just a little less engaging, it's also likely that he will be less of a potential embarrassment.

The drawback to guys who make no attempt to guard their thoughts or opinions is all those times when they say a little too much and create an uncomfortable moment. Shy guys are certainly harder to draw out, but they are less likely to blurt out a thoughtless comment because they most often think and then speak (unlike their counterparts, who have no such inhibition).

As a take-home-to-the-family or to-introduce-to-your-friends guy, shy men are often a difficult sell. Keep in mind, however, that a lasting, committed relationship goes well beyond the bounds of being in the company of Mr. Popularity. Your ability to trust and respect him, and his ability to do the same to you, is much more important. Sure, it's fun to be with Mr. Life of the Party—but is your shy guy a caring, thoughtful, and loving companion? In love that lasts a lifetime, those are the qualities that truly matter.

His Job Keeps Him on the Road

This can indeed be a difficult situation, especially if he's a great guy. It's an example of an issue that ranges somewhere between compromise and a deal-breaker. The choice of just where it falls on that scale is one only you can make.

In truth, certain partners appreciate the break from each other, particularly when they share a relatively small space. There is also a lot of truth in the idea that absence makes the heart grow fonder. Because you know that being together day in and day out is not your usual routine, you make much more of the time you do have together—thereby heightening all your relationship skills.

Whether you think this will work for you or not is an individual choice. You are well advised to consider it thoroughly. If two or three days a week, every week of the business month, is the maximum you'll accept in his not being there, it's important that you lay down that marker. Together, you can decide what works for the two of you and build your lives accordingly. It may, for example, be okay to travel extensively prior to starting a family but not okay after that. All things are possible when they are discussed from the start.

He Has Children From a Previous Marriage

This, too, can work, but whatever role these children play in his current and future life needs to be carefully considered from the early stages of building your lives together.

You would not want to share your life with a guy who was willing to enter into a new relationship and simply forgot about the kids he had in a previous relationship. Both of you should want these children to be part of your life. But if this is to be the case, you have to lay the groundwork from the start. Meet the kids. When you do, remember that, depending on their ages, this is often a difficult transition for them, too. Most children hold onto the idea that Mom and Dad will get back together, and meeting the new love of his life says to them that this is not going to happen. You may find yourself on the receiving end of blame for something that you may have had nothing to do with. Here, perhaps more than nearly any other tradeoff, a large amount of patience is required. Still, together you can get beyond this and help to forge a new family together.

He's Not as Well Endowed as You Had Hoped

This is just one way in which he comes up, shall we say, "a little short" of your expectations. There is much that substitutes for size, including romance, passion, and effort—before, during, and after lovemaking.

In fact, a host of physical issues can arise—and not just about his love instrument. He can be round shouldered when you have always admired broad shoulders. He can have a body that's not very well-defined. All of this comes down to your personal choices. Most of us consciously (or not) are looking for certain physical attributes.

Certain aspects we are willing to overlook, while other issues go beyond our willingness to compromise. It's a balancing act, and only you know what the acceptable tradeoffs are. Our suggestion, as with all other compromises, is to think outside the box. There might be more to this man than meets the eye.

He's Tight with His Money

This is a tricky topic because people can fall into so many different subsets when it comes to how they handle their money. Is he cautious with his money, or is he just downright cheap? Can he share his life and his wealth with you, or does he hold on to his money—and everything else he has—for dear life?

If the issue comes down to the fact that he's not a free spender, this (like being shy, for example) is a tradeoff that in time you may come to see as a benefit. Big spenders are not much fun to be around when the money runs out. So learn more about his habits involving money and find out whether he's cautious with his money and why.

He's Clueless About Your Needs

It's not uncommon for women to want their men to be all man but with the sensitive, caring capacity of a woman.

But perhaps your Mr. Right is a bit of a Neanderthal. Most men have a little or a lot of the stone-aged man lurking in the dark recesses of their minds. Generally speaking, if most women weren't open to bending on this issue, there would be a lot fewer committed relationships in this world.

While this is certainly a drawback and a tradeoff, consider it a challenge. Most men can learn to curb their Neanderthal tendencies when under the guidance of a loving—not to mention attractive—tutor.

Ten Deal-Breakers

With the passage of time, you'll get to know Mr. Right even better. You may discover he has some traits that will make you run in the opposite direction—and you should do so, without a doubt. Here are 10 that make our list.

He Can't Make Room in His Life for Anyone Other Than Himself

This is a polite way of saying he's selfish. When he has lived a life that is all about him, it's very hard to wrap his mind around the idea of "us."

You might try to change this reality, but most often you'll find yourself frustrated when you run head on into this behavior. In the world of me, myself, and I, there's often far too little room for you.

He Burns Through Money

This guy is the opposite of cheap. He might even make a good amount of income, but the problem is that whatever he makes, it goes out as fast as it comes in.

Can you change the guy? Well, as the expression goes, "Never say never"—although it's doubtful. And the pitfall here is that if he's on the road toward financial ruin, there's a good chance he's going to take you down that path with him. Misery loves company, and there will be plenty of that when his debt ruins your credit, too.

He's a Braggart

Tooting your own horn is a character flaw you can overlook some of the time. But when it goes on without end, you quickly run out of patience.

When confronted with a massive ego, you're going to want to bail sooner or later. So do yourself a favor and opt out early. A man who is deeply enamored with himself rarely has the room in his life to truly adore someone else.

He's Not Just Older, He's Also Inflexible

Earlier in the chapter, we discussed the possible unexpected benefits of meeting a guy who is older than you might have envisioned. That can be a tradeoff as opposed to a deal-breaker. It's problematic, however, when the guy is not only older but inflexible—more commonly known as "set in his ways." This is not necessarily a simple function of age. You can have a cheery, flexible 45-year-old and a grumpy, inflexible 35-year-old. More often than not, however, a certain degree of rigidity sets in as we mature and the issue of becoming set in your ways becomes increasingly more common.

This can clearly be a deal-breaker because you're looking for a guy who is willing to try some new adventures with you. An unwillingness to try whitewater rafting or travel with you to places you've never been will not be the deal-breaker. These are things you can do with other friends. However, inflexibility about having a family, or simply a guy who is unable to bend and see your point of view, gets to be too great a drag on your spirit. These issues are deal-breakers. Why? Because in any successful relationship, there has to be room for both individuals to grow. Growth itself requires flexibility, and when that's not there, the relationship's success is most likely in peril.

His Spiritual Beliefs Aren't in Sync with Yours

It happens all the time: a couple meets and enjoys the time they spend together, but if both are grounded strongly in separate faiths, it may well prove to be their undoing.

Faith is a matter of personal values. In issues of faith, you find the gamut of different views: from not at all an issue with either partner to it being a deal-breaker for one or both of you. Of course, many men welcome the opportunity to celebrate their girlfriends' religious customs and ceremonies.

And there are men who are willing to convert, just as many women are open to join their partners on their spiritual path. So yes, the faith gap can be closed, if the couple is willing to make the effort. But other times it's just not going to work. If either of you feel your different faiths create too large a chasm between you, the relationship won't last.

He Has Some Annoying Habits You Just Can't Overlook

Here again is something that you might think at first is not a big deal. But in truth, it *can* be a deal-breaker. Whether it's clicking his tongue or picking his nose, there are some great guys who have some very annoying habits. You can try raising it as a topic, but there's a good chance it's not going to change.

In one fashion or another, each of us has some habits that leave something to be desired, but they are not deal-breakers. At times, however, they can be. This is one more area where

> **He's a Keeper if ...**
>
> ... he senses your needs in bed. A man who makes it a point to be in tune with your body and your intimate desires is giving you physical proof that he wants you to be happy.

you—and only you—can decide which tradeoffs are acceptable and which ones are not. Ultimately, we have to be real admirers of the person we choose as our mate.

He's Dishonest

Most of us tell the truth as a matter of habit. Some of us are the exact opposite, however. You're not looking for a guy who thinks his nose will grow three inches because he told you an innocent lie. When you find yourself in a relationship with a guy who lies just as easily as he says "Good morning," however, run—don't walk—out of his life.

In reality, relationships have just one lasting currency: a basic sense of trust. When you're with a guy who lies with ease and aplomb, you will never be truly comfortable. Sleeping with one eye open is no way to get a good night's rest.

He Has Anger Issues

Guys in general—particularly younger than 35—often have flash tempers. Call it testosterone rage. It doesn't disappear over time, but it does mellow with age. That's one big reason why dads can be somewhat tough on their kids and grandpas are so much more indulgent.

However, out of bounds anger, or consistently showing anger that is out of proportion with the situation, is a clear and present danger. No woman in her right mind wants to live with a dynamite factory, and you should not want to share your bed with a guy who is ready to blow at the first note of upsetting news, or who hits, slaps, or shoves you. Take a pass, even though he'll be ticked that you called it quits.

You're Simply Not Adored by Him

It happens, but you don't need to like it. And why should you? A lasting, loving, committed relationship—at least, in part—is about being adored. It's not okay if you don't feel that. A guy can have a lot of shortcomings, not your ideal body type, short on cash, a little too shy, not quite the adventurer you hoped for … but does he adore you? Is he, at least in part, devoted to the idea that you should share a happy, fulfilling life together?

If you feel none of these qualities or desires coming from him, you're not on a ride to the land of happily ever after. Get off that train before your life together gets really unpleasant.

Physically, He's Coming Up Empty

Sure, there's more to a life together than hot, passionate sex. But if he never gets your engine going, that's a problem! Can you live without it? Absolutely. But that's not a tradeoff you need to make—nor should you.

Finding Mr. Right is in part the feeling of being happy when locked in each other's embrace—and yes, being more than just a little turned on as well. Compromise on the bedroom furniture by all means, but don't compromise on the passion. After all, you only have one life to live.

The Many Paths Toward Finding Mr. Right

By now, you clearly know that there is certainly no such thing as just one path toward finding Mr. Right. You'll make compromises that you never thought you would, and you'll walk away from relationships that in many ways looked like they were just what you wanted until you got close enough to see that they really weren't.

The bottom line is that there are many paths you can take toward reaching a more perfect union. Be careful but not overly guarded. Be thoughtful, but at times throw caution to the wind and see where it takes you. Most of all, be open minded. Relationships, like life itself, can involve many unexpected turns.

You're not really settling for less. In truth, you're opening your heart and your mind to the many possibilities that, when viewed in their totality, may well equal your ever-elusive Mr. Right.

The Least You Need to Know

◆ Settling for less all depends on your definition of the term "settling" and a realistic assessment of what you thought would be your ideal guy.

◆ Love, like life itself, is a series of tradeoffs—which factors are you willing to reexamine once you know more about the man who may indeed be your Mr. Right.

◆ In all potential relationships, there are deal-breakers. When you come across one, make the difficult but honest choice that this is not a compromise you are willing to make—and move on in your search for Mr. Right.

◆ More than likely it won't be a straight and narrow path into the arms of your Mr. Right. Perhaps you'll find him in the most unlikely place, or when you least expect it. He may not look like you envisioned, but the attraction is still there. One thing will stay constant: a mutual desire to live your lives together.

Chapter 20

The Heartbreak of a Breakup

In This Chapter

- ◆ Why some relationships fail
- ◆ How blame keeps you from moving forward
- ◆ Taking an honest look at your role (and his) in the breakup
- ◆ How a breakup affects your other relationships
- ◆ What you can do to get closure for your loss

One of the worst feelings in the world comes with the realization that the man with whom you presumed you'd be spending the rest of your life turns out to be yet another Mr. Wrong. At first, you feel incredible heartache. "What went wrong?" you wonder. How could this be happening yet again? All of a sudden, any feelings of doubt and insecurity rise up in you. You ask yourself, "Will I ever find my soul mate? Or will I end up alone for the rest of my life?"

Why Breakups Happen

The catalysts to a breakup are as varied as there are couples in this world. In fact, every relationship has one—if not many—reasons to fall apart. To put it into perspective, here are some of the most common pitfalls.

Financial Issues

If your guy is into toys—and if his spending eats into your joint nest egg—it will certainly be a cause of many arguments between you. And if he is also constantly asking to borrow money—from you, your friends, and even your parents—you'll come to resent his inability to support himself.

Now, if it's you who can't rub two nickels together when you need them most, he may resent bailing you out all the time—particularly if most of your discretionary income is put into stuffing your closet with all sorts of goodies. And then, when he finds out that you also hide your purchases from him …

No wonder it sounds like World War III at your house all the time.

If this relationship is going to last, the partner who seems oblivious to this financial situation needs a reality check—and fast. Denial is not an option. It is the catalyst for a breakup. And if it isn't addressed by the spendthrift now, it will repeat itself in future relationships.

If your Mr. Right can't quit spending, don't presume you can change him. He has to change himself. In the meantime, separate your finances as soon as possible. Otherwise it could cost you dearly in the long run.

Infidelity and Other Trust Issues

He flirts with other women—not casually, but aggressively. Or, maybe he goes off for hours on end and won't tell you why or with whom. You play the coquette with other men. And perhaps you look forward to working late with your hunky boss.

Even half-truths that you presume won't hurt anyone are sure to chisel away at the trust you thought you had between you. And once trust is broken, respect between partners dissolves. Hurt and anger take its place. The injured party must be open to forgive, even if the traumatic event will never be forgotten. The unfaithful partner must prove his or her devotion, every day. Counseling will help you through this. In the end, this effort will be worth your time.

He Said, She Said

Data from the 2006 General Social Survey, sponsored by the National Science Foundation, shows that, in any given year, an average of 10 percent of married spouses engage in extramarital activities. The gender breakdown for adultery is 12 percent of men and 7 percent of women.

Bad in Bed

If one of you is just plain lousy in bed—and unwilling to do anything about it in order to be more desirable to your partner—it's inevitable that this will affect the partner who seeks an ongoing, passionate connection. Life is short, and lovemaking should be an ongoing part of it. (See Chapter 17 for more on this topic.)

Personal Insecurities

If you're a positive individual, it's very difficult to be in a fully satisfying relationship if your partner is constantly in a gloomy state of mind or if he is paranoid about other people's feelings toward him, be they his friends, family, or his coworkers. What gnaws away at your feelings is that you are left in the position of having to constantly prop him up. You get down, too. Why is he so needy? When do you get a turn to cry on his shoulder?

Support has to be a two-way street. If you aren't feeling it, then eventually you'll be making a U-turn out of his life.

Of course, the same can be said if you are the insecure partner in your relationship. How long do you think he'll stick around your negative mojo?

Previous Negative Relationship Experiences

As much as we'd all like to presume that we could rise above the indignity of being kicked to the curb, that old adage is true: "Once burned, twice shy." (Or three times, for that matter.) Even if you're in a relationship that makes you completely happy, you'll always be looking over your shoulder, wondering whether your luck is too good to be true—that *he's* too good for *you*. And eventually, you're going to convince him that is indeed the case.

He, on the other hand, may have post-traumatic stress syndrome induced from his last girlfriend/wife/significant other. When you casually move your bangs out of your eyes, he remembers how *she* used to do that, too—and all of a sudden you are too much like her. He's projecting his issues regarding her onto an innocent bystander: you.

He Said, She Said

According to Emory University research, only 3 percent of mammals are monogamous, which is defined as "sharing the same nest and territory, where they are in frequent contact, and the male participates in offspring rearing." Besides mammals, this definition includes 90 percent of bird species. Only 15 percent of primates are monogamous (that is, faithfully bonding for life). Most are either polygamous or promiscuous. In fact, only one out of five "societies of humans" (also primates) is monogamous.

Who's to Blame, and Why?

When a breakup is eminent, it is oh so easy to find blame in your partner for the failure of what you thought was going to be a lifetime commitment.

But like the tango, a successful relationship takes two. So does a broken one. In other words, there is plenty enough blame to go around. For example:

If you …

- ♦ … are always looking to see whether the grass is going to be greener with someone else.

- ◆ … can't stop your own jealousies and insecurities.

- ◆ … can't drum up any passionate feelings when you're with him.

- ◆ … would rather lie to him than be candid, for any reason.

- ◆ … won't open up as to your concerns about him.

- ◆ … won't consider counseling to reconcile the issues that stand between you.

- ◆ … aren't willing to make the relationship your first priority in life.

If he …

- ◆ … can't be honest with you.

- ◆ … doesn't respect you.

- ◆ … won't share his feelings with you.

- ◆ … doesn't trust you.

- ◆ … puts others' feelings and opinions before yours.

- ◆ … isn't willing to make the relationship the first priority.

All of these issues must be important for both of you, if your relationship is to succeed.

When It's You Who Wants to Break Up

In Chapter 18, we covered those issues that should make it clear that he's your Mr. Wrong. By now, any sign of them should set off an alarm in your head.

That said, there are right and wrong ways to break up with someone. The most ideal example was seen in an episode of *Seinfeld:* Jerry thought he had found his soul mate because she seemed to be his female doppelganger. She, too, was just as picky in what she needed from a relationship—and just as uncomfortable with messy breakups. So when it came time for them to go their separate ways, they did it over lunch with a smile and a "See you around." It was the perfect breakup—for television, anyway.

Of course, in real life, being on the receiving end of a breakup is the worst feeling ever. That said, one of the hardest things to do is to tell the man whom for so long you called your Mr. Right that you no longer want to be with him.

When you break this news to him, you may see his face crumble in pain, and because you still have feelings for him, you feel his pain, too.

It's natural for you to feel some guilt over the fact that you've turned his world upside down. And while your reasons for breaking up are valid, he deserves to get answers to his questions about your reasons for wanting to leave. He deserves closure. That starts with your candid insights as to what went wrong.

The Wrong Things to Do

Our first instincts are to protect ourselves from hurt. But now, *you're* the one delivering the pain. Don't break up in such a way that you'll regret later; instead, do your utmost to treat him with the same respect you'd hope he'd give you if the shoe were on the other foot. For example:

♦ Don't wait until you're walking out the door to tell him that your feelings have changed for him and why you feel this has happened.

♦ Don't use some small blow-up as an excuse to get angry and leave.

♦ Don't do it in front of an audience. Your life isn't a soap opera, and breakups aren't entertainment (at least, they should not be).

♦ Don't give in to anger based on any taunts he throws your way. This is no time to get down and dirty and sling mud.

♦ Don't call him names and make him feel like a loser.

♦ Don't storm out without allowing closure for either of you.

♦ Don't leave a note, as opposed to giving him the courtesy of breaking up with him face to face. In this situation, that's the least desirable form of communication.

The Right Things to Do

You've made up your mind that there is no chance for reconciliation. Your reasons are valid, and you have no desire for a long, drawn-out goodbye. So here's how to make this breakup as painless as possible for both of you:

◆ Do let your resolution to have an amicable parting lead your every word and action. In other words, be graceful under pressure.

◆ Be honest and truly address your concerns with him. Don't beat around the bush, but lay it on the line. He'll need to know it before he goes into another relationship and finds himself making the same mistakes.

◆ Give him an opportunity to express his pain and anguish. It won't be easy to hear what he has to say, but that's part of the process. It is a necessary component of closure. Besides, you'd expect the same courtesy.

◆ If you can part as friends, try your best to do so. When the anger washes away, the memories you made together will still be there.

He Said, She Said

According to a 2002 survey by Market Fact, Americans under the age of 35 are twice as likely as those between 35 and 54 to have split with a significant other in the past decade, and nearly five times as likely as those 55 and older.

When It's Him Who Wants to Break Up

In most cases, a breakup is not pretty. When the realization sets in that you and The Man Formerly Known as Mr. Right are no longer a couple, you'll feel a range of emotions. Some of these will occur simultaneously while others will take place over time: over that first 24 hours—or perhaps even over the next 24 months.

Only when the dust settles on your emotions and you realize that you're still standing and intact can you candidly examine the issues that tore apart your relationship—and your heart with it.

First, though, you'll be put through the most heart-wrenching gauntlet of your life. Here's what you'll be feeling and why, in roughly the order it occurs:

- **Shock.** Even if there were some preexisting notions that a breakup was eminent, you are nonetheless stunned by his declaration: that he wants to end it *now*.

    First and foremost, close your eyes and take a deep breath. Your initial instinct is to panic. *Don't.* In fact, don't dwell on the past 24 hours. Instead, go out for a run, a walk, or a cup of tea with a friend or two. You need to breathe again. You'll do this more quickly by moving—be that your mouth, your hands, or your legs and feet. Be prepared, however, that the shock will stay with you for a few days.

- **Disbelief.** You took pride in being a couple, and now you're single again. Because this breakup isn't your choice, it's going to take a while to get used to the fact that half the closet (*his* half) is empty; that some friends (*his* friends) will drop you; that life as you knew it will be missing some very familiar components, and that you'll miss them—at least initially.

    Be honest: was what just happened totally unexpected? We're guessing that there were some obvious telltale signs that something wasn't exactly right between the two of you. Admit it: the friction was there already. That said, whatever disbelief you may be feeling now is embedded in your denial. Deep down inside, a part of you felt him pull away. You ignored some obvious warning signs.

- **Anger.** You're mad as all get out. And yes, you have every right to be! After all, you invested a lot of time and emotion in a man who, for whatever his reasons, no longer wants to be with you.

    Go ahead and get it all out. Yell, scream, and cry for as long as it takes. Then, do it all over again. Take a piece of paper and a pencil and start writing about why you feel the breakup was unjust, how badly it has hurt you, and how you feel about him now. Then, stick it in a drawer, because we'll ask you to look at it later.

♦ **Guilt.** Even if it was his idea, more than likely you'll presume that it was something that you did or said that drove him away.

Write down all the things you would have done differently if you could go back in time and change things. Again, stick that sheet of paper in a drawer, because we're coming back to it.

♦ **Blame.** You're obsessed with the urge to spread the blame, thickly and unevenly. He'll certainly get the brunt of it. And doesn't he deserve it? He never really listened to you. Obviously he never really cared. Your payback will be bad-mouthing him to everyone you know.

Yep, there is enough blame for everyone—and that means you, too. Take yet another sheet of paper. Label it "Blame." Put a vertical line down the center. On one side, write down the items he should be blamed for, and then take your lumps on the other side. Hold onto that page.

♦ **Depression.** When it comes to tears, you're all tapped out. You're totally drained of emotion. You feel numb. You know you'll never love another man as much as you loved him. You stay in bed for hours on end. You have no appetite, or you eat too much. You feel you have nothing to live for.

Get up out of bed now. Go take a shower. Put on your clothes. Put on makeup. Go for a walk. Go to the gym. Get together with friends. The goal here is to take that very first step in recovering from this devastating loss. You won't quit mourning, but you must start living again.

Dating 911

Depression is a natural response to a breakup. Symptoms of depression include sadness, hopelessness, loss of interest in your daily life, difficulty in making decisions, irritability, and trouble with concentration. Should your depression linger to the point that it keeps you from moving forward in your life, please see a licensed therapist without delay.

Getting the Closure You Need and Deserve

Remember all those feelings you've put down on paper to release your anger? All together, they make up the manifesto of your breakup with Mr. Wrong. They are the sum total of one of the most important life lessons you'll ever have. And because you've done it now, you are much better prepared for heartache should you ever suffer it again.

Our bet, though, is that you won't because you now know the mistakes you made. You have deeper clarity now in relationship issues that stop some men from being your Mr. Right: men like your ex. Finally, you are now better aware of where the pitfalls are, and you won't fall into another bad relationship.

Your last step: take those papers and burn them. They are old news. You, on the other hand, are ready for a new beginning.

If you have the urge to stalk him—that is, follow him, drive by his home, constantly call him on the phone or send e-mails, discuss him online with others—remember this: none of these actions will bring him back. Furthermore, there are both local and federal laws against harassment. All he has to do is file a complaint and have you placed on notice, and then your next act of obsession could place you behind bars and give you an arrest record.

Seriously, is he worth that? Of course not. A better use of your time, energy, and emotion is channeling it into something that benefits you, like a workout class or your career. Or better yet, put your energy into finding a Mr. Right worthy of your love.

The Least You Need to Know

- There is enough blame for both of you in this breakup. Whatever your role was in it, be honest and learn from it.

- After the breakup, you'll feel a flood of emotions that will ebb and flow for quite some time. Don't let it sweep you under a wave of anger, blame, and depression.

- If you're constantly looking backward, you'll never move forward. You must have closure on this episode of your life.

◆ If you achieve the closure you seek, you won't just move on; more importantly, you'll move *beyond* your heartache.

◆ You should consider yourself lucky that your breakup happened before you took that very important next step. And remember, if you don't break up with Mr. Wrong, you'll never find Mr. Right.

Part 5

Keeping Mr. Right

Meeting your Mr. Right is the first step in the process of finding love that lasts a lifetime. Long-term, successful relationships, however, are built on certain key elements—starting with a strong ability to communicate with each other. Also critical is finding balance during emotional highs and lows and the stresses confronted both as individuals and as a couple.

We support each other most effectively when we are both physically and emotionally intimate. How do we cultivate and protect that intimacy?

When commitment turns to marriage, another level of stress is placed on a relationship—beginning with the wedding planning. In this part, you find a guide to making it through those times of stress with your love still going strong.

Chapter 21

Communication Cues

In This Chapter

- ◆ The "Mars Venus" factor
- ◆ The failure to "hear" your Mr. Right
- ◆ The importance of good communication
- ◆ Pledging to reach out to one another

Bar none, the trait all happy relationships share is communication. It is the underpinning of trust, respect, love, and passion. If you or your Mr. Right cannot successfully express your thoughts and feelings to each other, eventually one of you will misperceive a tone, action, or conversation with the other. That can lead to hurt, frustration, anger, and distrust.

"But we both speak the same language," you think. "How hard is it to understand one another?"

Believe it or not, it's harder than you think. Words are only one way in which we communicate. With each sentence you speak, there are many other more subtle, subconscious messages you put out. The key to keeping you and Mr. Right in sync is to learn to decipher his covert code—his ManSpeak, as it were—so that he hears what you mean to say.

"The Mars Venus" Difference

In the early 1990s, couples counselor John Gray published a book called *Men Are from Mars, Women Are from Venus* that effectively delivered the message that men and women communicate differently. Or, to use Gray's memorable analogy, "It's as though men were from Mars and women from Venus."

Gray's book made an effective case for how we can get beyond our differences if we accept the fact that the emotional wiring of men and women is gender-specific. This causes us to communicate our feelings differently and to hear and react to each other in our own unique styles. This went a long way toward explaining why sometimes a man seems unwilling to listen and care: apparently he wasn't receiving what to her was a clear set of distress signals.

At the time of his book's release, Gray's message drew a fair amount of criticism from many corners. But it resonated so strongly with readers that the book became a cultural watershed.

It has been almost two decades since the book's publication. Since then, scientists from the Yerkes National Primate Research Center at Emory University have validated Gray's premise through their research of oxytocin, a hormone that stimulates the neuroreceptors in the brain that control lust, passion, and desire.

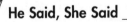 **He Said, She Said**

> Love is a game that two can play and both win.
>
> —Eva Gabor, actress

Let's all hope that it doesn't take yet another decade for them to find a ManSpeak decoder button. Until that scientific milestone occurs, you need to know how to decipher his communication cues.

Why Good Communication Is the Lifeblood of Successful Relationships

Any hope you have of keeping Mr. Right is going to depend heavily on your ability to pick up on his communication cues, and to effectively communicate to him as well, so that he hears and understands what it is you expect as your relationship grows closer.

To accomplish this, you don't have to become an expert in the intricacies of male communication. But you will need to commit yourself to the process of listening with an open mind and a giving heart—and to be accepting of the often-neglected fact that you may not be heard the first or second time that you have something to say.

To that end, we advise that you lay in a healthy amount of patience and appreciate the simple truth that communication between you is (now, and to some extent always will be) a work in progress.

So is it worth all this effort? Absolutely.

In the final analysis, more relationships fail because of an inability by one or both partners to make clear their hopes, fears, and desires. To that end, share your communication concerns when they arise. Keeping them to yourself and increasing your level of self-frustration is not going to lead to a positive outcome.

Remember that your actions speak for you, too. Better relationships are built through the actions that we take every day. Going to your own corner and sulking over communication failures will not get that important work done. On the other hand, improving your listening skills and working on your ability to communicate your needs effectively to him will. To help you accomplish that important task, let's start with ways to improve your listening skills.

When He Has "Knight in Shining Armor" Syndrome

One of the great frustrations nearly all women confront with their Mr. Rights is his "Knight in Shining Armor" syndrome: he wants to fix what concerns you, even when you are the only one who can do so. Forget why he has this compulsion to do so; just accept it as one of the many ways in which he feels he can demonstrate his love for you.

While you're thinking in terms of expressing your concern and simply wanting to be heard, his mind is locked and loaded in search of a solution. He senses your discomfort and assumes (rightly or wrongly) that your desire to unload your concerns with the love of your life is your way of making him responsible for fixing the problem just as fast as he possibly can.

He wants to come to your rescue, to solve your problem for you. You, on the other hand, want to let off steam or use him as a sounding board. Let him know upfront that just by giving you a shoulder to cry on, he's given you what you need.

You're saying, "Hold on ... you haven't heard me out!"

On the other hand, what he's trying to communicate is this: "I know exactly what you mean, and here is what we can do about it."

If through this exchange you become annoyed because you feel that he is shutting you down, he will become equally frustrated because he's dumbfounded that you don't want to rush into what he sees is a clear and easy fix.

As with so many other differences in approach, there is nothing sinister or mean spirited meant—at least, not until the point that you're clashing communication styles lead to frustration that then bubbles over into anger.

Here's a better approach to try: "Honey, I know that you want to help me find a solution, and I totally appreciate that. But I'd prefer you first hear me out, because I think the issue goes deeper than that." You will likely have to give him that message a few times. If you can do so without being patronizing, your Knight in Shining Armor is going to drive hard for a solution.

He's a Keeper if ...

... he's not afraid to talk about his feelings with you.

Remember: it's important that you hear his attempt to help, even if the help he is offering is not really the help you're seeking.

Dampening His Desire to "Take Charge"

Women commonly complain that, as a relationship gets more deeply committed, men lose the instinct to court their partner.

A woman loves for a guy to take charge now and then—perhaps suggesting a restaurant or a movie. Doing so for his lady fair is, in fact, a very common impulse in a man because it is yet one more reason for her to admire him. And that's what dating is all about, right?

So when a man appears to drop into what we think of as "auto pilot" mode, the special woman in his life rightfully feels neglected and becomes frustrated. What she may not realize, however, is that she unknowingly helped to create this situation.

Just about every guy loves to create success, but he hates it when he misses the mark. If your guy suggests a nice little Italian restaurant and you praise him for the suggestion, his self-approval rating goes way up. Tell him you enjoyed the movie he chose, and that will give him the same boost.

Most men do not trust their instincts when it comes to picking anything and everything that you may or may not want to do on your date night. Where a woman really misses the communication cue here is when she is critical of his choices.

Remember that constant desire to find a quick fix. The best way to stay out of trouble, he may well conclude, is to not make any suggestions—the theory being that no choice is better than the wrong choice. You, on the other hand, want to avoid his coming to this conclusion.

The best way to do that is to give him confidence about his choices, and for your added comfort you can help him subtly in making some of those choices. Driving past a restaurant you would like to try and mentioning something like, "My friend Karen said that place is good; maybe we should try it sometime" or, "I hear that film might get a lot of attention when the Oscar nominations are announced" are two good ways of dropping a hint.

Most importantly, if he has chosen (and chosen poorly), let *him* make that pronouncement. Then, make him feel better about his striking out by saying something like, "The best part of the night was spending it with you."

Is it a bit of a game? Sure it is. But if you like those date nights, you have to accept the bad choices that come with the good choices if you want to keep hearing those wonderful words, "I'd like to take you out Saturday night."

He Withdraws Emotionally

There will be occasions when your guy pretty much stops communicating all together. When this happens, you have to consider what you may have done to contribute to his cloak of invisibility. Somewhere in the primitive recesses of his brain, that's what he is trying to do. When a guy decides he can't say anything right, he stops saying anything at all. In that sense, he has willed himself invisible. Here's a good example of when you have to hear what he's saying—even though he's saying nothing at all.

This happens more than you might think. If you're relatively new to the business of long-term relationships, you may have to think back to a time when you saw your dad go into one of these silent phases.

Men have a strong instinct to lead. Your Mr. Right knows that his expertise isn't going to be welcomed *all* the time. Still, if it's steadily and faithfully rejected, it will drain his emotional battery. That said, while he doesn't have to be right 100 percent of the time, you have to give your guy *some* credit for being right 4 to 6 times out of 10.

If, in the past 30 or 60 minutes, you've shut him down about one idea or another, then you've probably heard this classic male lament: "I'm never right, so why try?" This tells you that you've turned down a wrong path in communicating with Mr. Right.

If you want your guy to find his voice in a hurry, just try saying, "I've been thinking about what you said, and you're right. We could give that a try …" and watch him come around.

The bottom line is that if you unknowingly send him the message "You have nothing to contribute," you'll create a self-fulfilling prophecy and spoil what otherwise could have been a successful relationship.

He's a Keeper if …

… he's willing to turn off the TV in order to ask you about your day.

Allow Him His Guy Time

Men need time to hang with their buddies. This is not all that different than you getting together with the girls to have some time to chat about topics that men have no interest in.

Unfortunately, this is an area where lots of couples get crossed signals. So if you think you're clueless as to why he needs so much time with his friends, it's not that difficult to understand.

Start by recognizing what attracted you to him in the first place: his masculine qualities. Oh sure, he had a sensitive side, and you may well have found that very appealing. But the real magnetism you felt was the fact that he was "a real guy." That doesn't mean you found him while he was playing football in the park (although you might have). Still, it's unlikely that you met during the semiannual shoe sale at your local department store.

It's interesting to observe how often couples fall into the trap of attempting to draw each into the other's world—when in truth, she is not seeking a more feminine male and he is not seeking a more masculine female.

If, for example, you're watching the Oscars, give him the option to do something else. While you live your lives as a couple, there is room inside the relationship for both of you to pursue your own interests. He's the last person on Earth who is going to want to dish with you on Angelina Jolie's gown. Save that conversation for a gal pal who knows the difference between Pucci and Gucci.

By the same token, give him some time to bond with his buds. Granted, for some guys this can get out of hand—where one poker game leads to the fishing trip which leads to the football game—and before long, you have a roommate rather than a partner. But in the relatively rare circumstances where we have seen this happen, the simple truth is that this Mr. Right was not ready for a committed relationship anyway. More often than not, it's a matter of maturity. He just can't get traction with the idea that a relationship means so much more than sleeping together and sharing breakfast.

Then, there are the millions of guys who have been disconnected from their male side and now have grown sullen and quiet. If that describes your Mr. Right, then there is a good chance that even he doesn't know what has him down. Once again, though, the good news is that there's a relatively simple solution: encourage him to have a night out with the boys. It can be a ballgame, a friendly poker game, or an overnight camping trip.

For a lot of women, the tough part is sending him off to have some fun. Their insecure side wonders whether he'll like life away too much. In the big picture, however, that's a rather silly concern: he doesn't need a night out with the boys to conclude that he's not happy in the relationship. In fact, in our experience, time spent by both of you in doing some same-sex bonding most often strengthens a relationship.

> **He Said, She Said**
>
> What makes women happy? Princeton University has figured it out. When rating the feelings of 900 women on a 7-point scale, the top 5 events that put a smile on their faces were (in descending order) sex, socializing, relaxing, praying or meditating, and eating.

If for whatever reason he won't pick up the phone to plan a night with the guys, get the ball rolling by having a weekly night out with your friends. He'll soon get the message, and you'll see him emerge from his quiet gloom into a guy who is more fully engaged in his life and in your lives as a couple.

Four Tips for Staying in Sync

Everything we've mentioned in this chapter allows you to learn a new language: that communication is a two-way street. As much as you're willing to give, he has to come up to the bar as well. Here's how to ensure you're both speaking the same language.

Pick Your Moments

There are times that he is ready to hear you and other times when you are simply driving at full speed into a brick wall. Don't do that to yourself. You know when he's more likely to hear what you have to say, so wait for those times and then make your move.

Remember, He Reads Subliminal Body Language, Too

When he either does not hear you or you're frustrated that he's not getting whatever it is you are trying to tell him, it's bound to happen that your frustration level will rise. You may think it doesn't show, but we're willing to venture a guess that it does. Men feel threatened when this happens and tend to become highly resistant to anything you want to express. In these situations, you're well advised to pull back. Your frustration is of course understandable, but it's only going to make it that much more difficult to communicate with him.

Be Positive, Not Negative

Men are more sensitive to positive and negative feedback than you would ever imagine. The great unspoken truth here is that every man at some level still wants to be that knight in shining armor for his sweetheart. Your negative feedback makes him feel like a jerk and a loser. Your positive feedback makes him feel like a champ. Men's egos are easily crushed, particularly when it's important to them that they impress you. Too much negative feedback and they'll just give up on trying to please you (something you hope will never happen).

Compromise

Sure, it can be fun for one partner or the other to consistently get their way. But be careful of what you wish for, because you might get it. When that happens, you find yourself living with someone who is demoralized and dispirited.

Women who do this to their partners are then regretful that they don't have "a man I can lean on." Typically, men who at least appear to welcome dominance have either given up on the relationship or given up on the idea that they have something to contribute.

As we suggested earlier in this chapter, remember to regularly say, "Honey, what do you think?" Even if he doesn't respond at first, keep doing it. He moves forward when he thinks his input is wanted and appreciated. Take that away and you have a noncontributing partner—not a happy outcome for either one of you.

The Least You Need to Know

◆ Men and women have different styles of communication and different motivating factors when they choose to communicate. Ignore this basic reality at your own peril.

◆ Successful relationships move forward based on the clarity of their communication. When communication breaks down, you begin to grow apart.

◆ Men give cues as to how, why, and when they are open to communicating. You can hear those cues even when they are not speaking, and there are tools you can use to reach the man you may have thought was unreachable.

◆ He wants to be your knight in shining armor, to solve your problems for you. But in most cases he won't be able to fight your battles. What he can do, however, is be a sounding board for you. Let him know you appreciate him in that role.

◆ To keep the channels of communication open between you, pick the best moment to broach a touchy subject. When you bring it up, do so without blame, and seek a compromise that works for both of you.

Chapter 22

Emotional Highs and Lows—Yours and His

In This Chapter

- ◆ Why our emotions cycle up and down
- ◆ Constructive ways to weather stressful periods
- ◆ When common problems become damaging disagreements

All of us are subject to highs and lows. We all have mood swings. Our moods are cyclical, lasting for an hour or two or a day or more. Additionally, we have low- and high-energy periods that can change with everything—from the amount of sleep we get to when and what we have eaten during the day. Stress is triggered by a variety of factors outside our control.

Stress and Relationships

The prospect of a job loss or a job promotion. A parent's health issues. A job relocation move. An accident. Money problems. Any and all of these issues can cause you to be irritable, grumpy, or depressed.

It doesn't have to be big issues that trigger stress, either. Traffic jams, long lines at the grocery store, and the howling baby in the seat behind you on an already late flight can put you in a foul mood.

No relationship is immune to times of tension. Regardless of how hard you or your partner may try, there are times when you just can't be in a loving, supportive place for your partner. So yes, there will be times that you're going to find it nearly impossible to keep your patience—and you will snap at your partner for no good reason.

He Said, She Said

Feel it's too late to get married? Don't fret. Perhaps women are waiting to get married longer at least in part because they are living longer. According to a recent article in *Time* magazine, apparently the rise in brides' ages exactly mirrors that of women's increase in life expectancy.

Like death and taxes, stressful times are inevitable. What is not, however, is a foregone conclusion to how we approach these high and low points. There is considerable room for variation. Most importantly (and most fortunately), there is room for improvement in all of us. If you have seen one or more relationships in your past crash and burn because of the failure to get through stormy patches, pay particular attention to this chapter.

The Roller Coaster of Human Emotions

A good place to start is by understanding why all of us are subject to emotional highs and lows. For most of us, our emotions are a rather fragile thing. You may think this is true almost exclusively in regards to women, but as you saw in our last chapter, when a man's ego is pierced he can drop into a rapid emotional descent. Just as the opposite is true, a few words of positive feedback can send a man's mood soaring.

But let's begin by looking at the bigger picture of those highs and lows that we are all subject to in one fashion or another. These highs and lows are not extreme (what mental health practitioners would call manic); they're just the swings that nearly all of us experience at various points in our daily lives.

No One Simple Answer

Any discussion of our daily emotional swings quickly gets derailed in today's culture and becomes a conversation about complex issues such as bipolar disorder, postpartum depression, and other serious mental health issues. But as we know from our own lives and from what we witness in the lives of others, we're all subject to mild mood swings that can occur with no readily apparent pattern at almost any point in the day.

An easy way to connect with the subject of our own highs and lows is to think back to our time as children or the observations that you have made of young children you know. Unlike adults, children don't start with a repertoire of techniques to hide their emotions. When young children are happy, sad, frustrated, excited, jealous, angry, or tired, it all comes through loud and clear. There are no adult filters to hide these emotions.

From the age of four or five onward, learning to "control our emotions" is a significant part of our maturation. Now, as grown adults, we have a good news–bad news outcome. The good news is that we have emotions that we have learned to control in the sense that they are partially hidden; the bad news is that most of us never learned how to properly dissipate those feelings. So what remains of that potentially negative energy that has not been dissipated? Well, that's simple physics: that energy can change from form to form, but it cannot simply vanish.

Here's one example. You're mad at your boss, but you can't say a word to him or her or to anyone at work about why you are upset. So you get home and bring with you all that bottled-up, negative energy that is going to be uncorked with the first person who crosses your path. More often than not, that would be your partner.

"Why am I always on the receiving end of your anger?" is the common lament from your partner. The answer is (although no one would be so blunt to actually say this), "You're a convenient target. I can't let loose at work, so I saved all that bad energy for you." Too often in relationships we become each other's whipping boys or girls. It's not fun, just an unfortunate fact of life. And that can be the source of a lot of pain and difficulty.

Stress Busters

So that you don't lash out at your beloved, consider the following stress busters:

- **Take a time out.** We all need quiet time. That means shutting out the world, even if it's just for half an hour. Take a walk around the block, meditate, do sit-ups, or turn on some music. The point is to get out of your head so that you give yourself a chance to regain your sense of balance and refresh your point of view.

- **Exercise.** The easiest release valve for stress and for the dissipation of pent-up emotions—particularly anger and frustration—is physical exercise. If you have no exercise regimen, such as working out in the gym, spending time at a swimming pool, riding a bike, or simply taking a brisk walk or jog, you really have no valve to turn to let off some of that steam safely. If you want to take a positive step forward in your relationship, encourage your guy to get out there with you. Those simple physical activities you do together can go a long way toward building a happy and lasting relationship.

He Said, She Said

A 2008 study of 3,000 couples conducted by the British wedding company Confetti is proof positive that constant physical contact leads to longer liaisons. In fact, those who were happiest shared a minimum of four kisses a day, as well as three hugs, and at least one "I love you."

- **Use sex to decompress.** Intimate contact is one of the greatest stress busters ever. Start by kissing, which is the most tender act of love. Feeling Mr. Right's arms around you will relax you, and making love releases "feel-good" endorphins in the brain, as well as the hormone oxytocin. All of this brings about the emotional balance you seek. Remember: when you're happy, so is Mr. Right.

Passing Clouds or Cataclysmic Storms?

Both you and your Mr. Right have traits that annoy each other but are not necessarily something to call it quits over. When stressed out, however, mundane issues which during less stressful times could be considered merely "passing clouds" in a relationship can suddenly billow into stormy disagreements.

Any of the following eight emotional weather patterns may be on your list. Let's look at why you may want to hang in there despite your angst—if he's willing to work with you on making a change or arriving at a compromise.

He Avoids Hot-Button Issues

What you should know about this: so he's not a great communicator. By now, that shouldn't be a big surprise. When it comes to emotions, few men have the verbal skills to reflect honestly on their shortcomings as an important first step before making any needed changes.

What you can do about this: when he avoids an issue, let him know that you see it as a problem that must be addressed as soon as possible and that you are willing to talk it out with him—that is, when he is ready to do so. If he avoids doing so for more than a week, take the initiative. Ask him for a day and time that works for him to talk it out. When you do, don't show anger or frustration. Ask questions dispassionately as you would if you were addressing any other friend. (Remember, he is your friend, too, first and foremost.) Your goal is to help him reason through his solution, not to solve it for him. Only he can do that.

He Wants to Know How Much You Spend

What you should know about this: most often, when people have issues related to money, it is something that took root a long time ago. It could have been that his mom, dad, or both were careless with money and as a kid he suffered because of that—or at least, that's what he has told himself. A need to control spending means that he is hoping to eliminate the persistent fear that he has of upcoming money problems—even though no actual prospect of that is even on the horizon.

What you can do about this: begin by saying, "We need to talk." Remind him of the fact that you are a responsible adult and that before he came into your life, you knew how to run your own budget. Remind him that constantly looking over your shoulder is an uncomfortable situation for you and not one that you will tolerate for very long.

This is an example of when you have to be kind but also fair. At the same time, you have to act in a loving manner because anger—as we have seen in past chapters—will not move you toward a resolution but instead toward only additional conflict.

With a loving approach, ask him to explain his real concern about money. We're willing to venture a guess that it started long ago. By putting it out there, he can start to work on the issue—and together you can move toward a resolution.

He Doesn't Know How to Talk to Your Friends

What you should know about this: first, realize that you have no cause for embarrassment. He's not the first guy who's inept at talking to females. Second, remember that your pals are there to be supportive of your hopes and desires. How he talks to your friends may have nothing to do with how he talks to you, and it is your satisfaction that is of paramount importance.

What you can do about this: begin by remembering the old physician's creed, "First, do no harm." You don't want to embarrass him in front of your girlfriends—or equally problematic, later on when you're both alone. There's a good chance that he already knows he's awkward around your girlfriends. What he's hoping for, but would never have the nerve to ask, is to get some pointers from you on what to talk about when in their company.

Do just that, and be sure to approach him with a good degree of subtlety. For example, "Did you know that Jane loves ice hockey? Both her brothers played, and she'd love to know about you being a big hockey fan." In other words, to get him started, push the boat into the water. When he discovers that he can connect on some level with one or two of your girlfriends, he will start to feel a lot more comfortable around all of them.

He Has Obnoxious Buddies

What you should know about this: he's not the first. Generally, the younger your partner, the worse the "brew crew." Many women would like to have their boyfriends' friends' heads mounted on their walls—and often with good reason. So take some degree of solace in knowing that you have lots of company.

What you can do about this: it's amusing to think how many guys get into arguments defending their buddies. If it weren't for the fact that they felt pushed into a corner, they might not come to their defense.

The most important step you can take here is not to push your guy into that defensive position. Your best path is to take a somewhat light-hearted approach. Say something like, "Gary is sweet, but he can be so silly when he puts those straws up his nose." Or, on a more serious note, "It would be great if Mitch could lighten up a little. I know he's just trying to make a point, but when he starts in, he just doesn't stop."

Here, like in so many other areas of trying to make a point with your guy, it's just as much *how* you say it as *what* you say. If you come down hard on your guy, he'll come out swinging—and we mean that figuratively, not literally. Don't make him feel that he has to come to their defense, and he won't.

Dating 911

Never discuss a hot topic until you've both had a chance to cool off. That may mean shelving the issue for a day or two, and that's okay. In the meantime, write down your thoughts about it. Go over in your mind how to make your point succinctly and respectfully. Be prepared to compromise, and you will both win.

He Hasn't Warmed Up to Your Family

What you should know about this: again, take comfort in the fact that he is not unique in having difficulty connecting with your family—particularly if you have parents who are, shall we say, overprotective.

Moms and dads run the gamut between open and laid back to uptight and suspect in their reactions to the guy you think might be your life partner. Whatever their behavior, you've had a lot more time to get comfortable with these two people than your potential Mr. Right has had. What you might just see as "Mom and Dad just being Mom and Dad," he might see them as unwelcoming—perhaps even hostile. He might also find their behavior toward you to be off-putting as well. It's a complex topic that has a long list of possible outcomes. Let's just say that when it comes to your guy and your parents, keep your sense of balance. A sense of humor is not a bad idea either.

As for siblings, that can also have its ups and downs. The good news is that if he has a prickly relationship with a brother or a sister, that's not the main event. Your parents are the much greater concern. Most siblings know that if they give your partner a hard time, they might be setting up the scenario for you to treat their significant other in the same manner.

What you can do about this: first, don't panic. A rocky start to his first time with your family is not necessarily a forecast for continuing problems. Second, be low-key with your expectations. If you like, express your concerns prior to their first meeting. Here are some sample comments: "Dad's a bit of a know it all, so don't get into a debate with him about politics. It's a lose/lose." Or, "Mom doesn't think any guy is good enough for me, so don't be surprised if she's not all that warm and welcoming to you."

This all comes under the wisdom of lowering expectations rather than raising them. It's better he should be a little uncertain of what he's facing and approach cautiously than go into the meeting overconfident and come out dispirited.

You know the situation better than we could suggest and will adjust accordingly. Follow, however, this one ongoing caveat: be careful of getting between your partner and your parents. It's a very slippery slope. Instead, be supportive of his feelings, and don't feel any overwhelming compulsion to defend him to any member of your family.

Hopefully, it will go rather well. Remember that you cannot control how people react to one another. Tread lightly and keep modest expectations, and you may well be pleasantly surprised to find that on your wedding day when he embraces your mom and dad, he really has taken them into his heart.

He Said, She Said

> I am that girl who goes off with the guy and then looks back and
> goes, "I have all these other relationships. Why did I neglect
> them?" The concept of always needing to be together—that's such bad
> advice. You need to keep your sense of self, your life, your background,
> your history.
>
> —Anne Hathaway, actress

He Forgets to Introduce You to His Friends

What you should know about this: talk about annoying! You probably just
want to kick him in the shins when he does that. Unfortunately, it's
something many guys do. Chalk it up to bad manners, shyness, or just
thoughtless behavior.

What you can do about this: letting him have it with both barrels is never
the desired path toward resolution of any problem. The old cliché about
catching more flies with honey certainly applies here. Later on in the
evening when you are both alone, in a low-key fashion, just tell him
how bad it makes you feel when he forgets to introduce you. Even if it
has made you angry, try to avoid expressing your anger because that
will only serve to put him on the defensive. Your goal is to modify his
actions, not create an argument.

If and when he does it again, apply the same approach. Old habits, particularly bad habits, die hard. He'll get the message, and he'll adjust his
behavior accordingly.

He Preaches to You About Your Bad Habits and Ignores His Own

What you should know about this: it's a human fault that's as old as the
Bible. Matthew 7:3 says, "Do not judge, or you too will be judged …
Why do you look at the speck of sawdust in your brother's eye and pay
no attention to the plank in your eye?" You don't need to get old school
on him, but this is a common wrong we all commit on occasion.

Most likely, he has clumsily raised an issue that irks him without stopping to think what he does that might just bug you. Again, it's a common human fault, but that makes it no less bothersome when you're on the receiving end of his criticism.

What you can do about this: don't start by pouncing on him, although it's tempting. Know going into this that it's a great way to fall into a bad argument if you don't handle the situation with care. Whatever your response, try not to say, "Well, it bothers me every time you ..." That's a certain route toward an argument. Instead, summon your patience and balance and say, "I never gave that much thought. Thanks for letting me know. Without honest feedback from a reliable friend, I don't suppose I would have ever realized that."

With that simple response, he might feel a little sheepish and want to know whether a trait of his is irksome to you. Undoubtedly there are one or two, but once again—save it for some other time. Tit for tat on the topic of "small" annoyances is an invitation to a battle royal.

He Wants to Make All the Decisions in Your Relationship

What you should know about this: it's a difficult problem that must be addressed: you could be facing a guy who formed some bad habits, either from watching his parents as he was growing up or from falling into this pattern in an earlier relationship.

Whatever the reason for his actions, you don't want to go there. Instead, you want to focus on changing—or at the very least, mitigating—this behavior.

What you can do about this: there are times in your relationship when a heart-to-heart talk is not only the best approach—it's the *only* approach. Do it when you're both relaxing, sitting by the fire, enjoying a walk in the woods, or enjoying a little cookout in the backyard. You need to take his hand, look him in the eyes, and then lovingly but firmly say, "I love what we're building together. Each passing day, our relationship means more and more to me. But I'm concerned that you seem to feel a need to make all the decisions for both of us. Don't get me wrong, I like a guy who offers some real leadership and has the confidence to say exactly what he's thinking, but you have to make some room for some of my concerns and thoughts as well."

There's a good chance that at this point, he's going to be insisting that he doesn't want to make all the decisions and that he'd welcome your input. In the final analysis, that may or may not be true—but having had this heart-to-heart conversation, you're now in the position to remind him of this talk the next time he jumps in to make a choice without finding out what you think first.

The Least You Need to Know

♦ Highs and lows are part of the landscape of human emotion and run a broad range. Part of the process of getting to know each other as a committed couple is learning how you both function during times of stress.

♦ There are positive and negative ways to relieve the burdens of stress and shifting emotions. If both of you use coping measures, you'll become a stronger couple and are far more likely to have a successful relationship.

♦ The potentially harmful nature of any problem can be either enhanced or diminished, depending on how you react to it. Learning how to keep small issues from growing into relationship busters takes thought, preparation, and skill.

Chapter 23

Relationship Stress Tests

In This Chapter

- ◆ When the intensity cools down
- ◆ Growing as a couple and as individuals
- ◆ When things go wrong between you: setting them right again
- ◆ The people and circumstances that pull you apart
- ◆ Keeping your bond strong

You and Mr. Right have a lot in common. You love each other and are totally in sync with your goals and desires. In fact, if it were just the two of you always, it would be a perfect world. Unfortunately, there are several hundred million other people on Earth, and each of them have their own agendas—some of which may put you on a collision course with Mr. Right. That is, if you let it.

Gravity and Anti-Gravity of Relationships

Most committed relationships begin white-hot. Like a new star, they burn with such intensity there is little room in either partner's life for anything less than total involvement with each other. But as is true with all aspects of our universe, intensity diminishes over time. That does not mean devotion to each other is less; often, that can grow with each passing year.

What happens as the intensity of this new relationship cools down is that both partners feel more of the pull of outside forces. Don't think of this as a good or bad thing. It is simply a normal part of the process of growing together in a committed relationship. The goal is to sustain your mutual passion for the long term, not to burn out on each other before you grow together in love. To that end, consider how outside influences can impact your life as a couple, bringing both good and bad results. Whatever the outside influences, the challenge is to remain strong as a couple. You'll find that, with the passage of time, this is a difficult balancing act. Still, with patience and practice, you can accomplish it.

The Love Bubble: Staying Inside as Long as Possible

The first and foremost rule: don't overreact to anyone else's opinions or suggestions. That should be easy to do, because—like most new couples—you and Mr. Right strive hard to focus on the best things about the relationship. For this short period of time, you have created an imaginary bubble of love and happiness around yourselves. How long can it last? Hopefully for a good while, if not forever. What keeps it impermeable is the passion you have for one another.

The intimacy you share also plays a strong role in keeping you committed. Beyond the bedroom, most new couples enjoy doing so many things together: from hanging out at the local coffee shop to going to the movies, the beach, the park, or on a beautiful drive. The list goes on and on. Think of it as a date that just keeps going. Joined at the hip? Sure, for now. That's typical. It's not unusual for a new couple to vanish from their friends' and families' radars. If someone calls you, you're "busy." And when someone does run into you, chances are you are hand in hand with Mr. Right.

Call it the "gaga" stage. It's sweet, it's adorable, and for most of your friends, it gets to be just a little sickening as well. But as we said earlier, this intensity diminishes, at least modestly—and there is nothing wrong with that. Think of it as running at the pace of a sprint when you're in a marathon. It's just not

going to continue at that pace. One day you're going to resurface, pick up the phone, and call a girlfriend. He's going to go out with the guys, play golf, or go to the ball game. You'll see a movie with a gal pal or two while he goes to an event out of town.

 He Said, She Said

> Gravitation is not responsible for people falling in love.
>
> —Albert Einstein, physicist

Pop Goes the Bubble! Staying Strong as Individuals

No two people are glued to each other, and we would never suggest that it was wise or desirable for them to be inseparable. We should grow as individuals *and* grow as a couple. It's possible and wise to follow both paths.

For example, you may want to pursue an interest in the visual arts while he may want to return to school to get a Master's degree in teaching. Having met these goals, what you bring back to the relationship makes your union that much stronger because you're more self-confident as individuals. Two strong people have the best chance of making a strong and lasting couple.

Whatever individual paths we follow, there should be no resistance on the part of either member of the relationship to grow and take on new challenges. To be worried that your relationship is too fragile to take on those challenges would be the same as owning a classic car that you keep in the garage for fear that out on the road, it might be damaged.

Relationships, like all things of great value, exist to be used. A strong and happy relationship is a place in which both partners can grow as a couple *and* as two separate people. If a relationship cannot stand up to the pressure of outside influences, then it is not as strong as the partners inside may think. Further, without the sometimes destructive nature and pressure put on a relationship by outside forces, couples would never be tested and therefore would never learn how to build a stronger and better relationship.

Stress Factors That Pull Us Apart

On February 1, 2003, the space shuttle *Columbia* streaked across the early morning skies over northern California. Framed against a sun rising over the East Bay hills, flying amazingly fast through a deep blue sky, it was a thing of beauty and wonder to behold. Minutes later, while passing over Texas on its descent into Cape Canaveral, the shuttle began to break apart. Later, we learned that a breach on the shuttle's wing, occurring days earlier at the time of liftoff, set the stage for the tragedy. Within a very short period of time, the ship began to break apart and spin out of control. We all know the sad ending of this story.

In some ways, relationships that move successfully through space and time do a similar thing. We've all heard of, or witnessed, a relationship that—as casual observers—we thought was "doing so well." "They seemed so happy," friends say when they get the news that Ted and Carol, Pete and Pam, or Mike and Dee have come apart.

He's a Keeper if ...

... he isn't dismissive of your thoughts and remarks.

Undoubtedly, their relationships fell victim to one pressure or another—internal or external—and most likely some combination of the two. Whatever the factors that brought the relationship down, the seeds of the disaster were sown a long time before.

Trouble Brewing: Relationship Breaking Points

The issues that could break up a couple are many. To paraphrase Leo Tolstoy's *Anna Karenina:* "Happy relationships are all alike; every unhappy relationship is unhappy in its own way."

As different as they may be, here are the most common hot-button issues:

- Attraction to another potential partner
- Financial pressures
- Interests that diverge too greatly
- Starting and building a family together
- The sometime corrosive effect of family and friends
- Persistent differences in critical life decisions

Let's look at five scenarios that can break up a relationship.

The Urge to Cheat

Considering that Mr. Right has certain qualities that you found attractive, it's safe to assume that other women would think so, too. Certain women would never dream of getting involved with a man in a committed relationship. Others have no such reluctance. And of course, that makes the somewhat dubious assumption that your guy doesn't have a roaming eye.

Trust is always a tough balancing act—one that presents a fair degree of stress. Does he have a cheating heart, or is he just a friendly, outgoing guy? Would he come clean or try to juggle you and another relationship on the side?

The answer depends on the man. Some guys have all they can handle when they're in a committed relationship. Others are happy with the steak but can't resist having the lobster tail on the side.

All straight guys like to look at women. The big question for you (and every other woman in a committed relationship) is whether it stops there or if he's tempted to touch and feel the eye candy, too.

What you can do about it: being cast in the role of the "jealous girlfriend" is a no-win situation. To avoid that (as well as the tummy aches that come from worrying whether you should express your feelings), start by having an open and honest dialogue with him about fidelity.

And yes, it's okay for either of you to express your thoughts about temptation—even if that temptation is more fantasy than anything else. If you find a particular type of man attractive or a celebrity gets you going, it's okay for Mr. Right to know that. And it's also fine for him to tell you that a certain type of girl always attracts his attention. Why is this okay? We are sexual beings by our nature. To ignore our sexuality is to play a false game that does both you and him a disservice.

That can be a dangerous game of hide and seek that leads to more "hide" than open and honest dialogue. Once the issue of your sexuality is on the table and it's no longer a great secret hidden behind a wall of "I only have eyes for you," you and Mr. Right can talk more openly about your fantasies. More importantly, you can make each other *part* of those fantasies. Or, many couples make the choice to simply ignore their sexual urges.

He Said, She Said

If he cheats, is it worth sticking it out? That depends on whether he plans on making it a habit. If he can't commit to an exclusive relationship with you, and that is what you want and need, then guess what? He's not your Mr. Right. If, however, he is willing to work hard to earn back your trust, love, and respect, you have to ask yourself if you're willing to take him back. You can't control what he or anyone else does, only what you do. Accepting this premise is actually very liberating. You are free to forgive. You are also free to walk away from a relationship that isn't right for you.

Money Makes the World Go Around

There's an old expression: when the money goes out the window, love goes right along with it. We don't think that is necessarily the case. But it's certainly clear that financial woes can put a great deal of strain on any relationship.

It can come in many forms, particularly in modern society when more often than not both partners contribute to the financial bottom line. Unfortunately, money worries put an additional relationship strain on Mr. Right. Why? Even if you're laid off and he's still working, the provider instinct in him is feeling inadequate that he is not able to provide a more successful life on just his one income.

When you were used to paying the bills and having discretionary money on top of it, life can feel less like a lark and more of a slog when, suddenly, there is just barely enough to cover the rent and pay basic bills. Occasional nights out and periodic weekend getaways seemed like the real fun in your life together. In the early days of your relationship, you would have been happy to share a tent and one sleeping bag. Now, your desires are grander than that, and you're both wishing you had the money to support at least some of those desires.

What you can do about it: start by recognizing the simple truth: money issues can—and will—destabilize a relationship. Commonly, people react to this fact by saying, "Not me!" But just about all of us are unnerved and stressed out by money problems at some point in our lives. And when times are tough, it comes with the territory: you're going to get more than just a little short-tempered with each other.

That said, don't hide from money issues. Face them head on. Half or more of the stress of financial worries comes from a lack of planning. As with every other tough situation you face, you're that much stronger when you can work through it as a couple. If a storm were approaching your home, you wouldn't prepare by planning an outdoor barbeque. What needs to be done, and what realistic financial projections can you make? When this subject is discussed, reviewed, and thought through, you'll both feel a lot better about the uncertain times ahead.

Remember one thing: great relationships are forged through the bonds built during tough times. That's because you've survived them together. No relationship that we know of was put in peril by trying to decide whether to spend two weeks or three in Maui. You can get by without the new Mercedes, the Lexus, or the BMW—whichever one you choose. What makes a relationship stronger is when you see how little you actually need to get through. When you finally emerge from that struggle into the sunshine of better days, you're a much stronger couple than you were when those tough times first arrived.

"That's No Way to Raise a Child!"

While disputes about raising kids don't come up for many of us in the first year of trying to build a relationship, they are issues for millions of couples who have children from a previous marriage. In fact, as tough as it can be to get a mom and dad on the same page about childrearing, it can be that much tougher when you're talking about the presence of one or more children in a new relationship. Whether it's Mr. Right's children or yours, or you've blended both your families into one big happy household, dual parenting can be an incredible source of tension between the two of you.

What you can do about it: begin by acknowledging that this is a difficult balancing act. Before you took the step of becoming a committed couple, you took the time and effort to meet his children—or you introduced him to your kids.

An important way to reduce the chance for disagreements is to discuss the kids with your partner *prior* to the merger of your households (or, if it's a temporary visit, before they show up for the weekend). What you're trying to do is reduce any and all emotional hot spots. Together, discuss discipline ground rules that have already been laid down. Ask questions. Be candid about the roles each other will play in your children's lives.

The goal is to move toward a respectful, civil relationship with all members of your new extended family, including any and all exes, in-laws, and even ex–in-laws. Some legal concerns may come up, including custody and child support. Emotional issues may also arise, including guilt on his part or the bitterness of his ex-wife. Your role is to show him your support and love.

Kids will test all boundaries and push all your buttons. Both of you have to be prepared for that. How will you react when this happens? Your children will presume that you're "choosing sides." It's Mr. Right versus them. They, too, should be allowed to express their opinions. After doing so, they'll be more receptive to what you have to say about Mr. Right's role in your life and theirs.

If one of his children is particularly stubborn and unyielding about your role in his life, avoid as best as you can the temptation to tell your partner that you were disappointed in the child's behavior. In the early days of a relationship, Mr. Right (and you, too) is bound to be an over-protective and overly sensitive parent who, unconsciously or not, lives by the time-honored mantra, "Love me, love my kid."

Keep it low key, and keep plenty of patience on hand. As time goes by, you'll have many chances to help shape the relationship and win the confidence and hopefully the respect (if not the love) of the children. Kids are as fragile in their feelings about a new mom or dad as you could possibly imagine. Tread softly here as you begin the process of building a new family dynamic.

Love is a complex emotion and we all show it in different ways, even if we don't always say the words "I love you." If you demonstrate concern, love, and respect toward the children, eventually you may get that back in return. Even if you don't, you'll know you did everything you could to open your home and your heart to them.

Dating 911

Because Mr. Right's ex-wife is the mother of his children, take care to talk civilly about her if the children are around. Harsh remarks about her will distress and offend them—and will only harm your long-term relationship with your stepchildren.

Mother Warned Me There Would Be Days Like This ...

There are days when everything goes right and days when just about everything goes wrong. Call it nature's balancing act. Just as it was true that a healthy flow of income can help reduce stress, good news is a stress-buster as well.

But on those days when your boss is being a jerk, someone broke your car's back window and swiped your laptop, and you're trying to beat back a bad cold, there's a good chance you're not going to have that top-of-the-world feeling. Our own rhythmic ups and downs can put us all in a sensitive state of mind, too.

Now he wants you to cheer up, and you're just not up for doing that.

Or, maybe you want him to get out of *his* slump. You try to lift his spirits by telling him, "You can get the car window fixed, you've got a backup for your computer files, and you were due for a new laptop anyway." But he's not open to your upbeat view of the world—at least, not right now.

This is just one of those times that life has beaten you down, has beaten him down, or perhaps has done a clean sweep and gotten you both in a headlock. Patience gets pretty lean, humor all but vanishes, and you're both at a point where you're not sure you can hold on to that loving feeling.

What you can do about it: you know how you got to this point. But don't ignore the cause of your down day. Instead, embrace it. We're not suggesting that you have a "Rotten Day" celebration, but rather cut yourself a break and remember that your mother told you there would be days like this.

It's interesting to consider that we are all trained throughout our childhood on how to deal with physical ailments. Got a cold and a fever? Get to bed, get warm, and drink some hot water with honey and lemon. Suffering from back strain? Slow down, get some rest, and give your back a chance to heal. Whatever the ailment, we openly talk about what you can do to make yourself better.

When it comes to our emotions, however, that's where the confusion starts. Here's a new approach: accept the fact that you've had a rotten day, be especially supportive of one another, and (most importantly) be kind to yourselves. Come up with your very own "blue day" cure— something that you both enjoy. Go for a walk in the park, eat some comfort food, see a good movie, make a martini, or do whatever acts give you some space and cut the tension. Giving it a silly name, like "blue day cure," is simply a signal to one another that it's time to take action and beat back the blues. Shared supportive rituals are one of the pillars upon which lasting relationships can be built.

"She's Just Plain Nuts" or "What Was He Thinking?"

This is the part where you're just fed up! At some point, we all get there. He's ticked because you thought it was a good idea for the two of you to go away on vacation for a week, and he claims that neither of you have the time or money to do that right now. You're upset because he thought it was a good time to invest in a tech stock that just tanked. Obviously, these are just two of hundreds of possible scenarios. The point is that you're both experiencing that old worry that we commonly verbalize as "I thought I knew him, and now he goes and does something like this."

In living our lives as singles, we all made some not-so-smart choices. But as a couple, we have someone to remind us that what we did was unwise, imprudent, or—if you prefer—just plain dumb. There's a good chance you already knew this, but you don't need him to remind you (or vice-versa).

You respond to his jumping on you about your ill-timed move by bringing up a mistake of his from the past. About now you're both ready to go into your own corners and come out swinging (figuratively, not literally).

What you can do about it: first, recognize that there is a good chance that you have both made some bad choices. There's a reasonable chance that he is feeling bad about whatever dumb choice he made, and your reminding him that he has made a bad decision causes him to defend his actions—something he may have never done if he hadn't been put on the defensive.

When your guy slips up and has a "what was he thinking" moment, try to think outside the box and consider what he might have been thinking *at the time.* As the saying goes, "Hindsight is 20/20." There are bad choices we make that can reveal a troublesome pattern of behavior. But more commonly, your partner made just *one* particularly unwise choice. Your anger and frustration is understandable, but don't fall into the reactive mode of "ready, aim, fire." Get your facts straight first, then have an open and honest exchange about what went wrong and what you can both do as a couple to keep bad decisions to a minimum.

Dating 911

If you're in an angry, abusive, or unhappy relationship, get out. Your life may depend on it. A 2008 study from the University of Utah shows that women in unhappy marriages are more likely to suffer from depression, high blood pressure, obesity, and high blood sugar.

Be Kind to Each Other

The one common thread that we hope you have seen in each of these five scenarios is that they call upon us to bring out the very best in ourselves.

Whatever the issue you are facing—from a patch of bad luck, a couple bad decisions, money worries, demanding kids, or fidelity worries—approach with caution, patience, and a loving heart. It doesn't take a lot of talent to come in, as the expression goes, "with all guns blazing." Remember instead the wise words, "Blessed are the peacemakers."

No matter how great your bond, there will be times that it will be put to the test. Not all relationships were meant to last or are destined to last for a lifetime. But a tremendous number of relationships crumble because of the pressure of one given moment in time—a moment that, if you can as a couple work through together, may well leave you with a stronger bond then you would have ever imagined.

True love is worth fighting for. Difficult times call upon us to be the best we can be. We encourage you, whenever possible, to rise up and answer that call.

The Least You Need to Know

- ◆ Relationships that appear so successful have forces both external and internal that can act upon them and pull them apart. Healthy patterns of mutual respect and love are our best defenses for overcoming those forces.

- ◆ Be aware of those events and issues that can put great stress on your relationship, and be prepared to think outside the box to find successful solutions.

- ◆ Honest and open dialogue carried out in a mutually supportive environment can help you overcome many of the difficult situations that wreck havoc with less-solid relationships.

- ◆ In all situations where you are both under stress, approach with care and resist the instinct to react out of anger.

Chapter 24

Intimacy: Physical and Emotional

In This Chapter

- ◆ Keeping sexual passion in a committed relationship
- ◆ What creates emotional intimacy?
- ◆ Strengthening your bonds of emotional intimacy

If we're lucky in our relationships, we learn to understand and appreciate the difference between physical and emotional intimacy. We also develop a relationship that is strong in both areas, securing the blessings of passionate physical and deeply emotional intimacy that will help enrich your relationship over a lifetime.

If you look at any relationship as it moves through time, you often see a pattern of physical and emotional intimacy that runs in opposite slopes. That's where physical intimacy starts high on the scale and tapers down and emotional intimacy starts comparatively low and moves up. In practicing the successful art of intimacy, this need not be the case.

In Chapter 17, we focused in detail on sexual intimacy and briefly discussed emotional intimacy. In this chapter, we're going to reverse that and touch briefly on physical intimacy and explore emotional intimacy far more deeply.

Sexual Passion: How to Keep It Hot

There are certain blessings that accrue to us in sharing our lives as a committed couple. None are greater than shared physical and emotional intimacy. One of the big questions that hangs out there for all of us as we enter a committed partnership is whether we can stay interested in each other sexually. You may ask, "He turns me on today, but will I still feel that way 10, 20, or more years down the road?"

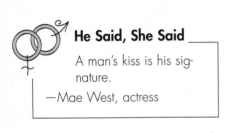

He Said, She Said

A man's kiss is his signature.

—Mae West, actress

It's a perfectly legitimate question. The answer more often than not is, "I sure hope so." Sadly, reality falls short of expectation. Here are two considerations to keep in mind if you want to keep it hot—whether your relationship is four months old or four decades old:

◆ **Keep the romance alive.** Start by considering a number of the aspects of physical intimacy that we discussed in Chapter 17. There's no rule that states that you have to stop romancing each other. In truth, most of us just get lazy. Just like it was a turn-on to be romanced by Mr. Right in the early weeks, months, and years of your relationship, it can still be that way much further down the road. Planning date nights, getting away from the kids just for an overnight, or enjoying a romantic mini-weekend break can all help rekindle the mood for love.

◆ **Place a premium on staying physically attractive to one another.** Putting on the pounds and letting our appearance go in other ways is a good way to say, "I'm not interested anymore." Too often, couples exchange passion for self-deprecating humor in which they all but surrender to the forces of time and nature and acknowledge that they no longer consider themselves to be physically attractive. This is an outcome you don't have to accept.

Although working to keep passion in your relationship can feel like you're going against the cultural tide, we encourage you to make the effort. As the years fly past, you'll be glad that you did.

Emotional Intimacy

Quite simply, emotional intimacy is the development of a close bond as a couple. Here's a simple example: say that today you lost your job, just got hired for a new job, or got a raise and promotion. Or, perhaps best of all, you just hit the lottery numbers for the week. Now, who are you going to call?

If your relationship with Mr. Right has developed into the close partnership you had always hoped it would be, you're going to grab your cell phone and speed dial him.

Good news or bad, a partner with whom you share true emotional intimacy is going to be more often than not the first person that you reach out to. Why is that the case? That person is your best friend, your confidant, and your partner on your journey through life.

Remember that sexual intimacy and emotional intimacy are connected. A couple who lacks physical intimacy will often see their emotional intimacy erode, and vice-versa. This makes perfectly good sense, because both forms of intimacy are about bonding as a couple. Without emotional intimacy, you lose the spark to engage your partner in conversations, decisions, and important moments. That said, it's reasonably unlikely that you're going to keep a healthy sexual relationship when you really are no longer connected emotionally.

In Chapter 17, we provided a list of which key elements help us create the strong bonds of emotional intimacy. Now, let's review that list and spend some time examining each aspect as it enriches our lives as a committed couple.

Two Hearts Open to Each Other

Having an open heart can mean many things, so let's break it down and get more specific. Opening your hearts to each other tears down the barriers of pride and ego. Often, this can be particularly difficult for your guy because it has a lot to do with revealing his vulnerable side, and it takes a while for a man to be able to say, "I could have done a better job in sharing my feelings." But in time, as he learns from you, he can see that opening his heart to you is the very best way of reaching you and of sharing his true self.

Another important aspect of communicating with an open heart was discussed in the previous chapter, when we exampled a number of scenarios that put stress on a relationship. Whatever that stress is, a good way to address it as a couple is to acknowledge the fact that you don't have all the answers—but that together, you can search for solutions. We become combative when we put ourselves in the position where we believe we have a monopoly on good ideas and our partner has cornered the market on bad ideas. If you're truly opening your heart, you know that you don't have all the answers and that you're better able to listen to your partner's insights.

> **He Said, She Said**
>
> The best and most beautiful things in the world cannot be seen or even touched—they must be felt with the heart.
>
> —Helen Keller, writer and lecturer who was blind and deaf from infancy

It's equally important to be open about sharing your fears or frustrations. After all, if we can't share that side of us, what can we share? In order to *really* share, you must open your heart as well as speak up. And he needs an open heart to listen to what you have to say.

Speaking Your Mind

We all go through some degree of self-censorship, if for no other reason than to strengthen our skills in communication. But when you're in a situation with your partner where you are constantly thinking, "I can't say *this* because he'll be upset; I can't say *that* because he doesn't like to talk about it" or, "I can't mention my job because he's not interested," then you have an emotional intimacy problem.

Sharing our day-to-day lives is a big part of being a couple. When you can't do that, you're denying yourself one of the fundamental benefits of being a couple.

Sadly, it happens all the time. Of course there are going to be times when it's not a good idea to communicate a concern. If he just had a blow-up at work, chances are he doesn't want to hear about your mother treating you unfairly. But these cases should be the exception rather than the rule.

When couples feel like they can't open up to one another, they start looking outside the relationship for someone else with whom they can share their hopes and fears. For obvious reasons, this can put the relationship in peril.

The freedom to speak your mind is essential for a happy, lasting relationship. You must have that in your life together if you're thinking that this relationship is going to go the distance.

The Ability to Accept What Has Been Shared with You

No one is going to communicate freely and openly with someone who is resistant to whatever it is you want to share. Opening your heart and finding the words to express your feelings becomes a hollow victory if you or he put up barriers to what you have heard. This is another way in which couples can deliberately show a lack of support for their partner as payback for an earlier time when they felt ignored. This is a destructive cycle of behavior that you want to work to avoid.

We're all going to make mistakes at times, and men particularly can be bad listeners—but try hard to always return to the ideal of being a supportive and engaged listener. Hearing one another is fundamental if we are ever going to have life partners that truly want to open up to us.

A Shoulder to Cry On

You're never going to have a life that is emotionally intimate if you can't cry on your partner's shoulder every now and then. Whether it's the illness or death of a parent, the promotion that you thought for sure was going to be yours and now it has gone to someone else, or simply you feeling overwhelmed by life, every now and then we all have a meltdown. Well, as the movie line goes, "Who ya gonna call?"

Hopefully the answer is your life partner.

Here again, if the reaction you get from your partner is something like, "Oh no, you're not going to cry about this!", then where do you turn for that need? If you're part of a couple who is emotionally intimate, your partner may not always be the pillar of support you were hoping to find—but for the most part, he should be where you need him to be: at your side.

We all know the classic wedding vow: "in sickness and in health." For a couple enjoying emotional intimacy, that list includes sickness and health. Other items, however, may also be times of stress and disappointment and times of loss and depression.

> **He Said, She Said**
>
> Love does not begin and end the way we seem to think it does. Love is a battle, love is a war, love is a growing up.
>
> —James A. Baldwin, novelist and playwright

If you're looking at a partnership that will last a lifetime, during that time you will together experience both joy and sadness. A strong bond of emotional intimacy will increase every joyful moment and bring you great comfort during times of sorrow.

No Regrets for What Has Been Done or Said

Building and maintaining strong bonds of emotional intimacy doesn't necessarily mean never having to say you're sorry, but it does mean that you trust in one another that you've given your best shot at whatever it is you hoped to accomplish.

Couples who don't have shared emotional intimacy are always wondering whether there's something the other partner is holding back. Did he or she really care to go that extra mile? Did he or she really take the time to listen to your problem or to think about a solution?

When you are truly bonded together, you have no regrets about the decisions you made—even when, as life would have it, they turned out badly. Did you sell that stock when the market was up, or did you hold it and see its value wash away? Did you let that house that would have been such a good buy slip away because you just couldn't make the decision to make an offer? In a shared life together, there will be plenty of opportunities to make mistakes. Often, the worst are the ones we see as negatively impacting our kids, such as, "We should have never put her in that school. She was so unhappy there." To that extent, sure, you have regrets—but you don't point fingers at one another because your bonds of emotional intimacy tell you that what was said or done was simply a function of not being able to foretell the future, not with the intention of ever causing harm.

Shared Lives and Separate Interests

Whether it's eating together on a regular basis, long phone calls when one of you is away from home, or simply sharing a ride home together, there are a variety of ways in which couples who are emotionally intimate spend time together.

The reverse, of course, is often the case for couples who do not have these bonds. Often, they are more like two people who share a space than share a life.

Obviously, we all have separate lives to some extent—and often, it is healthy to do just that. He may have no interest in gong for drinks with the girls, and you may have no interest in playing golf or going fishing with the guys. The idea of being "joined at the hip" is not appealing to most couples who have strong bonds of emotional intimacy despite these separate interests.

The ability to share in so many other ways, from dinner at home to a movie at the theater, is more a true measure of the state of your emotional intimacy then the sheer act of always being by each other's side.

Above All Else, a Basic Sense of Trust

We saved the best for last. It's hard to imagine a couple who is not going to tell an innocent lie to each other on a fairly frequent basis. Whether that's him telling you that he had to stay late at the office when what he was really doing was going for a beer with the guys to you saying you're meeting a friend for coffee when you're really out hunting for his birthday gift. Whatever the fib, they happen—and it's probably the natural result of always being on each other's radar.

But trust on all those substantive issues goes so much deeper than that. Besides the obvious, that he's not having an affair on the side, trust is about the basic belief that when needed, he'll be there. You just got word that your cat of 15 years is not going to pull through. You're pretty busted up about it. You know that when you get home, his shoulder will be there for you to cry on.

You're not sure whether it's wise or foolish that you put your time and effort into taking a class in website design although you've always had a great interest in it. You know that you can talk with him and trust him to give you his best and most honest opinion. He won't tell you just what you want to hear but instead what he thinks you need to consider.

Dating 911

Trust is the connective tissue that keeps all lovers together. When trust is not there, love never lasts.

As we're certain you know, trust has a thousand applications—and a day hardly goes by that we don't need a trusted friend. Through the bonds we build through the practice of emotional intimacy, we always know that a trusted friend is a phone call, an instant message, or perhaps just a pillow away.

Keep the Bond Between You Clear and Candid

Your bond of emotional intimacy should be kept and cared for through the years, just as you would care for anything precious that you have obtained and built during your years together. It's what gives you the ability in good times and bad to be able to say, "We need to talk. There is something that concerns me. There are times when it's wise to just simply say …" Or, "I just need you to listen to me for five minutes. I'm not asking you to do anything; I just want to tell you how I feel about this issue so you can hear my thoughts."

That ability to have an open line of communication is priceless in any relationship. It's particularly invaluable for two people planning to share a life—and very often raise a family—together.

The path toward shared physical intimacy as years pass by is your bonds of emotional intimacy. If you are to dance in the arms of Mr. Right as you share with family and friends the joy of your 50th wedding anniversary, it will be those same bonds of emotional intimacy that brought you to that day and put you on the path toward love that lasts a lifetime.

The Least You Need to Know

- While physical intimacy and emotional intimacy can take different paths throughout your years as a committed couple, you can keep both thriving if you put the effort and care into making that happen.

- There are many aspects of emotional intimacy, and no couple is going to get it right every time. Being open and honest with each other, however, is invariably the best path toward producing the happiest results.

- Safeguard and treasure your bonds of emotional intimacy. It is a cornerstone of a relationship well lived.

Chapter 25

He's Committed; Are You?

In This Chapter

- Why women get cold feet
- Determining your own feelings about your Mr. Right
- Breaking up gracefully
- Working through your doubts

You're in a committed, monogamous relationship. You may be living with him or even engaged to be married. But for some reason, you have begun to question whether you're doing the right thing to be merging your future with his. Where are these doubts coming from, and why?

Perception vs. Reality Check

Even after you've found the man you consider to be your Mr. Right, you may have several preconceived notions as to how this union will work out. These fantasies aren't based on anything other than your hopes, dreams, goals, and wishes—and, whether you know it or not, also your past experiences (both with other men and in observing your own parents' relationship and the relationships of other family members or friends).

None of this means these assumptions are right.

Yes, it would be ideal if indeed your Mr. Right were everything you'd hoped for. But the odds are there will be some compromises in the relationship as well as some areas of his life or personality that you won't agree with but will not be able to convince him to change. And if you can't learn to live with it, you'll begin to question whether you should move on.

Maybe you should also question why these issues concern you so much. Of course, any woman would be running out the door if the reasons had to deal with any of Chapter 19's "Ten Deal-Breakers." But not all cases of cold feet are induced by something he'll say or do. Your own reticence may be what's holding you back from fully reveling in this very special love. Here are our top 10 indicators that you're backing out the door:

- ◆ You still don't feel like a "couple."
- ◆ You don't feel as if you communicate well with him …
- ◆ … but at the same time, you avoid asking deep questions or giving candid answers.
- ◆ You still flirt with other men.
- ◆ He doesn't turn you on physically.
- ◆ You don't miss him when you're away.
- ◆ You are jealous of your girlfriends' relationships.
- ◆ You still think about dating other guys.
- ◆ You can't say to friends and family that you're in love with him.
- ◆ In fact, you question whether you actually love him at all.

The Commitment Quiz

Relationships ebb and flow, which is why both of you may feel varying levels of commitment at any given point in time. The following quiz can help you gauge your own level of commitment:

1. If you had a choice of staying in with him or going out, you'd ...

    a. Stay in and cuddle with your couch potato.

    b. Stay in but grumble as to why he won't take you out instead.

    c. Leave him a note that says he can fend for himself!

2. He wants to move in together. You ...

    a. Immediately start packing. It's your dream come true!

    b. Smile but tell him that grand plan needs further discussion.

    c. Shake your head. No way, no how!

3. He uses "we" when talking to other people. You ...

    a. Love it! And you start doing that, too.

    b. Grin and bear it, but it makes you feel uncomfortable.

    c. Tell him to cut it out because it makes you too uncomfortable.

4. He wants you to spend the holidays with his family out of town. You ...

    a. Pack your bags and pray that they'll love you.

    b. Thank him for the invite but beg off. You want to check with your own family first. Perhaps he'll join you there instead.

    c. Lie that you need to work through the holidays.

5. He doesn't take that job promotion out of state because of your relationship. You …

    a. Tell him not to worry about you because you'd follow him anywhere.

    b. Are flattered but want to have a serious talk about both your futures before either of you commits further to each other.

    c. Are angry and tell him that he's foolish for not taking it. And freeze him out for a week or two.

6. He wants to spend all his time with you. You …

    a. Are living the dream. No down time!

    b. Prefer to keep it fresh and tell him that periodic breathers make the heart grow fonder.

    c. Want to run away when you hear this. It scares you.

7. He assumes you will be spending the night at his place. You …

    a. Are so happy he wants that, which is why you brought a toothbrush (among other things).

    b. Are flattered but tell him you'd rather he just take you home.

    c. Roll your eyes. He's got to be kidding!

8. He wants to meet your family. You …

    a. Can't wait and schedule a meet-and-greet.

    b. Arrange it and then immediately regret you did.

    c. Make excuses why that won't work right now—and hope he'll give up on that idea.

9. He talks about when you have children together. You …

    a. Smile and start throwing out baby name ideas. You can certainly get into that fantasy!

    b. Frown. He's moving too fast too soon—and you tell him that.

    c. Laugh in his face and ignore the look of hurt that crosses it.

10. He's allergic to your cats, and you …

    a. Find them a nice home.

    b. Tell him to get allergy shots or just take a pill.

    c. Suggest that he not come visit.

11. He plans all his vacations around your schedule. You …

    a. Love the fact that he loves spending his down time with you.

    b. Are fine with this—but only if he's picking up the tab.

    c. Suggest separate getaways. Time to take a break!

12. When he nudges you for sex, you …

    a. Can't wait to undress and feel his arms around you.

    b. Oblige him … with a sigh.

    c. Pretend to be asleep.

13. He's already talking about venues for the wedding. You …

    a. Have a list of your own. Great! Let's get down to the details.

    b. Feel uncomfortable. You still see too many issues between you. Time to talk …

    c. At first, you laugh. Then, you get angry. Who does he think he is, anyway?

14. He gave you the password to his computer. You …

    a. Appreciate this, memorize it, but never read his e-mails because you trust him.

    b. Pretend not to care, then immediately snoop at his e-mail. You have trust issues, but you don't know how to ask him.

    c. Promptly lose it. You don't know why he wanted you to have it in the first place.

15. He says he loves you just as you are. You …

    a. Appreciate it. No man has ever expressed such acceptance of you.

    b. Think there's a catch. You've never felt that lovable, so he must be dumber than you thought.

    c. Know he's lucky to have you, and that just proves it.

16. He just wants to please you. You …

    a. Want to reciprocate because you appreciate him.

    b. Think he's lucky to have you and see no reason to dissuade him that he doesn't deserve you.

    c. Wish he'd stop fawning over you. It makes you uncomfortable!

17. His parents already treat you like their daughter-in-law. You …

    a. Act like it by calling them "Mom" and "Dad."

    b. Feel guilty about that because they are still strangers to you.

    c. Avoid them as much as possible.

18. He doesn't look at other women. You …

    a. Appreciate this because it means he only has eyes for you.

    b. Expect this. He's lucky to have you and shouldn't rock the boat.

    c. Couldn't care less. You're still looking hard at other men.

19. He has added your name to his car insurance policy. You …

    a. Immediately do the same for him. Somehow it says, "We're a couple now!"

    b. Think this is odd, considering that you have no intention of ever using his car.

    c. Call the insurer behind his back and ask that it be removed.

20. He never talks about past relationships for fear it would hurt your feelings. You …

    a. Do the same out of respect for him.

    b. Shrug because it's not a big issue in your mind. In fact, you'd rather know why he may have been dumped in the past.

    c. Laugh at this—and think nothing of teasing him about your old flames.

21. His friends tell him you're the one for him. You …

    a. Are so proud you've won them over.

    b. Expected as much. But to you, the real test is whether your girlfriends like *him*.

    c. Get chilled with a feeling of dread.

22. He gives you the key to his apartment. You …

    a. Feel honored because you know it's also the key to his heart.

    b. Leave it in a dresser. You probably won't use it all that much.

    c. Lose it. He'll never know because you'll never use it.

23. He wants to have a "talk" with your father. You …

    a. Are thrilled and get your dad on the phone.

    b. Feel things are moving too fast and say so.

    c. Get a cold feeling of dread but keep your mouth shut. It's better for one person to want you than no one at all.

Quiz Key:

If the majority of your answers are A, you are thoroughly in tune with your Mr. Right and see him as your life partner. No cold feet here!

If most of your answers are B, you have some important concerns about the relationship and are still questioning your own feelings. These issues aren't necessarily deal-breakers, but they are certainly going to come between you and your Mr. Right if you don't have a few candid discussions in which you hear each other out, set boundaries, and put some serious effort toward working out your differences.

He Said, She Said

Love doesn't necessarily mean marriage, but it may mean sharing the rent. According to the 2007 U.S. Census Bureau, currently 5 million heterosexual couples are cohabiting—a 200 percent increase since 1980.

If most of your answers are C, you're certainly not as committed to the relationship as your Mr. Right (Now). You're resentful of the obligation you feel toward him, and you are backing off quickly. However, you have not been honest with him as to your true feelings. That said, it's time you did some serious soul searching as to why you've let it go on this long and how and when you will break it off.

Back Out—or Work It Out?

Your feelings will lead you down one of two paths:

♦ You'll decide to call it quits.

♦ You'll take a good hard look at the issues that make you hesitate and see whether there is any way to salvage your love for this man who so obviously loves you, too.

Neither path is wrong. The goal is to take that best path for you, at this place and time in your life, without feeling guilt or obligation to do what is right for anyone else but you. Bottom line: If you are unhappy in the relationship for any reason, then he will be, too.

How to Say Goodbye Gracefully

If you've made up your mind that your cold feet aren't going to warm up anytime soon; that he truly isn't your Mr. Right; and you can't, won't, and shouldn't settle for less, then the only recourse you have is this:

♦ **Tell him as soon as possible.** There's no need to keep up a false front just because you don't want to hurt his feelings. If you don't come clean now, you'll be doing a lot worse damage to his psyche when, sometime in the future, you've solidified your relationship even more by living together, merging your bank accounts, getting married, or having children together.

◆ **Do so in a manner that demonstrates your appreciation and respect for him.** Whatever you say to him will have a shock-and-awe effect. That's a given. What you don't need to do, however, is lay blame on him for any of the reasons you've decided to call it off. Instead, use this time to describe how you're feeling and why.

◆ **Expect some angry blowback, both during your goodbye and afterward.** Give him the courtesy of answering his questions as to what went wrong in the relationship. And certainly allow him to blow off steam, too. You should be prepared for some accusations (and in all honesty, not unmerited, if your answers to the previous quiz are any indication of your feelings and actions toward him). Allowing him the time to speak his mind is allowing him to process his own hurt feelings over the breakup.

◆ **Ask him to forgive you for changing your mind but to also respect you for following your own heart.** Despite your breakup, you both still have intense feelings for each other and will for quite some time. Hearing you ask for forgiveness will go a long way toward allowing him to move on—and you, too. And hopefully it will allow you to stay friends in some capacity—that is, after the hurt subsides and you both get on with your lives.

> **He Said, She Said**
>
> According to a 2003 survey conducted by eNation, despite the fact that only 32 percent of men claim to have been dumped by their partners, 51 percent of women say they initiated their most recent breakup.

Embracing Your New Life with Him

You've worked very hard to find your Mr. Right. To use a football analogy, your cold feet at this stage are the equivalent of catching a long spiral pass, running toward the end zone, but freezing before crossing your opponent's goal line.

Why do you feel the urge to stop before crossing the threshold of your relationship happiness? Because, for whatever reason—and it's a reason that has nothing to do with him, but a valid reason nonetheless—you're scared of closing the deal. Those fears could be many: fear of this change in your life; fear of making a mistake; or fear of failing at happiness with a wonderful, sweet, caring, romantic, and considerate man.

Well, now is the time to confront all your fears, no matter what they are. And he's willing to be at your side as you do that. To move forward, consider couples counseling. In that venue, you'll be encouraged to express your concerns without judgment from him or from the counselor. You'll hear unbiased insights as to whether you're ready to move forward. And he will also be encouraged to express his own fears and concerns of building his life with you. Together, you'll break through the final blocks that keep you from finding happiness as a loving couple, and you'll move forward into the final stage of commitment: marriage.

The Least You Need to Know

- Women get cold feet, too, usually when the fantasy of their lives with their Mr. Rights doesn't match up to reality. Should this happen to you, be honest with yourself as to whether your desires are attainable in the first place.

- If you get anxious about the relationship, you should feel free to talk out your concerns with your Mr. Right.

- If the relationship isn't right, be honest to yourself and to him about it—and break it off in a loving and respectful manner that reflects the joy you had in the time you were together.

Chapter 26

The Happiness (and Stress) of Weddings and Honeymoons

In This Chapter

- ◆ Why you want to say "I do"
- ◆ Stress factors to avoid when planning your wedding
- ◆ Ensuring a wonderful and low-stress honeymoon

Having found Mr. Right and having committed to a shared life, your next step is getting serious about planning the wedding. The choices are huge. Big or small? Indoors or out? Modest or lavish? Spring, summer, winter, or fall? The list goes on. As silly as it seems, a lot of relationships have broken up over the stress of planning a big wedding. We say silly not because the stress is not a real problem, but simply how odd it is that a ceremony meant to celebrate and honor the love two people have found in each other should crumble over the plans to celebrate that love.

Moving Toward That Big Wedding Date— and Beyond

Today, most modern couples live together or virtually live together as they tentatively begin to approach their actual wedding day. Cohabitation long before you formally exchange your vows has overturned many of the rituals that previous generations partook prior to their wedding day. Even the formal act of having a guy on bended knee ask the question, "Will you marry me?" has changed.

Has it lightened that desire to tie the knot? Hardly.

Today, it's not until after several months (or years, even) that a couple makes the decision to take the step into having their marriage formally recognized and celebrated by family and friends. Statistics show that older couples who have established separate adult lives prior to meeting, and couples where one or both have come through a previous marriage, will wait longer to make the actual decision to marry than a younger man and woman who are marrying for the first time.

He Said, She Said

The odds of you getting married are excellent! Despite what the media would have you believe, Rutgers University's National Marriage Project shows that more than 90 percent of women have married eventually in every generation for which records exist, going back to the mid-1800s.

At whatever age and stage of life you find yourself, when faced with setting the big date, certain common experiences and stresses occur in the lives of most couples. So let's take a closer look at that turning point in our lives together when we approach the day when we say to the world, "I do."

Tying the Knot with Fumbling Fingers

It starts innocently enough: just the two of you at a special dinner that he suggested a week before. It's a splurge, and he's acting a little fidgety. You're thinking, "Is he anxious about the bill, or is he wondering whether I'm enjoying my meal?" In reality, he's nervous because he's about to pull a ring out of his pocket and tell you that the last year has been the best year of his life. He wants to know that every year to come will be just as great.

You always wondered whether you would cry when the man you loved popped that classic question, "Will you marry me?" And now, you find out that indeed you will cry tears of great joy that you have found each other.

Now you're ready to make that greatest commitment of all: declaring to the world that you are husband and wife.

That night is bliss, and you sit up talking until three in the morning. You joke about the cousins who you hope will make it to the wedding and ones you hope won't come. But of course, you have to invite everyone! How could you not? Before long, you're talking about the honeymoon—Maui, San Francisco, a cruise, a real adventure, a safari, or just a quiet beach. You have so many dreams that you just float on a cloud into a deep sleep.

You awake the next morning with a wedding to plan and at least 15 (if not 40) people to call and tell your big news. By that evening, you're exhausted. You've not only reached everyone, but half of them have reached you back and thrown out some pretty impressive ideas.

But like all things in life, great ideas come at a price. For the first time, you realize that a few possible options that you and your guy discussed in the wee hours of the morning are now 50 different options. For the first time, you feel a touch of the stress that weddings can bring. It's not necessarily a bad thing; it's just a hint of things to come.

What you don't want to do is go down the path of Kate Hudson and Anne Hathaway in *Bride Wars*, a film that played up the stereotypical crazed bride for every laugh it could squeeze out. Of course, picking the venue is top on the priority list. Just keep reminding yourself that from the venue to the caterer, from the florist to the band, there's always more than one choice. Here are four suggestions for keeping your cool when the wedding pressure starts to build.

Take Your Time Choosing the Venue

Sure, there will be those who gush at you about one site or another and tell you that they book up two years in advance and that you have to act today if you have any hope of scheduling a ceremony before you're both eligible for Social Security. Still, don't jump. Between the advice of family and friends, what you yourselves know as a couple, and the world of options you can research on the Internet, you want to take your time and choose wisely.

Set a Budget and Stay Within It

A lot of the stress occurs when one or both of you get into the common trap we call the runaway budget. "It's only this much, and that's only $300 more," becomes a mantra. It's one of those occasions that proves the point that "the road to hell is paved with good intentions."

Yes, we know that is very difficult to do. Once you are bumping up against how much you wanted to spend, when you add something to the budget, take something else out. Sure, it can be difficult, but ask yourselves this very important question: "Do we want to enjoy ourselves, or are we going to stress out over the cost and forget the fact that this is a celebration of our love, not a Hollywood production?"

We're guessing that answer is "no."

Any moment in your life that is supposed to be as big as your wedding and your honeymoon comes loaded with expectations. Unfortunately, with high expectations comes stress—and with stress, a lot of the enjoyment you're supposed to feel just goes up in one tense moment followed by another. People hoping to relish the happiness too often come out more exhausted than excited.

That said, if you're more concerned about the wedding than the years after, you're getting married for all the wrong reasons.

Too many couples are running up a huge debt preparing for one day that they're going to spend years paying back. Like all things in life, there's a limit. Decide at the start of the process what your realistic budget is and commit to that.

If you can't afford an expensive venue or a big guest list, do something simple like having an outdoor wedding or one in a small chapel. Invite just those you love most: your closest friends and family. Have a small reception afterward, with cake and champagne. Remember, it's the most important day of your life. Special doesn't mean "big"; it means "memorable."

Remember That It's Your Party

Weddings are a magnet for those who have too little to do in their own lives and too much to do in yours. If you welcome the daily (24/7) advice, no problem—but for most, it becomes a drag on their sense of enjoyment and anticipation of this very special event. Don't let that happen.

Whether you and your husband-to-be are paying most of the bills, or your parents are, or his parents, or some combination of all three, it's *your* wedding. Don't forget that.

> **He Said, She Said**
>
> I found the right man, got married, and just had to keep not reinventing myself, just deciding that it doesn't matter what you are if you are a good person.
>
> —Lisa Kudrow, actress

If you want to keep your stress levels down, give up control of only those things you're happy to give away (perhaps the seating arrangement or the choice of the band/DJ). But the overall event is yours to be as deeply involved in as you choose.

Finally, don't get so caught up in planning the wedding that it's all you can talk about. Make time for non-wedding-planning dates just for the two of you.

Keep Him in the Loop, but Don't Make Him Part of the Planning Committee

We can't stress how important it is for the two of you to stay close during this entire process. As a general rule, no matter how much of a modern man your Mr. Right is, most men are not too excited about being an integral part of wedding planning. Don't take it too seriously. It's like taking a guy to a chick flick: you're enjoying it, and he's probably trying to will himself to stay awake.

Yes, he'll want to know what's going on, if for nothing else to be sure that you're not spending the two of you into the poorhouse. Give him some clearly designated functions—perhaps the band/DJ, choosing his best man, and coordinating the other men in the wedding party.

Weddings can be big productions, or just two people standing at the edge of a dock at sunset with their guests close at hand watching as they exchange their vows and melt into each other's arms. Here's the most important thing to remember about your big day: it's about the two of you finding each other and celebrating the happy fact that you want to share your lives together. Everything else is and should be secondary to that fact.

Dating 911

Be open to his participation in your wedding planning—and yes, take his opinion into account. It's his big day too, remember? At the same time, if all the planning intimidates him, just assign him one task that is his to control fully so that he gets into the spirit.

The weddings we seem to remember the most fondly are those where the bride and groom and their immediate family were happy and proud, not tense and anxious. A certain degree of stress will be a part of almost every wedding plan and event, but both of you can cut that stress with a plan that prepares you for those most common pitfalls that put you on the path toward wedding tension as opposed to wedding bliss.

The Honeymoon: The Best Is Yet to Come

Honeymoons, like weddings, are rarely free. They can also range in size and expense. Here as well, it's the amount of high spirits and love in the hearts of the two principal participants that will really determine the success of your honeymoon and how well it sets you up for the hopefully many years of married life to follow.

What are the ingredients of a successful honeymoon, and how can you help ensure that you have a wonderful and memorable one? Start with these four tips for successful honeymoons.

Communicate Clearly with Each Other

From the honeymoon budget to your choice of destination, this should never be a battle of wills but rather a loving collaboration. In your years together, you may take a handful of trips or hundreds. But only one of those trips will be your honeymoon. Make it memorable, even if you just stay home for a week. Explore new venues, enjoy new experiences together, take lots of pictures, and make love every day.

Pick a Destination That's New to Both of You

There is a natural inclination for one of you to share with the other a past favorite spot from your travels. That could be a place 30 miles from where you both now live or a place that you love all the way on the other side of the world.

There are several reasons why it's better that this place be new to the two of you, but here are just two: first, you don't want to set up the "I love it, so you will too" dynamic. This can really backfire. The place may not be as wonderful as you remember, and now you feel the burden of having made the wrong choice and "ruining" it for both of you. Chances are it wouldn't be that bad, but why leave something like that up to chance?

Second, you're cheating yourself out of one of the great aspects of a honeymoon: discovering a new place together. Whenever you go to a place that is just known to one partner, one of you becomes the tour guide (or attempts to) and the other becomes the tourist. You're on unequal footing, and that's not the best ground to be standing on for a happy honeymoon.

Leave Yourselves Plenty of Time to Just Be Together

The bigger the trip, the more we tend to pack in as many events and as much sight-seeing as we can. This is understandable, particularly when the trip takes us somewhere exotic that neither one of us has ever been.

Gain from the experience of couples who have made that same mistake. If you're on the "If this is Tuesday, this must be Belgium" trip, there's a good chance that there will be very little time for romance—and romance is really what it's supposed to be all about.

An interesting trip? Absolutely! You can even climb a mountain if that's something special to the two of you, but don't forget to put in a couple of days back at the lodge with some scented bath salts, candles, and a bathtub for two. If your honeymoon is not for romance, then what is? Not the trip to Disney World or Disneyland 10 years later with the kids!

He Said, She Said

Here's an unexpected benefit of marriage: it keeps you fit! According to a University of Texas/Austin study that appeared in the September 2008 issue of *Journal of Health and Social Behavior*, those married couples report better health than people who have never married, or who are widowed or divorced.

Keep a Honeymoon Diary

Sure, it's a little corny—but if you make it to your 15th, 30th, and perhaps 50th anniversary, this little book might well be one of your most priceless keepsakes. It's incredible how fast our shared years can fly past. Being able to look back on the places and faces of your honeymoon becomes more special each year.

As opposed to your wedding album, you can keep your honeymoon diary filled with love notes and some sexy photos of both of you as your own private keepsake: something that just the two of you can take out on a special occasion—say, the anniversary of the day you first met, the day you got engaged, or that big wedding day—and reminisce over the fun and passion you shared during those very special days of your early life together as a couple. Best of all, if you want to retrace some of the steps of your honeymoon on a return trip 25 years later, that diary will be a great guide to everything you did back then.

Share the Moment; Share Your Lives

There are many ways to look at your life together during the early weeks and months that you step into the world of becoming a committed couple. Among the love and sharing, there are also the momentous occasions that bring joy and stress into our relationships. Truly wise couples know to cherish the adventure, celebrate their love, and create and safeguard beautiful memories that can last a lifetime.

The Least You Need to Know

♦ Weddings can be incredibly stressful events. Know that from the start, and come prepared with practical ways to reduce your stress and help ensure a successful event.

♦ Enjoy the process. In any event as big as a wedding, you'll have a few bumps along the way. Think of it as in-flight turbulence. You'll still arrive safely at your destination, so stop fretting and enjoy the trip.

♦ Great honeymoons are something you create together. Enjoy the collaboration, and create memories that you will treasure for years to come.

Chapter 27

A Lifetime of Love with Mr. Right

In This Chapter

- ♦ Through good times and bad
- ♦ Planning and execution of a successful relationship
- ♦ Nurturing that loving feeling
- ♦ Close or clingy?
- ♦ Appreciate your differences
- ♦ Continuing the story

There's *your* relationship, and then there's the *American sitcom version* of your relationship. Too often, people give up on the idea of a deep and meaningful shared life together and opt for the sitcom relationship, in which stereotypical partners quickly become bored with one another and focus on every aspect of their life other than the quality of the life they had once planned on building together. And as for sexual passion, romance, or cuddling five years into a committed relationship, the cynics tell us to just, "Fuggedaboutit!"

Of course you can resist falling into that all-too-easy trap, ignore the stereotypes, and go your own way. You can not just focus on the happiness of your relationship in its early years but also build for a future where you continue to share your highs and lows with your most trusted friend—your life partner.

It's something of a mystery why we so often settle for less. Love is like a powerful current that can flow abundantly through each of us, connecting our hearts and minds. Unfortunately, we can also short-circuit that current and disconnect from one another. When you disconnect, your frustration tells you to stop caring. From that point, your once-anticipated promise that you would live "happily ever after," spins wildly out of control.

It's Never Just Blue Skies

You can seemingly "have it all": money, good looks, and a wonderful personality. Even to those most fortunate, however, misfortunes will come: a family tragedy, ill health, financial disaster … maybe one of the above or possibly all.

To the "beautiful people" and to the rest of us, life—as the expression goes—can throw us one or several curve balls. These are the times that will test our character, our patience, and most of all our love.

This is why wedding vows declare devotion through sickness and health; good times and bad. To many newlyweds these are just words; to long-time married couples, though, they are words to live by. Only through life's trials and tribulations will you find your true commitment to a shared future. And with each test, your bond as a couple will strengthen. No one ever ran a marathon without first training to run a mile, then five miles, and so on.

The good times are great fun and put a smile on your face whenever you recall them. But as the years go by, you'll also look back at the disappointments you endured and the setbacks you suffered as a couple. These, too, will make you smile because you came through those trials with a deeper commitment to the life you've built together.

To keep your equilibrium during those times, good, clear communication between you both is essential.

Keep the Lines of Communication Open

As communication goes, so goes the marriage. Hopefully, and most likely, you built your love on good communication. You have learned early on the importance of compromise, and you continue to develop and practice those skills throughout your lives together.

Later on, however, too many couples settle into a pattern of growing slowly but steadily apart in their communication. Many couples silently drift farther from each other with each passing year. This by no means is destined to be your fate, and the number one way to ensure that it is not is to keep communicating.

Frequently, new couples ask, "After 5 or 10 years, what is there to talk about?"

"A lot," is the answer—that is, if you have continued to stay close. From a physical standpoint, just think of all the events that occur in a single day in each of your lives while you're away from each other. For example, one of you may be at school while the other is at work. One of you may be with your children while the other is on the job. Perhaps both of you are involved in different community projects, pursuing different hobbies, or traveling separately. All the more reason to communicate your love and devotion in a way that is understood and appreciated by your Mr. Right.

Even couples that spend most of their time together can grow apart emotionally. Why? Because they hadn't taken the time for personal growth, let alone to nurture their emotional growth as a couple. They've allowed other relationships or events to take precedence over their union. And they've lost the attraction and passion that brought them together in the first place.

But none of this will happen to you—not if you and your Mr. Right take time to do the following:

♦ **Talk openly and honestly with each other.** Feel free to exchange your thoughts on the various aspects and issues of your lives.

♦ **Listen, but don't judge.** A trusted partner who can do so invites candor and receptivity to any advice given.

◆ **When possible, give your verbal support and approval.** He lives for that, and this is a factor wired into his personality as much as your desire to have a partner who will simply listen and hear whatever is important to you.

Open communication is established in the earliest stages of a relationship. Like so many hallmarks of a good relationship, it's an invaluable touchstone that can stay with you through all the years you're together if you know how to care and cultivate the art of reaching out to one another.

No Matter What Else, Make Time for Each Other

Between careers and family, we have a countless number of demands on our attention. With all that consumes the minutes and hours of our daily lives, it's easy to forget that it was attraction and romance that made us a couple in the first place.

A date night at least once a month (and preferably twice) is an essential way to reconnect. We know that on a tight budget and with a young family, date nights can add an additional and seemingly unneeded expense. But even here, there are inexpensive alternatives.

For example, make Saturday night (or any night of the week that works well for both of you) your at-home date night. Have dinner after the kids are in bed (or even better, at a friend's house for a sleepover), and put on a movie that neither of you has seen before. Let him plan the date one week, and you plan the date the following week. Prepare the dinner or the snacks, get a bottle of wine, and maybe end the evening with a little candlelit romance in a shared bath. Now there's a date that's small on expense and big on romance, and you can come up with a lot of creative alternatives of your own.

He Said, She Said

Men benefit from just being married, regardless of the quality of the relationship. It makes them healthier, wealthier and more generous with their relatives.

—Scott Coltrane, author of *Gender and Families*

Being emotionally and physically intimate is at the heart of our partnership, too. Keep those qualities alive and healthy in your lives together, or they will simply vanish from sight.

Never Give Old Fights New Life

Television is filled with reruns. Your iPod probably has a whole bunch of favorite tunes that you enjoy hearing over and over again. But when it comes to old fights, never give them new life. It's one fight, and it's *done*.

There are several pitfalls that couples fall into, but one of the most common—and certainly one you want to avoid—is reviving an old argument. Perhaps, for example, you argued over picking the wrong color to paint the kitchen. "I would have never picked that color if you hadn't run out and bought that paint on sale," you say.

He, of course, feels that he was trying to be helpful—and he resents you for not seeing that. To make a very long story short, this relatively small issue in the scope of your life together escalates into a much bigger argument. But worse, it becomes a touchstone disagreement that gets reraised anytime you feel that he has ignored your input. Or, having not gotten any input at all, he runs out and makes a decision without you.

When you're angry about this, you say, "This is just like the time you picked that paint for the kitchen." In other words, you're having the same battle all over again. There is no doubt that certain issues where you both differ are going to be revisited over the years, but that is not the same as refighting the same fight.

It's time to make one simple pledge to each other: let old arguments go; and most importantly, never throw them on top of a current disagreement. If you don't want to be "one of those couples who argues all the time," this is one pledge you want to be sure to keep.

Dating 911

Never go to bed angry at your Mr. Right. Neither of you will have a good night's sleep until you resolve or compromise on your differences.

When It Comes to Housework, Play Fair

Whatever the chores, the days of "Daddy works at the office all day and Mommy keeps house" are as dead and buried as George and Martha Washington. Today's couples generally share incomes and every other aspect of maintaining a home and raising a family. If there's a question of fairness about the division of household chores, make a list and discuss how it can be fairly decided.

Too often, men show a real talent for talking their way around and out of their share of childcare and household responsibilities. In the long run, they will find that they won the battle but lost the war. Resentment over carrying an unfair share of the work is never worth whatever respite from labor may have been gained by not showing up for duty. Divvying up chores is easy: just make a list and take turns choosing what you're willing to do by the agreed-upon deadline. You'll have fun celebrating together when these missions are accomplished.

If you're the kind of partner who takes on more and more of the work of keeping a home and raising a family for fear that demanding balance means that you'll be rocking the boat, don't make that choice. Your resentment will only increase over time and create a toxic spill that can erode the very heart of any relationship.

Beware of the Money Trap

Too many new couples are unaware of the strains that money problems can put on a relationship. Don't let this be a trap that catches you and your partner in a downward spiral known as the Blame Game.

Living together prior to marriage can help prepare you for a lot of the aspects of shared lives, but unless one or both of you suffered a job loss or a financial setback, there's a good chance that you are in a money squeeze for the first time years after you became a couple. We don't mean a bit of belt tightening; rather, we mean, "Gosh, can we make the house payment this month?"

That kind of pressure can really put a scare into couples, and if you are in a situation where just one of you is responsible for the family budget, it can be that much worse. Why? The one who has been caring for the finances is going to feel like a failure, and the other partner is going to feel blindsided. Now you have a perfect storm out of which the troubled winds of blame can gather energy.

No one knows how many marriages have been blown away from the force of these troubled winds, but trust us when we say that it's very common. Your best insurance against this potentially destructive force is to make financial decisions together. That way, if you didn't sell the house when it was at the top of the market, or when shares in that great stock go in the tank, you can honestly point out that this was a shared choice that you made. Instead of one of you blaming the other, you can commiserate together.

When it comes to money, no one has all the right answers. Because ultimately you will both benefit from a good choice (or both suffer from a bad one), share your financial decisions. Regardless of the outcome, if you've been open and honest about your finances with each other, you'll both reap the reward.

He's a Keeper if ...

... he never equates your value with how much you earn.

Lead with Love, and Learn to Forgive

Unfortunately, there are times in which you and he will behave thoughtlessly. You'll say something totally unfair to one another. You'll allow your anger to get the better of you. Or you'll embarrass your partner in front of friends and family.

And, as you probably know, that's a short list of just *some* of the slip-ups you will make.

It's okay. He's going to screw up, too.

Because of this emotional tit-for-tat, it's very important to learn not only how to forgive but also how to grow in stature so that you can ask for forgiveness. To do so, you must find and strengthen that deep sense of caring and kindness that has always been there at the center of your being. Use it during those times when forgiveness and understanding is needed, and lead with love.

Mr. Right is that special guy who you hoped you would find, and you fell in love with him for all the right reasons. When you hit all those inevitable bumps, don't turn down a side road. Instead, get back on the path of partnership you worked so hard to build together. You know in your heart that the place you want him to be is there, by your side. After all, this is the man who has earned the honor of having you call him Mr. Right.

He Said, She Said

Does love spring eternal? Your brain thinks so. In 2008, while showing photos to subjects who claimed to be still madly in love with their partners after an average of 21 years, researchers from New York's Stony Brook University detected intense activity in the ventral tegmental or "pleasure-giving" area of their brains.

Great Sex Can Be the Gift That Keeps Giving

The cynics like to tell us that a good sex life is to be expected for only the first three—or at most, five—years of marriage. Nonsense. Don't buy into that. All couples will see their sexual activity rise and fall over the years. Too little sleep during a new baby's first months or some major stress at work can put a dent in our pursuit of a rich and rewarding sex life. But when those pressures relieve themselves and you once again have more time for each other, your sex life should come back up to a level that you both find satisfying and meaningful.

Sexless marriages, or ones where physical intimacy is a twice-a-year event, is not the outcome either of you wanted when you decided to become a committed couple. If you do find a real and steady diminishment in your sex life, talk about why and then do something about it—whether that's a romantic weekend or just seeing a romantic movie. Don't rule out that couples counseling may be needed. Sex is important. If there is something that is keeping you on opposite sides of the bed, the sooner you find out what it is, the better it will be for your marriage.

A healthy marriage is not just about shared goals and mutual admiration; it's also about an active sex life in which we stay attractive to and passionate for each other.

The Distinction Between a Close Bond and Clinging

We are not suggesting that he share every detail of the baseball game he just saw with his pals or that you share every scene from the chick flick that you went to see with your girlfriends. Living lives that balance independent interests while maintaining close ties is a healthy and essential balance.

Partners who are needy for each other's attention because it is the only social contact that they have outside the workplace have set up a very unhealthy dynamic. It's even more problematic if one partner wants a healthy degree of independence and the other partner tends to cling. Supporting and keeping a circle of friends that are largely unique to you and you alone can be greatly beneficial to your marriage.

Whatever separate interests you pursue, when you come back together, give some brief details of your weekend, day, or evening outing and ask about his event as well—even if his answers are usually brief (which for most men, they are). This touching base is a symbolic reminder that we're always interested in the lives and interests of each other.

Your attraction to each other was based on the individual who you were before you became part of a couple. You don't want to lose that individual. You're life partners, not two halves of the same whole.

You're Simply Different

Speaking of being two different people, you would be wise to always cherish and celebrate that fact. Men and women are different from their heads down to their toes.

Here's a small, silly difference, but it illustrates our point. Josie leaves for an overnight trip in which she will be sharing a room with a gal pal, so of course she shaves her legs before she goes. Martin thinks, "Gosh … I've gone on overnights with guys where I shared a room. It never occurred to me that I should have to shave."

But isn't that the point? *It never occurred to him because it's just one of the many ways in which we're different.* At times, it can be confusing or confounding, but most often it's just amusing. The French probably say it best: "*Vive la difference.*"

There are times that the differences between the sexes amuse us and other times when they drive us to distraction. But without our differences, our shared lives would not be as interesting or nearly as much fun!

Writing Your Private Sequel to Finding Mr. Right

It wouldn't be fair to take you to the end of this book without giving you a preview of the next book. Only this time, the sequel is all yours to write. Here's your working title:

> *Sharing My Life with Mr. Right*

We took you this far. Now you'll have to write that book on your own. Will your story have a happy ending? We certainly hope it will, but you and Mr. Right will have to work faithfully and continue to care deeply about one another if that is indeed going to happen. (You're not alone: we, along with hundreds of millions of other couples, are still working on writing our own happy ending.)

When you have met your Mr. Right, he has met his Mrs. Right, too. And you've both been blessed by the good fortune of having found each other. When difficult times come along, just remember how you felt when you first met, when you first fell in love, and when you first knew you wanted to share your lives together.

We wish the greatest gift you can ever find—a loving partner who is worthy of your love!

The Least You Need to Know

♦ Relationships in the long run are always part bliss and part struggle. Establishing the ground rules for what makes a successful relationship can forever change the quality of the life you share together.

♦ Successful couples monitor their relationships and communicate concerns to each other whenever they sense the relationship is getting off track.

♦ We're never going to get it all right, but if we lead with love and find forgiveness in our hearts, our chances of living happily ever after improve dramatically.

Resources

Knowledge is power, and the following books and websites will connect you with all the ideas that you need to be current on the topics of dating, happy relationships, living wisely, and so much more. Jump in and start soaking up the ideas that will make your life complete.

Books

Behrendt, Greg, and Liz Tucillo. *He's Just Not That Into You: The No-Excuses Guide to Understanding Men*. Simon Spotlight Entertainment, 2009.

Brown, Josie, and Martin Brown. *Marriage Confidential: 102 Honest Answers to the Questions Every Husband Wants to Ask, and Every Wife Needs to Know*. Signal Press, 2003.

Casey, Whitney. *The Man Plan: Drive Men Wild ... Not Away*. Perigree Trade, 2009.

Coleman, Paul. *The Complete Idiot's Guide to Intimacy*. Alpha Books, 2005.

Coltrane, Scott. *Gender and Families*. Pine Forge Press, 1998.

Findling, Rhonda. *The Dating Cure: The Prescription for Ms. Picky, Ms. Eternal Bachelorette, Ms. All About Me, Ms. Can't Let Go, and Ms. Matrimony.* Polka Dot Press, 2005.

Gray, John. *Men Are from Mars, Women Are from Venus: The Classic Guide to Understanding the Opposite Sex.* Harper Paperbacks, 2004.

———. *Why Mars and Venus Collide: Improving Relationships by Understanding How Men and Women Cope Differently with Stress.* Harper, 2008.

Harvey, Steve. *Act Like a Lady, Think Like a Man.* Amistad, 2009.

Kirschner, Diana. *Love in 90 Days: The Essential Guide to Finding Your Own True Love.* Center Street, 2009.

Lenderman, Teddy. *The Complete Idiot's Guide to the Perfect Wedding Illustrated, Fifth Edition.* Alpha Books, 2007.

Locker, Sari. *The Complete Idiot's Guide to Amazing Sex, Second Edition.* Alpha Books, 2002.

Page, Susan. *If I'm So Wonderful, Why Am I Still Single? Ten Strategies that Will Change Your Love Life Forever.* Three Rivers Press, 2002.

Rose, Barbara. *Stop Being the String Along: A Relationship Guide to Being THE ONE.* Rose Group, 2005.

Websites

Dating.About.com   Relationship tips and dating advice, including online dating, date ideas, seduction techniques, and a body language guide.

www.DatingWithoutDrama.com   Dating tips for women, relationship advice, dating rules, understanding men, dating communities and forums.

www.FindingMrRightBook.com   The official website for this book, complete with tips and information on current dating trends.

www.Love.iVillage.com   Love advice for any relationship, including dating etiquette and sex tips.

www.MarsVenusLiving.com   Hundreds of articles, based on Mars Venus wisdom, from dating to starting over to living a full and healthy life.

www.oprah.com/topics/relationships   Get health, beauty, and relationship advice to live your best life.

www.PlanJam.com   Find, plan, and share fun things to do with others, including unique and romantic date ideas.

www.SinglemindedWomen.com   Dedicated to women's issues. Find articles, blogs, and forums that cover issues such as dating, health, beauty, and travel.

Index

G

2/11

Rogue Waves

The Canoe Caught Unawares

We think our lives smooth basins,
glassy as summer rivers,
placid as captured lakes.
We assign actuarials to random events:
lightning strikes, falling satellites,
Jesus coming back.

It takes a disturbance,
a lurch, a wobble.
Maybe an accidental meeting,
a brushing of hands,
a closeness that lingers
and then emerges later, deeper, larger
in an unrelated conversation.

Maybe it's a baby kicking a bathtub,
the waves conspiring around the rubber duck.
Maybe a bird bathes in a random puddle
and blesses your car with splash.
Maybe a current remains from a dammed spillway
and journeys over submerged abandoned bicycles,
piles of mossy old tires, scoured Indian points.

It can turn into a question to which
we cannot accept the answer:

to walk the dock, the wind barely kissing our cheek,
only to find our canoe submerged
and sitting on the bottom, looking up,
its rope barely rustling on the steps,
the thwarts holding its mouth open
in permanent surprise.

Typeface

This poem is set in a typeface
called Apocryphal Hominid 10 point.
Its curlicues and unexpected angles
may be confusing.
It may seem as if
you have been submerged in lines
or reduced to mere symbols.
You may begin to think too much about the presentations
and too little about what they represent.
As if when you see a beautiful woman on the street
and your mind begins to wander.
You might imagine yourself walking beside her.
You might call her Estrella
and she might call you *mi roble, mi momento.*
She will have a slightly chubby bottom,
heels half an inch too tall.
In 1611 a slightly deranged monk
had too much wine and found a way
to codify both pleasures of the flesh
and a rather horrific cataclysm in
marginal letter-endings and stylized curls.
It was a secret all about sound and image
and, especially, symbol congruency, easily
translatable once you knew the key.
Mi momento. No tree lives forever,
not even Yggdrasil. You will want Estrella
to choose what you will do, as if she will know.
You will want her to know.
She will unlatch the watch from your wrist,
and say it is all about the sounds
that will happen next.

The Hardy-Weinberg Law

*The Hardy-Weinberg principle states that genetic
frequencies in a population remain constant from
generation to generation unless outside influences are
introduced. In nature these outside influences are always
in effect. Therefore, the Hardy-Weinberg principle is an
ideal condition that can never be achieved.*

If Columbus and La Salle
had not sailed until
their sails were perfectly ironed
then today we might
be working for the Aztecs.

Some poets will not submit their poems
for public consumption
until the lines are exactly right.
Their notebooks end up
bulging with cabochons.

It's the messiness of things
that makes them perfect:
the sugar falling
from the cinnamon roll,
the ice cream melting in the cone.

Flood waters rise
and kiss against doorways.
The fire comes
down the mountain.
The wind pushes trees into yards.

When I was much younger
I wrote the characteristics
of my perfect girl

on a piece of paper,
did a little chant,

then burned the list in a coffee can,
sending my wishes to the universe.
Now you are sleeping in the crook of my arm,
and maybe you are drooling a little,
and definitely snoring,

and I am thankful for all bugs
that will ever land in my coffee,
grateful for all nails
that will ever make my tires
breathless.

BRONTOSCOPY

The ancient art of divination by listening
to the sound of thunder.

Thunder on Thursday is a good omen
although I think this might border on phrenology
and what I have bumped into recently.
Perhaps if we didn't already have Madame Cleo and
Oprah and Facebook
then we would spend more time
looking for signs ourselves
and less time expecting directions.

In a small town in Mexico
someone, in the midst of remodeling,
found an image in the vague shape
Of Our Lady of Guadalupe
in their sheetrock. It was never questioned
why Our Lady was hiding
beneath old wallpaper.
Instead, the story centered
on how all the candelarias
had flown off the shelves of the local markets,
regardless of whether the saints
were applicable or not.
People wrapped themselves
in candlewicks of holiness
in case drywall had the ability to foreshadow.

It was as if all the kids
in grade school in the Roman era
were given the assignment of
"Go home tonight and create a divining system.
And remember this will count toward

one-quarter of your final grade."
Some less bright kids counted chicken eggs,
some referenced Delphi,
some counted Grandma's aches and pains,
and some actually looked truly outward
trying to comprehend a larger measuring thing.
They might have understood
they were wrapped in holiness every day,
in every dark storm,
if they would just light a candle,
and listen.

WHEN ALEXANDER THE GREAT'S MOM HAD
HIS PHOTO DONE AT SEARS

She constantly chided him.
"Don't fidget. Stand up straight.
What will the Persians think?"
She had a coupon so she wanted to try him
in as many outfits as possible.
He was always so dour, even posturing;
far too grim for a five-year old.
But he was no more grim than she was smart:
she was going to take advantage of this phase,
the tilting of his head,
the puffing of his infantile chest.
Of course, he did keep talking in the
          third person
and that bothered her some.
"Alexander does not like this background.
These shoes pinch Alexander's feet.
Alexander will comb his own hair."
And when the bow tie came up he simply said,
"I would not be Alexander."—and refused to put it on.
He tried the cowboy outfit, under duress,
sitting astride a wooden horse
(which still bore the 'Made in Thessaly' label—
she could have died.)
He seemed relatively comfortable—
but kept calling the conchos 'girl's baubles'.
When he tried on the tiny pin-stripe suit
he only quit scowling when he realized
the matching tie had a picture of Aristotle.
It was when she relented, finally,
and allowed him to stand, bare-chested,
one foot propped up on a carpeted step,
a fist clenched and close to his body,

the other arm extended like a spear,
that she dared followed his eyes
that were looking through,
and past, the cameraman,
and for a chilling, pride-filled second
she believed, as only a parent can believe,
that he could crush the world
beneath those sandaled, dimpled feet.

¡Mis Amoebas!

This child's toy should have
better enunciation.

It's as if God said, "Let there be Light"
and the second vice-president
he was shouting the command to
across the galaxy heard instead "Let there Delight!"
and he ended up just shrugging his cosmic shoulders
and re-interpreting the command
to suit his own agenda.

And chicken lips. We should never pay attention
to overheard conversations while we stand in line
for street lights.
From then on we can only imagine
pullets pulling on cheap cigarettes,
a brim pulled low over one eye,
a feathery Sidney Greenstreet in the background.

In college sheer plod made plow down sillion shine—
but a telemarketer from Ceylon
interrupting me at dinner
can turn it into mere wad make billion
faster than I can hang up.

Sometimes the syllables come out cleanly
and we only mis-hear.
But sometimes the words are as thick
as slow, muddy water over mossy boulders.
It seems like it might be a language we know
if only the sending lips would form it correctly.

So I am left with this lingering image

that haunts me at the most gay of times:
An innocent Hispanic girl,
with a mouthful of rocks,
thinking only in the moment,
as she blithely leads a herd
of giant, one-celled organisms
to a tacqueria, a fiesta,
or some strange and wonderfully bizarre quinciñera.

Famous Poets Trading Cards

These are the small packets
snuggled with slabs of gum
you will never find.

"I'll trade you two Robert Frosts,"
(who is rather common), "for a Rilke
or an Auden."
You can't give away your Wordsworths
but your Shakerley Marmions
and Stephen Ducks are like gold
(even if no one knows who they are).
You always treat your Amy Lowells
and Emily Dickinsons with respect;
you have no trouble at all sticking
Carl Sandburg in the spokes of your bike.
Then there are the team cards
(the post modernists, the beats,
the romantics, etcetera):
The faces are so tiny and you never really believe
Li Po wore his baseball hat backwards.
Of course, every card
has a library of information on the back:
how many double dactyls they wrote,
their sonnet sequences, their favorite topics,
their count of books published, their Nobels won—
all their metrical runs batted in,
how much they tinkered with classical forms,
how many times they rhymed Heavens to Dale Evans,
how often they alluded to
the connotations of chance.

DEAR YOURS TRULY MY LOVE

My beloved tax collector—
as you can see you are special to me.
Have I not written you checks larger,
and more painful,
than alimony for year after year?
My special, my one and only.
Yours truly.
Salutations can be as meaningless as saying
that something is On Sale!
Or the deal is Once in a Lifetime!
The woman says "You will never know
any one like me again!"
That is, of course, correct if you
totally accept that something must be
A and Not A to be true.
When you have washed
your Grateful Dead t-shirt over and over,
and it's thirty years since the last concert you went to,
you've finally noticed that the black thread,
blood, and skeleton
have all faded and washed into gray
and Easter-bunny pink.
You give in one morning,
shrug the way your father used to,
and you use that shirt to wash your car.
It's the same shirt—but you're not the same man.
Nobody cares but you
how many times you wear a pair of socks,
how many times you get married,
how many times you give up smoking.
Your closure is your own, as many times
as you want to use it. Say it again:
Tell me the story of how you ran into Marilyn Monroe

at the bus depot
and how she called you "Honey"
and how it changed your life,
how you're sure she meant it just for you
no matter how many times she had said it before.

Gasping

They haunt you afterwards
when you discover they aren't rhetorical
or aren't solved with a simple
yes or no.

Paper or plastic?
What does this red button do?
What political party are you?
Left or right? Regular or unleaded?
Are you married?
Cream or no cream?

Mostly you can stumble through,
flail around, claim lack of sleep, distraction,
change the subject.
You hit yourself in the head later
when you come up with the clever answer,
but once your mind is prone to disengage
then that gear tooth is broken.

For instance,
one day your wife asks
"Does this dress make me look fat?"
and your cognitive functions
are left standing in neutral,
spinning like crazy but generating no sparks.

Shrugging and grunting won't do,
you can't caveat,
and "I don't know" is absolutely the worst.

It's like being alone on a skiff
and hearing the clacking

of chitinous nails against the boat side,
a mossy hand on the gunwale,
the sibilant, burbly hiss of air
drawn over gills and larynx
not used to human speech.

Maybe it will be the moss draped like a boa,
or the way the color of her eyes
shifts constantly from blue to green.

It could be any of that,
as her eyes will lock yours,
but more likely it will be that
she will ask the question
she has asked countless sailors before.
She will wait,
then swim in closer in her serrated impatience,
this time grabbing the oar,
and ask just one more time,
"Is Alexander the King alive?"

AS MARTIN LUTHER WALKED
ALONG THE ROAD ONE DAY

his best friend beside him was struck by lightning.
Naturally, the whole 'Sal to Tarsus'
thing came to mind
and, sure enough,
Martin immediately turned it into a sign.
He never seemed to question
why his friend was the target;
he just immediately
made the event about himself.

I know a man who gave his wife a hammer
for her birthday
because one day he had seen her lift
a cookie sheet of cookies hot from the oven
with one big, mittened hand
and he thought she might appreciate
something else that was practical
and had such good balance.
As certain as steps on a ladder
he felt he owned a piece
of the holiness
of personal equilibrium.

When you drive past
small, frame churches on rural roads
there is always a lawn for after-service discussion,
a gravel parking lot, a swing-set painted red,
and a sign in front, usually painted white as a lamb
with big black letters.
And on that sign you can expect to see
hours of worship, maybe an alert about a revival,
some quote from Corinthians at the very least.

But on one particular sign it reads:
"We Kill Fire Ants".

You will not be a mile down the road
before you will begin to feel
a vague, unreachable itch.

Rogue Waves

The slight tremors
create ripples in your coffee
and belie impending trouble underneath

We're doomed, of course,
so why does it catch us by surprise?

The car has leapt the curb
and we still insist on spending a moment
in contemplation.

It's like watching the re-enactment of Krakatoa
over and over, the slow-motion replay,
the rocks spraying out,
the ocean rising,
the villagers looking up from the net-mending.

We think ourselves omniscient,
calculate angles,
create quick metaphors in our head,
search for buoys to grasp like a faith.
We try to ground ourselves in questions.
"Why here and not over there?"

There's no divining.
Scientists can only guess.
The dogs won't bark
and the cattle won't stampede.
Even John the Baptist and Nostradamus
would have to scramble.

Some moments don't leave time for questions.
Not like stacking stone blocks

and you pull the bottom one out.
Even a slave could see that grief coming.

This is that piece of debris from the sky
smashing through your roof and into the recliner
where you just told your husband to sit
but he wasn't yet because he couldn't find
the remote. As the upholstery smolders
you both immediately start rewinding
past prayers in your head.

This is the windborne trash
that clings to your windshield
and blinds you in the rain.

This is being in line at the bank on hold-up day.

This is being swept along
on a ley-line of circumstance,
one event angling off another,
an airborne twig shearing
the final thread that was holding the
sword you did not know was there.

This is the keystone that dislodges,
the chain that breaks, the distracted wasp,
the mountain lion out of range,
the intercepted letter.

This is God tripping on a phantom stone
and using you to break his fall.

TO EVERY SOCIAL STUDIES TEACHER

Here is the poem you cannot
pass on to the junior high students.
They are still trying
to get their heads around Flanders Field.
Now Pasternak eludes both them and Russia.
And good luck dealing with the school board
regarding that Ginsberg thing.

Social Studies is all about
believing in the temporal intimacy of a moment.
Like those unguarded sentences
your mother told you when you were five.
She was sipping her coffee
and didn't really seem to be talking to you.
She was talking about that man,
The Marlboro Man,
that man who was thick as a tree,
and inscrutable as Joyce.
That man who was handled and tooled.
That man who would look at you and say
you could give him any name you wanted.
That man who would wake up before you,
cook your favorite eggs,
then bring them back to bed
and feed you both with just one fork.

CHOKING AHOGO

Poor Ahogo.
Someone has put up a sign
on how to end him.
It seems amazing no one has caught him yet.
Based on these instructions
it does not seem as if he will put up
much of a struggle.
He must be relatively famous
if he is only known by his first name.
"Hey! Ahogo! We told you
your jay-walking would get you in trouble!"

Certainly Miss Daisy needed driving,
and records indicate that Cain was raised,
(and I have heard that members of the Fit family
are not opposed to being tossed),
but I suspect you will not find
a sign in a post office or grocery store
that instructs you on how
to Free Gratis or Poison Sumac.

No one else is paying attention to this sign.
I will forget it too
and hope Ahogo never crosses my path.
Let Fate grant him the same invulnerability
as his wildly gyrating cousin
Slippery Cuidado.

Strong Bones

Now that he's grown
he might still be searching
the cosmos for it,
blue x-ray eyes
peering into every corner.

True to its origin
It must have been
set on its own
extended journey
from the faraway planet
called Kansas,
propelled like a orphaned rocket
from Fate's launch pad.

How could little Clark
have lost this?
Maybe he sat it down
absentmindedly
when he heard a far-off kitten
mewing for help.
Maybe he got distracted
by the infinite microscopic universe
of a very earthly grain of wheat.

This would not have been a thing
he would have abandoned lightly.
Destiny might just have set it rolling
along a dusty road,
then into hands which might, or might not,
have been villainous.

Regardless,
now Superman's lost thermos
sits quietly on the shelf
of this thrift store,
its insignia throbbing
gently in the dark.
It waits, in its alien way,
to again keep milk cold forever,
its metallic skin
perfectly
unbroken,
undented,
unscratched.

JESUS STOPPED BY AND FIXED MY GRILL

Jesus stopped by today
and raised my grill from the dead.
It made me question the whole
divine spark of life issue.
I started mourning for all the toasters
I might have tossed too soon.
And blenders. And piece of junk lawnmowers.
Maybe they could have been reclaimed.

I can't honestly say the parts on my grill
look new. I mean, consider
that it's not as if the people
he raised from the dead
came back as babies after all.
It wasn't a do-over, a start-again at go.
And no one was made immortal.
No, it was only a pause, a deferral,
a holding off of the imperial inevitable.

My grill just works now. It's still rusty.
The shelves are loose. But it fires up.
I offered Jesus a beer in thanks,
if he had a minute,
but he smiled and declined,
said he was on his way to some
carburetor a few blocks over.
I shook his hand, turned up the flame,
torn open the franks,

just like Lazarus must have done
after all the hosannas and news-spreading
and re-tellings.

I'm betting he ran off
somewhere privately with his wife
checking to see what parts still worked.

THE PIPES OF PAN

When we,
quite by chance,
ended up standing
side by side
watching some
delicious nymph
bounce her bosom
down the street,
with only an acknowledging
nod of our heads
we both knew
that on him
immortality
had been
misspent.
He was as shaggy
as a derelict Hasidic
and he leaned
on a worn and gnawed
cane.
He put his shoulder
against a light-post
and started beating
on his crotch
with his stick.
He looked up at me,
shook his head,
and shrugged his shoulders
as if to say nothing, nothing.
He pointed me up street.
He turned the other way.

TIME BOUNDED

Sometimes it's all about how
curiosity drives our steps
and how we set our goals.
How might things have changed
if the Mayans had sailed east?
Of course, the Europeans
already had a continuity
and were pretty sure their
empire and arts habits
had carved their place in history.
They might not have been able
to grasp it when the Mayans said,
"Don't worry.
Look past these turquoise amulets and jade knives.
We're not really into
the whole conquering thing.
Oh sure, there's some tribal disagreements
but we'll keep them in our backyard.
You've got some mighty fine buildings here.
Just keep doing what you're doing.
We just came over to let you know
that we've done some checking and,
well, there's an expiration date coming up
and you might want to do some planning.
Now, we gotta go. Long voyage home and all that."
How many fair-skinned people
standing there on the pier
would be waving farewell to the harbingers,
their brows furrowed, debating whether to believe,
deciding to pay more attention
to all stops on the way back home.

TINKERBELL IN TROUSERS

Mighty Mouse,
Steve Canyon,
Buck Rodgers.
We want these to be temporary.
We do not want them to have back-stories.
We do not want them to like blackjack,
or have appeared on Jerry Springer,
We don't want to see their baby pictures.
We don't want to meet their children.
We don't want to watch
the Justice League grow old.
We don't want to read how
Tinkerbell has lesbian tendencies.
We want them all to be in and out and done,
as temporal as ourselves,
as complete and perfect as Christmas gifts.
We don't want to know
where the boxes came from
or where they go.
We don't want to know
what powers or drives our fantasies.
We just want to see them fly.

DELEGATION

Sometimes delegation just won't do
and it's all about performing the task yourself.
Like in the middle of the night
when Persephone pushes Pluto out of bed
with her insistent (and guilt-inducing) toe
and says Get Up, Get Up, I think I heard
a noise out there close to Rome,
maybe Athens. So he rolls out of bed,
climbs in the chariot,
and does a cursory drive around all the stalagmites
(he even has Cerberus growl into the darkness).
But if Persephone still hears the noise
she's not going to like his answer
until she checks things herself,
her bunny slippers glowing like spring
down the stone hallways.

You hand the task off
and the message gets garbled.
Rosencrantz and Guildenstern end up
vacationing in Sweden,
or someone shows up with
a lock of Grendel's hair instead of his arm.
It just leads to more trouble.
It lengthens the process.

You pay to have a secure stone wall built
but afterwards you discover holes so large
Pyramus and Thisbe could have
crawled through them
and started a family.

Sometimes you wish you were the person
in charge of calendars and watches.
But alas, that job has been delegated already.
You have looked in the mirror in the mornings
and been surprised,
and reach the conclusion that man
is doing a poor job,
letting things burn through so quickly.

Those old gods, you decide, must be
given special dispensation,
near the top of the decision tree,
never getting older,
given enough authority
to frighten or satisfy mortals,
but not necessarily
other gods.

Why Being Fifty-Plus Is the Best Age

There are always at least
four older people in horror movies:
two that die early because they don't believe
that a spider as big as a tractor
was running across their yard,
and two that die next-to-last
trying to protect their grandkids
from the rampaging mummy.
(There's always an alpha teenage couple left alive
for sequels.)

It's best to always believe
in the extrapolated unreality of things.
You learn to duck, be fast on the draw,
be able to tango on command.
You learn to cope, accept the scars,
bend a branch, leave a sign.

Maybe, after your adventures,
you write your memoirs.
Maybe you write a list:

"Being Fifty Plus Is the Best Age
because all but the slowest dinosaurs are extinct;
because we got those pyramid thingies built;
because we survived the Black Plague;
because I painted her name onto a stone, there,
right there,
along the river. "Ooaug".
Well, maybe I didn't use those exact letters,
the Phoenicians haven't come along yet
so the whole symbolic thing hasn't gelled.

My mark for her is more like an auk or a deer.
I'm sure she'll know herself when she sees herself."

No geologic plate is ever stable.
Earthquakes lift and reefs are exposed
and pretty soon there's an island
complete with natives that want independence.
They start keeping track of history,
honoring elders,
always listening to hear
if the ground will shift again.

And here we are, listening to Elvis
(the best music EVER)
spreading out our picnic
on the stones of the river bed.
We accept that around that corner
there might be a meteorite
that might contain an omnivorous alien.
But until he shows up
I am going to scratch your name
on this rock and this rock and this rock
and set them in the river
so the water,
through the minutes, hours, and years,
will say your name again and again
and every time you hear it
you will know it's you, it's you.

His Next Task

After Michael told the Virgin Mary
the glorious news
he returned to heaven to,
"Well Done, Faithful Servant",
a slew of seraphamic high-fives,
and an unending chorus of,
"Who's the Angel?"

But it's the problem with any plan
be it five year or five eons.
After the big project was done,
like everything else corporate,
the vision got diluted
and the hierarchy got rearranged.
Michael was consigned to lesser tasks
like holding swords over battlefields,
greeting saints as they came and went,
standing in for Jesus during the visitation
on an occasional taco.

THE POET OF DISHWASHERS

In this era of specialization
would our gods get more selective?
Would they save only people
who were left-handed, those people
who were color-blind, those people
who were only four foot two?

I heard a poet called
The Poet of Households
and already I suspect we have become
too selective.
The Poet of Lawnmowers.
The Poet of 8-cylinder engines.
The Poet of People Who Only Have G.E.D.s
The Poet of People Who Like French Roast Coffee.
The Poet of Small Appliances.
The Poet of People Who Like Chocolate.
I suspect that last one would be appealing
to most ethnic and age groups,
but over-all
what would those poets talk about?
What would their message be?

And here is the latest volume from
The Poet of Dishwashers.
Here, just read the cover blurbs.
Do you feel universally included?:

"Best thing dishwashers have seen in a long time."
"I trust this poet's vision, his voice,
his grease-cutting power."
"I was delighted. I was amazed.
I let him scrub my pots."

HALLOWEEN

Casper, Superman, Batman, Peter Pan,
ridiculed presidents
all species of cats, dogs and bears—
and whatever comic character
is in theatres at the time:
they will be waves of them in the neighborhood,
thick as high-fiber cookie dough.

I guarantee you will not find
a poet costume anywhere.
Someone could make one
and give it the title 'Poet'
but the poor urchin would always
have to identify himself.
"How cute! What ARE you?"
                              "I'm a poet."
And the parent at the door
handing out the candy will laugh, maybe nervously.
The poor miniature bard will, of course,
be dragging a wagon-full of rejection slips,
have a flagon of day-old coffee on his hip,
and carrying a pen made from a
dingy white feather.
To complete the look he will need
tattered MFA's poking from his pockets.

At wakes you always wish
you had known the person better.
You find out he had studied
to be an anthropologist,
he grew orchids at his summer house,
had an addiction to kung pao chicken.

Our lives, as we walk through them,
are not as clear and well-stated.
Maybe we should all wear name tags
that state our occupation and desires.
We might feel like centerfolds though.
Perhaps just an indicator
on our driver's license would be better
(since we have no clear idea what we want to be
until we at least get to sixteen anyway).

At parties, bars, social functions, we could just
whip out our neurologist tag
('likes peanut butter and long walks on the beach')
and it would instantly break the ice.
And strip away all pretense.

Instead of waiting for one day a year,
or one final day,
when people discover who we really are,
while we pause there waiting for their approval,
dragging our lives, like an apology, behind us.

SOMETIMES I IMAGINE ALL REALITY IS A BALL

but it's my ball.
You might have a pyramid
or a square.
The spatially-challenged might only
have a handkerchief.
But it's really only like
the astronauts
going to the moon.
They always want to
see what's on the dark side.
What is your big box hiding?
What is waiting
on the other side of that hill?
Something grim, austere, foreboding—
or flappy and cartoony with big arrows
and signs for a drive-in?
It's always a future that spins slightly
out of our reach, places we know
we need to visit.
Quick Lube, Great Tacos, Home of the Runza.
Or maybe someone else's
face in the darkness
that our hands don't really know.

No Soliciting

I am going to have a bar installed
on my front door.
You know, the long medieval kind, on a hinge,
or maybe just an old-world beam
that sits on brackets.
Of course, such a system depends on someone
always being home
to lock up after me
when I go off to work.
So maybe I should just add iron plates
to deter hewing axes, Jehovah's witnesses,
and girl scouts selling cookies.
The key, of course, would need to be humongous,
for sheer intimidation purposes.
I would need something much more effective
than a lock on a diary any older sister can pry.
I need to at least have
a sprinkler system for a moat,
or a Chihuahua to substitute
for a spike-encrusted dog.
I need a "No!" that people will believe,
something as clear and undeniable as fate,
something that will repulse even the man
who attaches pizza coupons
to my door with a rubber band.
I want to have an indication so clear
that when I'm old and less able to recall
clever literary retorts
to ward off unknown knocking
that my device or sign or whatever it is
could drive off even Death.
He will read the unwelcome doormat
a letter at a time with his bony finger,

realize I am really serious,
and move on to the neighbor next door
who has high cholesterol anyway.

That Satellite

carries a plaque
with music and words
and pictures of two humans.
It is optimism of the highest cosmic proportion
that that would be all the information
a starry visitor might need
to pique his curiosity.
It might make him at least steer in our direction
and look down on our blue-green ball.
But whoever sent our satellite up
should have considered
that photos are only captured light after all.
When those photos are turned face up,
even something as innocent
as leafing through an album,
or displaying on a screen,
then all those struts upon the stage
will shine up into space
and those all-powerful, light-year-bending aliens
will measure our intelligence
from those billions of photos
shining back up at them,
which will include
my family's faded Christmases,
our starched Easters,
and our summer cookouts
with our mouths dangling hotdogs,
our faces anointed with mustard,
me and my brother wrestling,
my fingers held in a V behind his head.

BON MOT

My mind is not content
with short lines.
Like a description
of a pair
of cardinals
perched around the woodpile
yesterday morning.
No one asked them
if they were related
or married
or simply friends
living together
to cut expenses
to get through
the current economic
downturn.
I have heard
a poem should not contain
a question.
So, declaratively,
I have named
my salt shaker Eunice
and the Pepper Roger.
They knew
my grandparents.
Eunice and Roger
considered divorce once.
They had a big falling out
when Eunice was lost
in the land of stove.
While she was gone
Roger took up
with the sugar bowl,

aptly named Cindy.
But Roger fell one day
and chipped his foot.
There are more stories here
than short lines will allow.

They old ones—they knew suffering.
They needed long lines.
The cardinals forage on
through their sinful state.
Though injured
Roger still keeps
his head held high.

THE FIFTH KIND OF CONFESSION

*There are four kinds of confession: talking to God, writing
the sin down, talking to someone else, and the confession
that comes with the passage of time.*

There is a fifth kind of confession,
the kind where the sin is passed
through the fingers and lips
onto other objects:
the twisted cup,
the unsettled door,
the catawampus chair,
the gelatin that will not set,
the tea that never gets hot.
I know a beautiful woman
whose eyes hint of secrets
but the last joint of her pinkie finger
has more bumps than a phrenologist
could decipher.
These are subtle errata,
the kind you hope no one notices
but you know, by their very origin,
they must be seen.
It is why the dog barks
at the mower that cuts in patches.
It is the insight of a torn seam
on the black sofa
where you offer your guests to sit.

Scientists Have Discovered Crabs Can Feel Pain

Scientists have discovered
crabs can feel and remember pain.
Does the same hold true
regarding mailboxes on country roads?
Does the soda can
tossed out the car window
feel abandoned
(and frustrated because it has no legs
to find its way home?)
When we first open a box of cookies
do they imprint on us?
There are some things
it is better not knowing.
Sometimes we don't want to carry
so much guilt.

OMPHALOS

This is a place
no one cares about.
No presidents have slept here.
No famous people have stopped by.
It was never threatened by a 100-year flood,
knocked akimbo by a tornado,
or even had a tree fallen on it.
It is simply a room in a rather common house
where I used to smoke a pipe
but through the years
I have evolved to coffee.
The silver cutlery box collects dust.
The cookie jars on the shelves
have not moved for a decade.

Perhaps it is the center of something,
a balance point for something larger.
Some Balinese native walks better right now
because his center, thousands of miles away,
is stable. If I move the napkins he may stumble.

The weight of the sunlight pouring onto
the cushion in the chair the cat likes
is essential for a polar bear
balancing on an ice floe.

Oh, if I spill salt
what calamities! What volcanoes!
I may read of an avalanche,
surprised skiers digging out.

Words like to live here where it is quiet.
They stop by, as sure as fed cattle.

Their ethereal mass maintains things.
They hang from invisible branches,
buoyant in the balance.

If Sophia Loren
decides to stop by
then she can sit in the chair
next to me
as long as she is respectful,
as long as she writes.

FOCAL POINT

Behind the speaker at the conference
there is a wall of movable panels.
If it turns out he is no good
will the wall swallow him up?
A trap door, some summary judgment
propelled by manic applause, or the lack of it?
What do those doors open into?
Another ballroom, another speaker?
Shall we exchange, compare entertainment value?
Is it a mirror-version of us, all books
with author's signatures in the back?
These tiles above our heads,
these seemingly benign vinyl squares below our
feet.
What did Persephone think as she walked
the vernal hills that morning?
Was she only concerned with gathering flowers,
listening to the songs of birds?
Or did she question whether
she had been a good girl,
whether that cracking in the earth
was her fault after all?

FREE T-SHIRT

When the famous writer
came to speak
the venue gave away
commemorative
long-sleeve t-shirts.
Why long-sleeve?
Was he a biter?

When I went to vacation bible school
every summer I would get a little metal button
with a clasp in the back I could bend
so it would hang on my pocket.
And on this button was a picture of Jesus
with his arms around a bunch of children
and the caption said "Jesus love me."

My grandma likes to drink her coffee out
of a mug shaped like a donkey.
From the 1960 election she has told me,
the last Camelot.

This hawking of paraphernalia,
These baseball cards,
These movie posters,
These tears from the saints.
Buddha is coming.
Here is your small box of souvenir rice.
And tomorrow Jesus will be in town.
Here is your free goat-skin bag.
Inside you will find a commemorative crucifix.
Keep it. It might have some value
later.

ON EACH TOMBSTONE

there should be a forenote.
It should be government mandated.
Something by Dickens, Pound, Thomas Gray,
or some other words
that have outlasted us.
When you are writing your will
it will be gently recommended
you should pick your phrase.
The importance will fall right below
disbursement of funds
and right above
who gets the piano.
If you don't do it
then the relatives will be compelled
to work with the funeral home.
It will be another book for them
to page through
when they are picking the guest register
and type of lining.
"Longer quotes will be more expensive, of course,"
the director will pat your hand soothingly.

Many quotations will become stock, so to speak,
and will be seen over and over,
as common as reincarnation.
Angels will be replaced with ostentatious script.
Large stones, bearing essays, will
be the mark of wealth.

Perhaps it would be best
to be a member
of a less literate family,
forced to used snippets

from the newspaper,
fulfilling the requirement,
regardless of applicability.
"Good machinist available for hire."
"Big train wreck in Chicago."
"Tender Rump Roast. Eighty Cents A Pound."

QUICKENING

I saw him playing in a patch of gray clay
down on the riverbank. He had already made
a dozen gray birds out of clay: rudimentary things,
roly-poly, sticks for legs,
wings outlined with a thumbnail.

I would have guessed he was eight, maybe ten,
and as focused on his task
as if he was reading a comic book.
When I came up to him to watch closer he looked
up to me with the clearest eyes
I have ever seen and said,

"It is exactly as you have always suspected:
It is all about the form."
He made a few more efforts on his latest shape
then sat it down. I saw his lips move,
just a few silent words, then one by one he touched

the head of each clay bird. Like an exhalation,
for each, there was a burst of gray wings,
white flashing, beaks gasping,
then they lifted into the sky, anxious for the air.

The boy smiled, washed his hands
in the flowing water. The strength left my legs.
I sat down on the stones. He straightened up,
walked over to me, leaned in close.

His breath was like roses. He whispered,
"Breathe life into everything.
Isn't that why you're here?"

He looked up into the sky, once, then turned,
and walked downriver, disappearing around a bend.

A mockingbird flew down to the stones beside me.
He tilted one eye up at me and began to sing.

WHEN CATS WALK UPRIGHT

The dog was as big as a pony
but when the cornered cat turned
and stood on its hind legs
the dog understood the dynamics
of the whole chasing thing had changed
and now the universe was out of kilter.

The universe is all about balance:
What did that cat have to give up
to learn to walk up tall?

Will he now develop affectations,
a monocle, a cane,
a baseball cap pulled low over his eyes,
a t-shirt that says, "I'm with stupid"?
Instead of running his neck against your ankle
will he now shake hands?
Suddenly he will not have to
look up quite so far
to be disdainful.
But where is his proud profile,
the questing tail,
the secret of hiding behind things
only foot-stool high?
Where is the horizontal stretching,
the total lack of need for pockets?

Did he have to give up the reassuring holiness
of being able to land squarely
on all four feet?

SIGN ON A TRASH CAN

"Temporarily Out of Order Sorry."
I had no idea the universe was so fragile.
I have grown to depend
on the sturdiness of physics
even when I did not include it on
my Christmas card list.
But now, this sign on this trash can
changes everything.
If trash gravity is out of order
It makes me question where previous trash went,
the tossing out of refuse.
the indecision of destination.
Ancient monks would measure time
with a water clock,
striving for precision out of arbitrariness.
They had only a broad and vague notion
of a final brimstone-laden and sin-fed tabulation.
Still, those cloistered people believed
that a bucket measure was always the same
and water would always fall.
So imagine the look of fear on their face
when they came in to check the time
and saw instead an illuminated sign that said,
"Sorry. Clock out of order.
Doom is Coming.
Do you know
where your prayers went?"

Noodling Catfish

The largest danger posed to noodlers are other forms of aquatic life found in catfish holes. Far more dangerous than catfish are alligators, snakes, beavers, muskrats and snapping turtles, who will take over abandoned catfish holes as homes of their own. These animals are always on the mind of experienced noodlers. —Wikipedia

Agnes, at thirteen, learned to tie cherry stems into a knot with her tongue. She was as homely as her name but determined to be popular. She had only a vague notion of what this lingual skill might do for her but at a rudimentary level she had the faith that said happiness followed the smallest of ambitions. The faith of Agnes. It's why we tie words together and then wad them up into syllabic bundles and throw them into the editorial darkness.

Noodling catfish is all about going underwater, full of faith, and then coming up, hair in your eyes, covered in muck, with your hands throbbing. If you get baptized and the preacher's hands start throbbing then he suspects an angelic agent. But with noodling you just don't know what those agents are.

It's a condition we reach for every day. Taking a different route to work, trying a different flavor of coffee, dating a different guy, trying the special of the day, vacationing to a different resort. We weigh out what we are willing to lose. We think we have a sense of where we are going but that's why palm readers get paid—the water's too murky for the rest of us and we're just sticking our hands in holes.

Cousins! Send us photos of nine-fingered Bob!
Agnes, tell us again how many stems you've tied
into knots over the years. You—there—on your
third cup of coffee! Tell me how many words you
have written, how many times you called on the
Muse, and who exactly really showed up.

CLOCKS IN CATHEDRALS

are generally concussive things.
They want to remind you
Doom is impending
and God is watching.
Nursing home clocks are
quiet things
like watches.
Should we get to choose the music
of the events of our lives,
like at a wedding?
Vivaldi, Beethoven, some Gregorian chants?
Perhaps something from Queen
when you wife runs off with her lover?
Something tympanic and menacing
when you get divorced, lose your job?
Perhaps, like poetry, it is all about the sounds
and how we connotate them with what we
say and do and feel.
People in a nursing home
do not want to hear the seconds slipping away.
When the angels visited the shepherds
with the world-changing news
they announced it
with trumpets and a heavenly host.
When succubus come in the night
we want them to whisper.

Guiseppe Verdi Tuscano Bertilucci

did not do anything particularly great
that we are aware of.
He did not perfect the alchemist stone.
He did not create an exquisite painting technique.
He strode the streets
of Verona unobserved.
He might have come from some bucolic background
and spent his time writing eclogues
that no one read.
He might have worked at a printing press,
a vineyard, a mill, some other smudging job.
He might have been as unique as a sunrise
which today is coming in my window
from a slightly different position
than it did the day before.
Perhaps one day Guiseppe
turned left instead of right,
crossed this bridge instead of that,
misread a Pharmacopoeia,
bought a glass of wine, did not buy a glass of wine.
And tomorrow
the pitcher of flowers on my table
will cast a slighty different shadow
as the sun rises again
in a slightly different position
from the day before
as it rolls and spins and burns
on its glorious, indifferent way.

BEFORE YOU DISAPPEAR

If you're squeamish, don't prod the beach rubble.

—Sappho

you are allowed to look back once.
You always harbored the secret wish
you would be lifted at the last possible second
out of harm's way
and dropped into someone's swaddling arms.
But instead you are drifting, looking down,
bemused and detached.
You know the French have a phrase for it
(and now you know what the phrase is):
the name for things that are left in a person's pocket
after they die.
While you were walking around
the objects were like little moons,
circling in and out of your gravitational sphere.
Now a man is reaching into your pockets,
digging, holding his breath, looking away,
and pulling out the pieces
that no longer have a need to orbit.
He will stir them with his gloved finger,
turn them over, catalog them.
Maybe he will pat your head tenderly,
fold your hands over your chest.
This was not what you expected.
You could have worn better shoes.
Your haircut made you look old.

The only thing that matters really
is moving forward
and leaving all that debris behind.